FRONTLINE TEAMWORK
One Company's Story of Success

FRONTLINE TEAMWORK

One Company's Story of Success

LOUIS W. JOY III, CFPIM
JO A. JOY, CMA
Foreword by Donald E. Wilson, Jr.
1992 APICS International President
Illustrations by Martin Kozlowski

The Business One Irwin/APICS
Series in Frontline Education

Business One Irwin
Burr Ridge, Illinois
New York, New York

© RICHARD D. IRWIN, INC., 1994

This publication is designed to provide accurate and authoritative information in regard to the subject matter covered. It is sold with the understanding that neither the author nor the publisher is engaged in rendering legal, accounting, or other professional service. If legal advice or other expert assistance is required, the services of a competent professional person should be sought.

From a Declaration of Principles jointly adopted by a Committee of the American Bar Association and a Committee of Publishers.

Sponsoring editor:	Jean Marie Geracie
Project editor:	Gladys True
Production manager:	Irene H. Sotiroff
Compositor:	The Wheetley Company, Inc.
Typeface:	11/14 Palatino
Printer:	R. R. Donnelley & Sons Company

Library of Congress Cataloging-in-Publication Data

Joy, Louis W.
    Frontline teamwork : one company's story of success / Louis W. Joy III, Jo A. Joy ; ill. by Martin Kozlowski.
        p.   cm.
    ISBN 1-55623-955-6
    1. Group work—United States—Case studies. I. Joy, Jo A.
II. Title.
HD66.J69   1994
658.4'036—dc20   93–16923

Printed in the United States of America

1 2 3 4 5 6 7 8 9 0   DOC   0 9 8 7 6 5 4 3

To the spirit of Howard Roark

THE BUSINESS ONE IRWIN/APICS FRONTLINE SERIES

Supported by the American Production
and Inventory Control Society

OTHER BOOKS PUBLISHED IN THE
BUSINESS ONE IRWIN/APICS SERIES
Attaining Manufacturing Excellence *Robert W. Hall*
Bills of Materials *Hal Mather*
Production Activity Control *Steven A. Melnyk and Phillip L. Carter*
Manufacturing Planning and Control Systems, Second Edition
Thomas E. Vollmann, William Lee Berry, D. Clay Whybark
The Spirit of Manufacturing Excellence *Ernest Huge*
Strategic Manufacturing: Dynamic New Directions for the 1990s
Patricia E. Moody
Total Quality: An Executive's Guide for the 1990s
The Ernst & Young Quality Improvement Consulting Group
Forecasting Systems for Operations Management
Stephen A. DeLurgio and Carl D. Bhame
Common Sense Manufacturing *James Gardner*
Purchasing Strategies for Total Quality: A Guide to Achieving
Continuous Improvement *Greg Hutchins*
Logistics in Manufacturing *Chris Gopal and Gerry Cahill*
Computer Integrated Manufacturing *Steven A. Melnyk and*
Ram Narasimhan

Foreword

Frontline Teamwork is one of those rare books that crystallizes and simply settles the debate of how to cure America's manufacturing dilemma. It's about time! What makes this book unique is that rather than rely on the old cliches and ivory tower theories on Teamwork, it takes a different approach. Unlike many Teamwork applications, this book stresses that the blue-collar line worker must be included in any kind of team application. If that goal can be affected, then manufacturing can be a pleasant working experience for all.

Business should take heed! As this book makes its impact, it will take the reader on a journey that will eliminate all of the excuses for continuing to operate a business as has been done in the past. Business owners and managers will be forced to open their eyes to the fact that people are their most important resource. When you open the door of communication and trust, the "blue-collar-force" becomes your true guide on the crusade toward the end of the rainbow of excellence, increased productivity, and profitability.

The rewards do not lie solely at the end of that rainbow. There are many rewards, "pots of gold," encompassed within the challenges along your path. This book makes it clear—we need to focus on people and their abilities rather than their jobs. Careers define much of what we are, but not everything. Management has historically been short-sighted about their work force. Line workers are *not* just cogs in the wheel to be manipulated. They are people who want to make a difference: people who pay bills, balance check books, raise children, attend religious services, and strongly desire to contribute to providing excellent products and services for the customer.

Perhaps some historical perspective would be appropriate. What we learn from the past helps us make the right choices for the future.

Henry Ford is remembered as a pioneer in mass production of the automobile. But it was the lineworkers who put the Model T together and made it work who were an important part of Ford's success.

Historians extol American industry's ability during World War II to make the conversion from the production of domestic goods to war materials. We accomplished this task within six months after the attack on Pearl Harbor. It was the dedication of the line workers that made America the "arsenal of democracy" and produced the tanks, ships, aircraft, and weapons that defeated fascism.

America's golden age of manufacturing lasted for more than a century, until its precipitous decline began in the 1970s. To revitalize American manufacturing and prepare it for a new golden age in the Twenty First Century, management must be willing to be patient and open the doors that have been closed in their minds. There is a treasure of information residing in the minds of the people who operate machines, assemble products and maintain facilities. This book points out the need—in no uncertain terms—for management to find out what their workers know. Not just what they know, however, but *who* they are as well.

Think about it. How many years have you asked your employees to come to work, do their job, and check their brain at the timeclock? Have you ever asked for their suggestions, really listened, and given them the respect they deserve? Have you explained the problems at hand and then given them the tools and encouragement to solve it? For the most part, the answer is a resounding *no*!

This impersonal disconnection between management and line workers is counterproductive. I have been acutely aware of that and have fought it through an organization that I have been associated with for most of my professional manufacturing career.

APICS, (American Production and Inventory Control Society), the international educational society for resource management, has for over 35 years stressed the need for structural changes in business operations. Teamwork is an essential component necessary to affect these changes critical to revitalizing the manufacturing sector.

Using sports metaphors is the best way to describe it. You have players, coaches, and owners. Employees are the players, the supervisor is the coach, and all are employees of the owners. As with all teams, each member has a specific assignment. Each player, however, must also know the overall objective of each play, and the roles of the other players in order for the team to win.

The process that leads to successful teamwork in manufacturing will not be an easy one. Someone once said that "success is going from failure to failure with great enthusiasm." The road will not always be well-lighted and smooth, but this is a handbook to guide you on your journey. It is a handbook that reads like your favorite attention-riveting novel.

Travel through the evolution of a manufacturing plant operating with outdated management styles to a vision-

driven organization where employees participate and become true stakeholders. Use this book as a living
document. Share it with your employees. You can, you
will, and you *must* make a difference!

Mr. Donald E. Wilson, Jr.
International President
American Production and Inventory Control Society

Donald E. Wilson, Jr., CFPIM, is the 1992 international president of the American
Production and Inventory Control Society, an international not-for-profit society
for resource management.

Mr. Wilson is presently the product manager for the systems/materials programs
division of the Siemens Energy and Automation Inc., distribution equipment
business in Charlottesville, Virginia. His specialties include the technical and
business management of the design and implementation of integrated computer
network systems.

Preface

During the last 10 years as both a manager and consultant, I've worked closely with people at all levels in organizations, from the board room to the shop floor, to find ways to improve business performance. It's been an incredible journey. It's fascinating to observe people respond and react to new ideas.

This book describes the typical emotional reaction to change and will help people better understand themselves and their company members. The intent is to prepare the reader to properly deal with the challenge of Teamwork. Artists, philosophers, and scientists all seek to understand and describe the world we live in, and by doing so help us better understand ourselves and our role in the universe. There's a yearning in each of us to know who we are, and who we aren't. And we must identify both our strengths and weaknesses to achieve real progress. Like a mirror in the bath, this book will provide an accurate, real-life reflection.

Today's business literature is filled with organizational behavior theory, Teamwork models, and explanations of

how to apply specific techniques. The business fable has
gained popularity, playing over and over a theme of quality
or leadership. All of these are useful and make an important contribution toward understanding the new world
order in business.

But this book is different. It is not strictly a "how to" book.
It's not a rehash of old ideas. It provides an answer to the
question on everyone's mind when faced with Teamwork,
quality, or any other major change: How's this going to affect
me? Skepticism abounds, and usually increases with our
years of service. So when a new system is placed in front of
us we don't always embrace it. This book shows how people
often respond to these changes, and reflects the impact
Teamwork will have on you and the people around you. Our
objective is to help you better understand the trials, tribula-
tions, and accomplishments that lie ahead when you become
a Team-oriented organization.

The skeptical workforce that has been beaten up and
holds management in contempt. The traditional plant
manager who is a destroyer of new ideas and thrives on
power. The supervisor who plays king of the hill and just
can't let go. The senior executive whose proud military
leadership style doesn't meet the needs of his workforce.
These are some of the players in *Frontline Teamwork*, and
are common figures in most traditional organizations.

You'll also meet the people who lead the company out of
the darkness. The general manager willing to risk his
career for the principles he believes in. His partner who
works in the trenches and facilitates the needed changes.
And the workers who volunteer to take on the pressures
and blaze the first trails. Success requires these heroes to
live and breathe on your shop floor and in your office.

I've seen organizations that sincerely believed they were
on the cutting edge of empowerment. But upon closer
inspection they had gotten no further than a traditional
company decorated with the slogans, banners, and buttons of Teamwork. The question facing these organizations

is: How do we get managers and supervisors to really change their management style and behaviors and listen to and empower the work force? As this book points out, most people *can* make the transition to coach and leader. But they will need help and lots of persuasion.

And there will be those people who will fight it, struggle frantically, and not make the leap. One's degree of patience with such resistance will vary with each person, but should the company suffer for the sake of a handful of stubborn people? Renegade managers and supervisors can quickly destroy the worker's perception of management's undying commitment to change. If you are the one who is mired in tradition and can't get over these new hurdles, then admit the problem to yourself. Talk to your friends and business leaders about the dilemma. This book will help you recognize the condition.

So how should you use this book? Our objective in writing this book was to present simple rules and guidelines for supervisors, facilitators, and Team members. Don't take these guidelines lightly! I urge you to carefully consider each of the rules. You are likely to meet with added frustration if any are ignored. Surely, there's more than one way to conduct Teamwork. But think carefully about changes to these guidelines before making them.

Over the years, we've searched high and low for a book that could be used in the start-up phase of Teams that would serve to catalyze discussion. *Frontline Teamwork* serves that purpose. At the end of each chapter are pointed questions that reflect the issues the characters are working to resolve. Your Team can compare its situations with those facing the Team in the story. Talk about each question. Use these points as a checklist to ensure that important issues are uncovered and decisions facing the Team are resolved.

Frontline Teamwork is intended to be fun to read! We believe that you'll quickly relate to these characters, and enjoy your time spent with this book. It's entertaining, and this helps the reader grab hold of the message.

A powerful technique presented in *Frontline Teamwork* is a new and proven shop floor scheduling system called Production Sequencing. Materials Requirements Planning (MRP) was designed and presented by the experts over 17 years ago. How many of our companies have a formal MRP system used to schedule and prioritize production at workcells, workcenters, or departments? The answer is that MRP and the software industry have let us down and not provided a system that the average company can use with ease. They've created software products that are perfectly logical, but equally impractical and unusable.

Production Sequencing is a simple, manual pull system for make-to-order and make-to-stock plants. It only requires a master production schedule. No black box. No MRP, shop floor control, or other special software is needed. But Production Sequencing does require discipline, organization, and common sense. The book briefly explains the response of Work Teams to the concept. Read the appendix article to learn more about this Team-based scheduling system.

The fit of Teamwork with a labor union is often questioned. Please know that this book neither advocates the formation of unions nor does it suggest the two are incompatible. We've seen success and failure with and without the presence of a union. The only guideline to keep in mind is that the company must show respect to union leaders and involve them in all phases of Teamwork design, development, and implementation. Only a working partnership between labor and management will result in successful, large-scale change.

One more thought about a crucial component of Teamwork: Pay systems in a Team-oriented environment must take on a new look from the old, feeble techniques presently used. Let me say this without hesitation—piecework rips the soul from a company. It pits worker against worker, and personal compensation against meeting the schedule and quality performance. That's not to say that the pay system must be changed before Teamwork efforts are begun. In fact, experience has demonstrated that a viable approach is to pursue Teamwork-type improvements with piecework or other traditional systems in place. You'll find that the weaknesses of the existing pay system become readily apparent, and there is a groundswell of support for a better system. Seize the opportunity to involve workers in the process of pay system design. But what should the pay system look like?

We've found that for Team members, a combination of supervisory and peer performance evaluations to determine hourly pay increases and bonuses works best to motivate high performance. Who should evaluate a worker's performance other than the people working side by side, day in and day out with that person? This is true empowerment, and finger-pointing at pay systems as unjust and unfair is quickly dissolved. It's hard to discount an evaluation that is the aggregate of your peers.

Teamwork by itself will not result in improved productivity and quality. It is not the end, but the means to implement change. It is the way to not only find the best solution, but also to give the people tasked with implementation an opportunity to gain ownership and buy in to the solution. This book strives to make clear the need for participation on the frontlines, on the shop floor. All people, regardless of race, education, language, or culture, want to help. They want to be listened to and respected. This book is written to help us all better understand how to make that truth a reality.

Louis W. Joy III

Jo A. Joy

Manufacturing Excellence, Inc.
19 Top View Court
Newark, Delaware 19702
(302) 737–3603

Acknowledgments

Make no mistake. This book is truly the product of Teamwork. John Selden once said, "Old friends are best. King James used to call for his old shoes; they were easiest for his feet." It was with the greatest pleasure that I worked closely with an old friend from my early childhood, Mr. Martin Kozlowski, of Lucida Studios, New York City, to mold and shape this manuscript. Even with today's pressures of family and business, this project allowed precious moments to once again join together and engage in a creative undertaking. There is a magic in schoolboy friendships, and this effort rekindled the laughter and good-natured banter that old friends can share. Koz is truly a talent. We are indebted to him for his work on this manuscript as well as the illustrations that enhance and illuminate this story.

We are truly grateful to those companies that have allowed us the honor to participate and assist in their Teamwork and Total Quality efforts. The many executives, managers, supervisors, and workers have touched us deeply, and we admire and recognize your work.

Many thanks to our parents, teachers, and business leaders who have encouraged and inspired us. Kind words, a pat on the back, and a kick in the fanny have all helped us through the more difficult times and pushed us ahead.

We truly appreciate the efforts of Rick Hoberg and George Brasher of Hewlett Packard, and James Stautzenberger of Wing Industries, for their time spent reviewing and evaluating initial drafts.

We are grateful to Jean Marie Geracie, our acquisitions editor, and the good people of Business One Irwin for their faith and unending support and patience. And we thank Don Wilson, 1992 APICS International President, for his belief in this project and in people.

And we acknowledge each of you who fight the good fight to make your lives and businesses as they ought to be.

L. W. J.
J. A. J.

Contents

Illustrations

The following were drawn by Mr. Martin Kozlowski

Chapter One

Introduction

"We didn't know what to expect."

I t was 4:30 P.M., and the machinery hummed soothingly in the power supply workcell. The Work Team members were preparing for the shift change scheduled for 5. Immersed in their work, the day had seemed to evaporate and one could sense the mood of satisfaction in the air. Suzanne, who was the assigned Team Leader for the next three months, was completing a chart titled "Performance to Schedule." A working mother with three kids at home, she was also a kind of mom on the job, offering a sympathetic ear and genuine concern to any co-worker who needed them.

Glancing up at the clock, she said to no one particular, "What a difference three years makes. I'm always amazed how much better my work life at this plant has gotten."

Dave paused thoughtfully, rubbing the back of his burly neck. They called him the Big Man because of his physical resemblance to that of a pro football linebacker. He wondered aloud, "Yeah, it's too bad someone doesn't tell our story. I'm sure there are a lot of employees out there who would like to know how Teamwork *really* works, what it's like to be a successful Team member. We didn't know what to expect when we made a commitment to Teamwork. Remember how scary it was when we heard we would be involved in the decision-making?" He walked over and patted a small plaque the group had hung by their work area several years ago. It read:

> "A **Team** is a group of individuals, bonded together, striving to achieve a common purpose through mutual cooperation."

Bobby picked up the ball, "We were very frustrated for so long before we started on our Teamwork journey. Deep down, though, we always felt that our company was a good one. Despite all the problems, there was a strong feeling of loyalty, and a sense we owed a lot to the ownership and management. For many years, the company gave us a shot at earning a fair living, to raise our families, educate our kids, and enjoy a decent lifestyle." Bobby was the senior Team member, and the person others most looked up to. He was a quiet guy, but firm in his convictions. He always said the right thing, and could dance around the toughest subjects without stepping on anyone's toes.

Suzanne added, "We always knew we could be so much better. Let's face it. We were lucky to get a new general manager who created the atmosphere that allowed us all to constructively criticize the way things were done, and to offer solutions. Remember when he first arrived?"

Dave grinned and shook his head, "Whoa, do we ever."

Suzanne continued, "Today, the person who criticizes and

is just negative and doesn't present a better idea, will be told to put up or shut up." It was a reminder to both her fellow Team members and herself.

Jane, the youngest Team member and a petite, vivacious woman who could pass for a highschool co-ed, was within earshot. She smiled, remembering the sad state of affairs at her previous job. "Do you think Teamwork could have been successful here without a new GM?" she asked the group.

"I've heard stories where existing managers learn the ideas of Teamwork *and* give the employees the space to make it work. The stick-in-the-mud managers here would have had a tough time. They weren't open-minded. Mostly, they didn't have the guts to admit the problems in the plant may have been their own fault." Dave was the son of a staunch union man and being tough on management was in his blood.

"If they ever do tell our story, they shouldn't sugar coat it. They should include all the mistakes that were made. It was making the mistakes that showed us how it really should be done. Of course, it would have been easier if someone had warned us." Suzanne finished filling in the chart, placed it in its folder, and began to straighten up her work area.

"Our biggest boner was when we let the Big Man join our Team," Bobby kidded. "I taught him everything he knows, and look at the thanks I get!" Bobby nodded toward a framed photo on the shop wall of Dave in a sport jacket and tie shaking hands with the corporation president. Last year he had been honored for his leadership skills at the annual awards dinner sponsored by the corporate headquarters.

Dave turned his back on Bobby and muttered "old dog" through the faint, proud smile on his lips. Catching Jane's eye, Dave adopted a stern tone as he said, "Think back to when you joined us two years ago. You didn't know there are two basic types of Teams, and what your responsibilities on each would be, did you? You weren't ready to deal with your new supervisor in a new way, different from how you did at the old, fuddy-duddy company you came from, were you? And you didn't know how coordinators work on the Teams, how to conduct the meetings so time isn't wasted, and how to be sure your Team makes progress and implements the right solutions, right?"

"Right!," Jane cried in mock guilt.

"You were just a young pup, and us old-timers took you under our wing," Dave continued, with a sly smile. "But we knew you had potential."

Jane looked at Suzanne and rolled her eyes, appreciating the good-natured ribbing. She said, "Yeah, you've all been great to me, and I appreciate the camaraderie. It feels like a second family here to me."

To Suzanne, the word *family* was a reminder of a missing friend. She said wistfully, "Sometimes, though, I kind of miss Keith, you know?"

The group fell silent for a moment, reflecting on her words, and they all gently nodded the agreement they felt in their hearts. Finally, Bobby returned to Suzanne's original point. "You know, Suzie, you're right. Teamwork helped solve basic problems in our company and made our work lives easier and made us better and more qualified employees. Fact is, I think we all look forward to coming to work these days and we find the work more satisfying. It ain't perfect, but I guess you'd call it pride in the success of our company and our Teams that we're feeling. It sounds a little corny, but I wouldn't change it too much."

They all grew quiet again, and each completed the tasks that would prepare the work area for the next shift. This was a pretty typical bunch of "Joe Average" American workers toiling away in an old urban center, but there was a unique feeling about them. The feeling of being in the middle of something special, even extraordinary, a very human yet almost heroic experiment that would test the ultimate potential of both their workplace and themselves. It was a journey that they were committed to fully, one that they would not let fail.

KEY POINTS FOR DISCUSSION

(1) In this scene, we meet Team Members who belong to a company that improved performance and the quality of the work lives of the employees. Discuss the extent to which you believe the quality of work life in your plant can be improved. What is the probability a scene like this will occur in your company three years from today?

(2) The Team members were uncertain and afraid of the changes Teamwork would bring to their work lives. Discuss your expectations of Teamwork. Based on your perception of Teamwork, what aspects do you consider the most fearful and intimidating?

(3) This company recognized Dave, the Big Man, for his leadership skills. What are the characteristics of leadership? Why is it necessary in a Team-oriented organization for leadership to exist within both the management and worker groups? Identify several people in your organization who are strong, positive leaders in your company.

(4) What aspects of Teamwork do you wish to better understand? List three questions about Teamwork.

Chapter Two

The Workers Speak Out

"If only they would wake up and listen to us."

"Every working day for the last 10 years I have driven the same blue Chevy Impala across this bridge that links the interstate highway to the city. I used to get a thrill at the sight of this sprawling urban mass, with buildings that reach up from the ground like monuments to some great dream, carefully placed and positioned to send a message to God and anyone else who cared to notice. Now, when I look out at them, I see the field of monuments at the cemetery where I visit Ginny.

"From this vantage point, I always wonder about the people you don't see. You sense the city is alive—vibrant and full of purpose, but you can never see a single living soul. Where are they hiding? Or does the concrete have a life of its own?

"At the toll booth, the collector welcomes me back to humanity, but I can't even force a smile to meet his. Within another five minutes my destination is within sight. It's a huge, dark steel structure, its windows now covered with brick and metal grates. The complex blots out the horizon at the dead end of the street. It looks run-down and tired, and only the cars in the parking lot suggest there might be life inside.

"This neighborhood has changed. From the bridge, the city still looks pretty glamorous, but, like they say, you should never judge a person's looks from across a room. Up close, you can see the decay and gradual deterioration of the gray buildings and the cracked streets. Lately, all I can fix on is the rust that's everywhere. It really never does sleep.

"On the right here are the four large manufacturing plants that were active not so long ago. I got my start in #2 plant. Even after they locked the doors, I couldn't accept its fate. I always hoped to see the big, neon sign relit, see Smitty back on duty at the security booth, see the crews back on the job. But it's gone now and you can't ever get some things back."

* * * *

Keith Dawes pulled into the parking lot to his regular space. A skilled factory worker, he walked towards the rear entrance of the plant, merging with the hundreds of others on their way to their jobs. The shrubbery along the walkway that once beautified the lawns now barely survived each season. The stream of people, nodding hellos and muttering sleepily, headed inside from the autumn morning chill, gritting their teeth, preparing for another work day.

Keith, like most everybody, had a morning routine that made coming in bearable. A routine that provided comfort in its predictability. Many of the workers went to the cafeteria 10 to 15 minutes before the 8 A.M. start time. This was a chance for a cup of Joe, some chat among friends about the family, politics, sports, and the business of the shop floor. Managers and supervisors never entered this place. The cafeteria had 16 picnic tables lined up in two parallel rows. Against the back wall stood the vending machines. They were vintage models, but could still provide edible snacks on request. Dave said the candy bar machine looked like the condom dispenser in the bathroom of Flaherty's bar. The walls lit by harsh fluorescent lights overhead were painted a sickly green that hadn't been retouched in years. This was not the sort of place you would be proud to bring your spouse or friends. But the workers ignored the dinginess because it was their escape and refuge.

Keith entered the cafeteria. It was Wednesday, and he had taken vacation days Monday and Tuesday to spend with his daughter. In days past, he would've been anxious to catch up on the latest news and gossip. Now, it was the meager comfort of a hot chocolate that he craved.

But when he entered the cafeteria this day, he immediately knew something big was up. Major change was on the way. He felt an unfamiliar tingle at the nape of his neck. The voices of his friends were at a high, fevered pitch. He could see they were nervous and unsettled.

As Keith neared the knot of his co-workers, only Bobby looked up to greet him. "Hey, Keith, how's little Crystal doing? Or not so little—which birthday was this?"

"Her sixth. She's just fine, thanks," Keith answered distantly. He was pained that he had to leave his daughter behind with her aunt each morning before work. He focused on a strident voice in the crowd. "Here we go again. Now it's Teamwork! Another bright idea that will solve all our problems. We've seen so many fixes, from robots and computers, to QC circles and time studies. If only they would wake up and listen to us. I mean really listen to us."

Another voice added, "I've been with this company for over 17 years, right here on the factory floor helping make our product. Back then Old Sam knew all 400 of us. Let me tell you, we put out the best product in the world. Nobody could touch us. The Japanese and these other foreign companies couldn't even come close to meeting our quality. Hey, there were problems then, and of course, you always felt underpaid, but I still wish we could get back to the way it was."

Keith hung back from the group, not all ready to dive in. As he hovered, Suzanne looked up and called, "Hey, Keith, welcome back to the nuthouse! Did you hear they have a new system coming? We're all going to work in Teams now. Can you believe it? What else are they going to come up with?" He shrugged his shoulders and listened intently to the news. An older fellow gibed, "Do you think they'll give us Team uniforms with numbers?" One of the women at the table retorted that he'd wear a big goose egg if numbers were assigned.

* * * *

"So here I am back two minutes and I've already stepped in it. Maybe I shouldn't have returned. Just picked up Crystal and hit the road heading west. But instead, here I am, in it up to my neck.

"These days, all of us in the plant and office are frustrated. I'm sure that management is not having a picnic either. There are so many problems—bad raw materials, poor equipment maintenance, even simple hand tools that don't get the job done. Who needs it?

"Out here on the floor, the answers always seem obvious and the solutions easy and cheap. But, management doesn't seem willing to look the situation in the eye and tackle the details. I just don't get it.

"Many of us feel that we don't get the respect and trust of managers. They act like we're trying to take advantage of them. And we feel the same way about the managers. Sure, there are some deadbeats who don't give the company a fair day's work, but they're only a handful. The tension between the managers and the workers, between them and us, just keeps rising in a vicious circle.

"Our problems really started seven years ago when Old Sam sold the business and the corporate professional managers came here. Computers and robots that none of us understood soon followed. They hired engineers to work the fancy equipment, but they didn't understand the product. These people acted like they had all the answers. It was too bad, because all we could do was sit back and watch them make major mistakes. There is some pleasure in saying, 'I told you so,' but who needs the hassle?

"Old Sam listened to us.

"Sam knew everybody in the plant. He was tough, but he was fair, and he and his managers knew what was going on. There were definite standards for product quality and for our behavior. We all knew that if you fell out of line, Old Sam would pay a visit and provide encouragement at high decibels!

"It was personal then, and we were more than an employee number and paycheck. Looking back, we didn't appreciate what he was doing for us. But you don't miss your water till the well runs dry. And our pride in our product and ourselves is as dry as a bone.

"Now they are talking about Teamwork. Where were they seven years ago? And why am I here now? Yeah, I should've taken off, but that old Chevy probably wouldn't have made it past the state line."

*   *   *   *

A female worker added to the discussion, "Well, if they ever ask me for my opinion, I'll tell them I see several major problems. We have to improve quality and reduce rework, scrap, and bad product going out the door. We have to meet our schedules and our promises to our customers. To do this, we need a leader that can gain our trust and can motivate every person to be their best. We've lost our pride.

"Sam would always say, 'We made that customer a promise and if *we* don't keep it, *we* will all be out of jobs.'

"Look! Over the last seven years we have had four different general managers, each with a different approach, attitude, and management staff. It seems like every time we finally learn to go left, they tell us to go right."

Keith listened further. "How can we be successful when we're forced to do things that are not in the best long-term interest of the company? They try to make the current month's profits look good. At the end of every month we ship product that we all know is not right, but we ship it anyway so that our shipment numbers are higher. Either the goods come back, or we lose another customer, or both. Keep that up, and we'll all be looking for work."

The bell signaling the beginning of the shift interrupted the bull session. Reluctantly, the workers got up, slugged down their beverages, and slowly filed out of the cafeteria. Bobby and Dave were the last to leave. They looked at one another and the Big Man sighed. "I saw on the news last night that a group of business executives went with the president to Japan. It seems to me they could've better spent their time in their own plants talking to their own people. I wonder when was the last time any of them did that?" They got up and went to work.

* * * *

Eight weeks ago, yet another general manager had arrived at the company. Still young enough for idealism, yet toughened up by several years in the corporate wars, Pat Forte was determined to make a difference. A personable guy, Pat liked people and was as level-headed as they came, but he hadn't lost his imagination on the job. His first order of business was to spend time in the trenches talking to the workers. He talked up cooperation between management and labor at every opportunity, although he didn't expect them to fully grasp the concept at this point. How could they, after years in a rut?

Pat knew that suspicions ran high on the floor. Everyone knew change was inevitable, but what form would it take? Even he didn't know for sure. And could this fresh-faced outsider provide the leadership? A lot of people didn't think he would last a year. Taking bets on his fate soon grew more popular than the football pool.

The incident that sparked the commotion in the cafeteria had occurred two days before when Pat was talking to Frank, a machinist next to Keith. Frank was usually pretty quiet and easy to get along with. He took it as it came. However, while talking to Pat about what had been going on the last few years, Frank nearly lost it.

"How can the front office expect us to be competitive without the tools, equipment, and materials we need? Maybe you, Mr. GM, should come out here and try to do this job. You'll see what we have to put up with every single day. It's ridiculous." Frank, not a talker, was just getting started. Surprised to hear the edge in his voice, those around him perked up their ears.

"It seems that as soon as a person puts a tie around his neck he loses his senses. Maybe it cuts off the blood to the brain. It doesn't take a Harvard degree to see that we aren't going to make good parts when the dies we use are worn and don't make tolerances. These machines need mainte-nance. You wonder why productivity is down. That's not to hard to figure out. The machine is down waiting for repairs 8 to 10 hours each week." Frank was really cooking now, and he had the full attention of about a dozen surprised co-workers.

"That's okay though. Just go back to your office and turn on your computer. Stare at your colored lights and play with your numbers. Everything will get all better." Frank looked straight into Pat's eyes, and expected to see fire.

Pat was moved. He understood how years of frustration and disrespect grind a person's dignity and self-worth into the ground. He was the son of a first generation immigrant millworker, a man whose pride survived his job, but whose health didn't. There wasn't a thing Pat could say in reply. They stood in silence for several minutes, as the tension dissipated into the air. That silence spoke of a mutual respect and Frank sensed that Pat truly understood him. Something in his eyes signaled that this man was different from all the rest.

Pat broke the spell. "We really are going to need the help of everyone in the plant to fix the problems. I can't and won't promise that this will turn in six months. But I'm going to make the emotional commitment and do everything in my power to make this business the best it can be."

"Look, I'm real sorry. I know it's not your fault. We've got good people out here. We just need some of the basics and this place can work as well as any." Frank turned away and started up his lathe.

"I know that. The key to success will be cooperation between the Management Team and the workers. We are going to build Teams of workers to solve problems, and to produce the product. We may or may not be world class, but I can tell you that we're going to be the best we can be." With that, Pat turned and walked off. He knew that it was time to take his message to the troops and to create some tangible results. Yet the scene with Frank had already left an indelible mark on those who had witnessed it.

First thing the next morning, a memo on bright yellow paper hung on the lunchroom bulletin board. In less than an hour, it was covered with hand-scribbled graffiti addressed to management. The memo announced the time and place of a series of four company meetings to be held the following week. Each would be 90 minutes in length and held in the cafeteria. The memo read that Pat and the Management Team would discuss the "Teamwork Strategy" and explain the changes that were to come. At the bottom of the page was written, "Attendance Mandatory for All Employees."

* * * *

"I'm not sure why but I can't get too worked up about this shakeup they're trying to sell. Not much will get my mind off my troubles.

"Teamwork! That word's on everyone's lips. Most people just laugh and say 'Here we go again.' That's the big joke these days, but the laughter sounds a little hollow to me. I think they're all afraid of getting their hopes up too high. And they're even more scared that if this fails it might mean our jobs.

"This time it may be different. But something about this guy Forte seems awfully smug. What's he in it for? Trying to be a hero, or was he sent here to do the hatchet job and get rid of this place? Anyhow, why should I care? I just want my time, my breaks, my check, and my hot chocolate. I'm not looking to switch gears even if we're all heading downhill. Let me be miserable; it feels comfortable."

KEY POINTS FOR DISCUSSION

(1) The company was founded and managed by Old Sam for many years. When he finally left, professional managers were unable to maintain the performance of the business. Why do you think they were unable to successfully implement new technologies and methods? Briefly discuss the history of your organization, focusing on the relationship of labor and management in each time period.

(2) Old Sam was a dictator and ran the business with a firm hand. What do you think were the problems and complaints of the workforce during his reign?

Chapter Three

The Big Meeting

"The people, especially on the shop floor, must work together."

T he day finally came, and at midday the workers were ushered into the cafeteria by their supervisors. There were over 100 gathered at each meeting, a sea of workers in their plain work clothes with smatterings of the gray, blue, and black of their suited superiors. While waiting for the meeting to begin, the supervisors stuck close by the vending machines. It was as though they were prepared to seek shelter behind them should the crowd get out of hand. They were out of their element and felt outnumbered and overwhelmed by the apparent strength in numbers of the workers.

The workers sat silently or spoke in whispers to each other, careful not to be overheard. They waited edgily, knowing that their world was about to be forever changed. The old-timers said their day was done, thinking that they would have to leave to make room for the younger workers, or just leave to reduce costs. Several of the younger workers hoped that the end result would be that certain supervisors would be fired or forced to leave.

Pat entered the cafeteria right on time. His sleeves rolled up and his tie loosened, he was smiling, almost grinning. There was an unmistakable bounce in his step. He beamed, and everyone saw it. The eyes of all in that room were glued to him, each person trying to read his expression, to imagine his thoughts.

After some initial joking comments to the workers in the front of the room about the "cheery green walls," he sat down on a picnic table top, one foot up on the seat. He addressed the entire group with a steady gaze. "Welcome. Glad you all could make it. Not that you had much choice." He smiled, continuing, "I know that everyone here is anxious to find out what the future holds. That's why we are here today. Before we get into that, I want to start by describing what I think are some of the problems you are up against each day. We are going to be a company that focuses on quality through empowerment. In other words, we, the managers, are going to start to listen to you, the workers. Pretty unusual, heh?

"I don't expect you to believe all that I say today. But I need you to listen to me, and listen carefully. Solving these problems is not my responsibility. These guys, your supervisors, can't solve these problems. Only you can. Our job is to get you the resources, the tools, and the cooperation of everyone you need to get this place back on its feet. Our job is to put the ball in your court.

"Let me tell you where I think we are." Pat turned to an easel with an oversized pad on it, and uncovered a sheet that listed the "Seven Deadly Sins of Our Company." "This list is different for every company. Let's look to put our own house in order." He proceeded to explain each point.

ILLUSTRATION 3–1

SEVEN DEADLY SINS OF OUR COMPANY

1. Lack of trust and respect by management.
2. Production schedules change daily/hourly.
3. Poor equipment maintenance.
4. Pay system provides little incentive for individual or group effort.
5. Sloppy product engineering.
6. New equipment not usable.
7. Lack of leadership and Teamwork in plant & office.

"First, there is a lack of mutual trust and respect between management and the workers. I see it here every day in the way the supervisors talk to you *and* the way you talk to the supervisors. Over the years both sides have lost a sense of respect for the other. Previous GMs were dictators, telling every single person here what to do. Didn't work too well, did it?

"Nobody likes to be told what to do without having a chance to voice an opinion. It also didn't help that previous management made some rotten decisions. It's hard to respect incompetence.

"Next, production schedules change daily, and sometimes even hourly." He paused for effect and scanned the room knowingly. In the silence, the whole group smiled as one at the obvious stupidity of that system. "Don't worry, we have more computers on the way. They should be here by week's end." This brought outright laughter. He had begun to thaw out the chill of fear in the room and to show that they might all, workers and supervisors alike, want the same thing.

"Where's Peter Horner, our beloved maintenance manager?" Pat saw a greasy hand go up in the back row.

Pete thought to himself, "Here it comes again. Now I'll get chewed out in front of everyone."

"I don't think I have ever met a more competent, harderworking fellow in my travels. You're a Florence Nightingale with wrenches. You use more bandaids and bubblegum than the local hospital and grade school combined." Pat stopped for a moment, and lowering his tone, said, "And it's because that's all you've been given to work with. If anyone else were in your shoes, this place would have fallen apart years ago."

Pat understood the traditional conflict between the maintenance group and production managers and workers. In every plant he had been in, these two functions were at odds. Maintenance is disgusted with the abuse of the machines by the workers, and the workers don't respect the ability of maintenance to repair and maintain the equipment. It becomes a vicious cycle perpetually feeding itself.

"We need to get everyone here, through Teamwork, to accept responsibility for the equipment. How we do this will become clear over time, but let me just say that maintenance is a priority on my list. I know that it is on yours." Pat saw a number of heads move up and down. He knew that his message was being considered.

"Now, let's talk about the matter closest to our hearts: money." He stopped to see the eyes of everyone focus directly on him. Pat knew that money motivates, but that traditional compensation systems have provided little incentive for people to work hard *and* to cooperate with each other.

"I will not lower wages or lay people off until we have exhausted all other possibilities. We are all in this together.

"Today, each of you are paid an hourly wage. That's it. Your performance is rarely evaluated; many of you are at the top pay of your wage classification. In other words, whether or not you work hard and put in a good day's effort, your pay is the same and is guaranteed. There are a lot of you who see others getting paid the same amount and, in your opinion, they do half the work you do. To make matters worse, the opportunity to advance is negligible. Most of you are just glad to have jobs. You've given up the hope that there will be fairness *and* a chance to do better."

A hand went up and caught Pat's attention. A supervisor tried to signal not to interrupt, but Pat indicated it was okay to ask questions. "We have heard over the years that the company was considering profit sharing. There were some other types of systems brought up also. We don't want anything other than what we have. We wouldn't trust the company to tell us the truth and share the real numbers. Besides, sharing nothing gets us nothing." Everyone waited for a response.

"Let me say this. We have a lot to do before we change pay systems. The long-term answer is a combination of hourly pay and some simple, easily understood way to share the benefits of hard work and success. Meaningful performance appraisal is also a key part. Any changes, and I mean *any* changes, will be done with the participation and approval of the Management Team and each company member. Once we get some positive results and each of you trust me better, then we will tackle this issue."

Pat continued, "Any other questions?" There were none.

"Next, we have sloppy product engineering. This includes a lack of communication between our design people and our manufacturing people. Design changes are often late and poorly documented, and product specifications are often difficult to meet on the plant floor. You can't build it if it isn't designed to be built.

"Next, we have a number of monuments to our purchasing department and management. At times, the company has invested in new equipment. Unfortunately, it often

ILLUSTRATION 3–2

wasn't the *right* equipment. A lot of this machinery was large, technically advanced, and automated, but inflexible for the job we needed it to do. They tried to automate low-volume, poorly defined production processes. *You* would have selected smaller, less sophisticated equipment."

Pat heard a voice say, "Big bucks wasted." He acknowledged this, and went on. "The people who know most about the production process will be involved in the evaluation and selection of new equipment. We must move toward automation, but only where it makes sense."

Peter Horner, the maintenance manager, broke in, "Some of that equipment could work, but there are two problems. One, no one knows or wants to learn how to operate the machines. Second, we don't have the expertise to maintain and repair that stuff."

Pat responded, "I understand. You, I, and the *Teams* will have to work on that one." He paused, having gotten everyone's attention when he emphasized the word "Teams."

"Which brings me to the last point. In order for this company to be its very best, the people, especially on the shop floor, must work together to solve problems and get the job done. There are two types of Teams that we will use." He flipped the page of the pad, and it read:

* Improvement Project Teams
* Self-Directed Work Teams

"All you need to know for now is that each of you will be involved in solving these and other problems. *You* are going to participate in decision making. We all need to pull together. I can't do it. I don't have the answers. You do.

"The news isn't all bad. Don't feel that you are responsible for these problems. The good news is our strength, which is the character of the work force. We are here today, the lights are on and business continues as a result of your persistence and determination. You should feel proud of that accomplishment."

Pat paused, and grabbed the glass of water on the table next to him. His mind briefly wandered off to the phone call he knew awaited him after this meeting. He was skilled at visualizing his opponent at the other end of the phone line, at anticipating the demands that would be made. This would be the challenge of his career, and he was betting the minds, hearts, and jobs of the people that now sat in front of him that he could bargain for more time and hold off what most of the corporate officers thought was inevitable.

Pat began again. "Let me quickly explain what we are going to *do*. I've got three mottos that we will live or die by. These are the most important points. He turned another page, revealing his message titled "Our Keys to the Future."

ILLUSTRATION 3-3

OUR KEYS TO THE FUTURE

- Evolution, not revolution.
- Continuous Improvement via Teamwork and Total Quality.
- The customer is king.

Pat circled the first point. "The changes to the plant, office, and to your jobs will come slowly, at a rate that everyone should be able to accept. Don't be frustrated, change has to come slowly, so don't expect to come to work next week and find all our problems resolved. But, you should expect to see immediate progress. As a starting point, the first Employee Teams will attack simple problems like housekeeping and tool management."

"Keep in mind though, that we need to quickly achieve meaningful results for our customers and our corporate office."

An old-timer sitting in the front row raised his hand. "What will change the most? I've been here since the beginning of this place, and the only thing that ever really changes are the faces."

Pat looked at the supervisors standing by the vending machines. "Building Teams and giving the workers here a voice in the improvement process will be the basis of all we do. This new way of working will at first be hardest on the supervisors. For so many years managers were rewarded for being tough, and for making all the decisions. Now, they must learn to ask questions, get your ideas, and then help the Team make decisions. Be patient and help your supervisor evolve.

"Almost all the supervisors and workers will learn these new ways, but there may be a handful of you who will resist. You'll be given every possible chance to get on board, but if you don't make it, you'll find yourself pounding the pavement, looking for a new job."

"For the sake of this business, I am committed to Teamwork, and will let *no one*, not executives, managers, nor employees get in the way.

"Later, you'll see a movie about other companies that have used the same strategy, and you'll hear plant workers talk about their experiences. They all say that it isn't easy, that it can be almost painful at times, but that the benefits are worth it. For most of these companies, it took several years before they could say they had dramatically improved their performance and had really stamped out the big, major problems.

"Remember. We need to *evolve* quickly."

Pat turned and circled the next point. He spoke in an upbeat tone. "Okay. Someone explain Total Quality. What do you think it means?"

Pat could see people turn and whisper to their neighbors, testing their ideas. Maureen, a machine operator, stood and said, "Doing everything the best way." Another added, "No rejects to the customer." And another said, "And no errors in the plant." They understood instinctively what Quality was and knew they were not achieving it.

"You are all right. To achieve no defects we're all going to evaluate every single step in the manufacturing process and improve our machining, cutting, winding, stamping, assembly, and tooling procedures so that we can easily avoid making errors. Only 10 to 20 percent of our defects are because a worker isn't paying necessary attention. The majority are because our manufacturing processes are set up to create enough variation so that parts are made out of specification."

Frank spoke up, "Like those lousy, no good, garbage dies we use. You never know what you'll get out."

Pat added, "Just like those dies. Now, what about this 'Continuous Improvement' stuff?"

A voice blurted, "You keep gettin' better."

"So, in other words, every single day we find ways to improve our quality. We have to challenge the way we do things, and be willing to accept new ways. In some cases, you may even have to do extra measurements and record keeping, but you'll need this data to evaluate variation in the process."

Pat continued, "There is another part to this. Continuous Improvement also means that performance will be measured and that everyone will be shown the numbers, even some financial numbers. You're expected to always show at least some small quality, performance to schedule, or productivity improvements. You need to know how well you're doing to know whether or not progress is being made."

The workers sat silently, thinking about this point. There was a sense of uneasiness, like something needed to be said, but people were afraid to say it.

Bobby stood up slowly and said, "There are always rumors about how much money the company makes, about sales, and about the cost of scrap and rework, but I'm not sure we have ever been given that kind of information before. Neither Old Sam, nor any of the managers after him, have shared any of the financial information. How can we trust the numbers the company shows us?"

Pat responded, "First of all, most of the important performance numbers you'll need each day will be kept and determined by the Teams. Measures of Quality and Performance-to-Schedule will be displayed by each Team for everyone in the plant to see. We'll share the financial data monthly, and this will include numbers that are relevant and meaningful to you, such as profit margin percentages, sales dollars, etc. Whether or not you *trust* me is another matter. Each one of you must draw that conclusion in your own mind."

Pat continued, "One of our goals is to make this a *fun* place to work. We could easily become a company that people in the community consider as the best employer, and one that you could be very proud to work for. Success is really the responsibility of each of us, and not just our manager's job. We all have to work at building the level of trust needed to achieve these goals.

"Let me briefly show you the key performance numbers for the last several years." He turned several pages, and exposed graphs. For the next 15 minutes, he explained profitability, inventory turnover, estimates of the Cost of Quality, and productivity measures. There were many questions, and Pat knew that his credibility was on the line. He had to demonstrate his integrity. By the end, they seemed satisfied.

On each graph, he marked a point that represented the six-month goal. "We have to achieve these levels in six months, otherwise we could be in for some tough times." He didn't want to frighten or intimidate them, but he had to emphasize this point. The audience didn't seem to comprehend the vast changes that would be necessary to achieve such significant bottom line results.

"Which leads us to the last point. The customer is king. Your goal and my goal is to beat our competition by doing a better job of servicing the customer. Price, quality, and delivery. We need to be the best in all three to win back and keep our customer base.

"We're going to set up meetings that will teach you about the use of our product and about our customers."

Dave, who at 6 feet 4 inches and 270 pounds earned his Big Man moniker, called out and grabbed the attention of everyone in the room. "Sure, we need to know about our customers, but first, maybe we should learn more about what goes on in our own company. We build many different products that are sold to a variety of companies in several different industries. I don't think there are many workers who can explain all the production steps in the plant necessary to build even the basic products. We each just do our little piece and don't really have an understanding of the big picture. For example, I've never even been to our final assembly plant across the street. And I don't think too many people over there know what we do here. This has created real conflict between the two locations. I mean, it's to the point where the two plants have separate Christmas parties."

Everyone agreed. It was suggested that short tours be scheduled to familiarize everyone with the various aspects of production.

Pat brought the discussion back to the customer. "I have scheduled the vice president of purchasing of one of our largest customers to come here next month and talk to you about our products and about the opinions of their people about the quality of our work. You might hear some stuff that's not pretty. It seems they are having continuous problems with what we send them."

Pat scanned the audience to see how this was playing. He sensed that their minds were generally open and searching, this audience was hungry for answers. In that sea of expectation there flashed two angry eyes that Pat fixed on. They were Keith's, and he looked as though he were trying to stare Pat down. Pat asked the group even as his eyes met Keith's glare, "Can you imagine what the customers are saying?"

Keith couldn't help himself from spitting out, "Yeah, they're saying don't sell us a pack of lies!"

Pat couldn't mistake the challenge in that voice, but he knew that it wasn't the time to argue and debate. "Yeah, that and a whole lot worse," he concurred for the sake of the presentation.

Other workers expressed a strong desire to learn more about the customer and about the marketplace. They said that almost everyone in the plant felt the same. There wasn't a clear sense of who the customers were. The employees felt as if their completed work was being sealed in a bottle and tossed into the sea. Knowing the customers would make the work more meaningful and would make doing a quality job more personal. The questions asked during this session included, "Who are the most important customers, and why?"; "How much of our total business is done with each customer?"; "Why do customers buy from *us*?"; and "What do the customers complain about?".

Pat concluded this part of the discussion by again hammering home the point, "The customer is king. And we are his servants."

KEY POINTS FOR DISCUSSION

(1) Pat uses the Big Meeting as a way to explain his views of the current situation and to present a short-term action plan. What are the benefits of this type of companywide presentation? What are the risks of publicly announcing a new program? How should your company announce and communicate the initial Teamwork efforts?

(2) Pat lists the Seven Deadly Sins of Our Company. Why does he do this? How would this list read for your company? What are the strengths of your organization?

(3) Pat lists his three mottos for the Teamwork and Total Quality Program. Discuss what each of these should mean to your company?

(4) Pat emphasizes the importance of performance measurement. What are the performance measures presently used and communicated on your shop floor? Are there other measures the

plant should maintain and make available to the workers? Describe each, especially as it impacts Teamwork and Quality Performance.

(5) The workers highlight the need to learn about the entire manufacturing process, rather than just know about a small area of the plant. To what extent do people in your company understand the total production process? Why is it important, and what impact does this have on Teamwork and product quality? What steps should your company take to improve the knowledge of the workforce in this area?

(6) The workers in this company express a strong desire to learn about the customers and the end use of the product. To what extent is the shop floor in your company "close to the customer"? What steps should you take to improve this area?

Chapter Four

The Action Plan

"Give it a chance."

A t this point the lunchroom doors swung open noisily on their rusty hinges as a tall, casually dressed figure walked in. Clark was considered well-spoken and matter-of-fact, and people gravitated toward him due to his openness and to his ability to immediately make people feel good about themselves. Even though his thinning hair and horn-rimmed glasses gave him a bookish appearance he was widely accepted as one of the guys. He was a persuader and a charmer, a kind of natural born leader. Most of all he was a man of integrity, who had proven his ability to challenge traditional thinking and create solutions that stood the test of time. Clark rarely sought the spotlight, but rather took pleasure in seeing average people excel and get their share of the credit.

He was, however, impatient and unable to muster the inner strength to withstand bureaucratic processes. Life had led him to believe that his personal mission was to wreak havoc on bureaucracy whenever it stood in his way. He and Pat were old friends, and each brought a skill and a talent that the other needed for business success. They had worked together since they met some 10 years ago. Both were working at the corporate headquarters of a major steel corporation and had promising careers. Perhaps it was a mid-life crisis, but as they came to know each other they shared the realization that their career paths needed to drastically change.

Their careers had moved quickly and really skyrocketed, and the money was more than either could have hoped for. But, they shared a deeper sense that they were not directly affecting change, that they could not point to any one specific thing and feel a sense of accomplishment. Yes, they made day-to-day decisions that affected tens of thousands of lives, but those lives seemed so distant, and so impersonal.

They had become the enemy. They were the dreaded well-oiled bureaucrats and slick corporate politicians, spending most of their time defending turf and being loyal soldiers in the camp. Time had let slip away the hope they had held at the start of their business careers to be great leaders and masters of change. They had sensed that the world existed for them to mold and shape. And now, after all those years, they had no one who looked up to them. Some staff assistants did because they had to, and this was feigned affection. Instead they craved sincere personal respect, the kind that only comes from shared values and successful leadership. They looked behind them and saw no one in their own long shadows. They had touched no individual lives. The air was very thin in their self-made vacuum.

They decided to leave, and to give up the trappings of Fortune 500 senior management. Instead, they sought opportunities to turn around industrial business. During the last 10 years, they had directed such efforts at three midsize businesses. Two successes and one failure, that business lost to a customer base that had been stolen away and was impossible to get back. The highs were high, and the lows were off the scale. And they liked it that way. The rollercoaster fed them dizzying doses of adrenaline and self-respect.

And now they once again had the chance to transform a company and to make a difference.

*   *   *   *

"And speaking of servants, this fellow has arrived right on cue and is here to serve you. We're ready for you, Clark. Clark Ford joined our Management Team six weeks ago, and I know some of you already met him. His official title is "Director, Total Quality and Teamwork." As you might guess, he will be the chief coordinator of our Improvement efforts. He has already spent several weeks guiding our Management Team through education and discussion about these new concepts. Clark will explain what we're now going to *do*." With that, Pat thanked the group and made a quick exit from the cafeteria, heading toward his office. He felt all of those eyes on his back and wondered how much had sunk in, how much they'd believed. He knew he'd given it a good shot, but even as he shut his eyes to recall how it went, the only image in his mind was that of a ringing telephone. He knew that the next hour would test his patience and push his worst fears to the edge.

*   *   *   *

Clark stepped up front and turned to a new blank page and wrote in bright red magic marker:

* Improvement Project Teams
* Self-Directed Work Teams

As he addressed the crowd with a yardstick in his hand as a pointer he looked every inch the college professor. "Usually after a meeting like this, you leave not sure who is going to do what. Traditional managers will say that we need to improve, but they don't tell you what the game plan is to fix the problems and get better."

A voice shot back, "Sounds like you've been here for the last 10 years. How come you didn't introduce yourself sooner?" Everyone laughed. The ice broken, Clark knew he had safely made it over the first hurdle of acceptance.

"We'll use Improvement Project Teams to solve major problems that affect many different areas of the company. Workers from different departments in the plant and office form a group and recommend solutions to the stated problem.

"Self-Directed Work Teams will include approximately 85 percent of the workforce. These Teams are self-managed and Team members work together on a continuing daily basis, and are responsible for the day-to-day performance of their work areas.

"We are going to start with three Improvement Project Teams, and each will have approximately five Team members. These members will come from the plant, maintenance, the office, from anywhere in the company. The first project is housekeeping on the receiving and shipping docks. These areas are always a mess, and you can't expect quality performance when the place looks like a tornado just blew by.

"The second project is to improve the timeliness of the product design change notice information to the plant. The plant doesn't always get product design changes in time, and this results in rework, returned products, and unhappy customers. We can really help ourselves in the short term if we can reduce these errors to our customers.

"The third project is to improve the procedures for using the stamping dies. There are hundreds of die sets, and it is

ILLUSTRATION 4–1

THE TWO TYPES OF TEAMS

I. Improvement Project Teams

   * Solve major, companywide problems.

   * Include workers from different departments to recommend solutions.

II. Self-Directed Work Teams

   * Group of self-managed employees working as a Team on a continuing basis.

   * Responsible for the day-to-day performance of their work area.

---

extremely difficult to find the dies you need for the job. They are often scattered throughout the plant, and even when you find them in the die room, you cannot be sure the dies will perform correctly. Let's see, I was told a fellow named Frank might be interested in being on this Team."

Frank was there and stood up. He said, "I'll gladly be of assistance. Those things are so screwed up it'll take an army to get it straightened out. But I do think we can make progress." Frank changed his tone from conciliation to one of anger and doubt. "The big question is whether or not the company is really serious about all this."

Clark knew his response to this would be crucial. His strategy was to look them in the eye and tell the truth. He blinked just once before he said, "There isn't anything I can say that will convince you that there is a total commitment. Give it a chance. Participate on the Teams, and work

ILLUSTRATION 4–2

THE INITIAL IMPROVEMENT PROJECT TEAMS

- Housekeeping on receiving and shipping docks.
- Timeliness of product design change information.
- Procedures for using stamping dies.

---

to solve the problems. The only way you'll know whether or not all this stuff is for real is to put the ball in the company's court, tell us what needs to be done, and then see if we respond. That's all Pat, I, and the rest of the managers here are asking of you."

Frank said, "Fair enough," as he sat back down.

Clark continued and explained that these projects were selected because each would be relatively easy to carry out and serve as a successful trial for Teamwork as the workers and supervisors learned the process. He told them that they did not have to be on these initial Teams if they didn't want to be. Joining a Team in those early stages would be voluntary. Team members would be invited, and it would be fine to decline the offer.

"If anyone here would like to volunteer, then come and see me." Clark closed the meeting, and thanked everyone. It was time to get things done, to implement change, and he was anxious to help the people that sat before him solve problems that had plagued them for years. He also knew that many old-timers would struggle with change, resist the new ways that were necessary to improve quality. He would do everything in his power to help each person through the process. Some people would not make it, and they would have to find new jobs. That was the part that hurt the most, but they couldn't let the company suffer because a handful resisted. He had resolved himself to these realities and looked at the crowd departing the cafeteria with a mixed sensation of great anticipation and some small sadness.

*   *   *   *

The cafeteria emptied, and Keith remained staring at the dingy blank walls. "I can't believe I said that! What's the matter with me? Mouthing off like that when I know it's for nothing. I mean that guy is full of it, but that's no excuse.

"These last several days there's been lots of talk and debate about Teamwork. The majority are skeptics and nonbelievers. We simply don't trust this company. Just look at their record.

"Most of us don't believe anything real and meaningful will change, though deep down inside we really want it to. I guess it's fear of emotional commitment. And that's what Ginny would always accuse me of. She teased me about how such a big strong macho guy could be scared of a little gold ring. And of course, she was about 80 percent right. Well, I got over my fear, and committed every inch of my heart. And now every inch of it is in pieces.

Despite all the resistance, almost everyone agreed to give it a shot, and said they would be Team members if they were asked. In fact, a lot of them will probably be angry if they're not selected. Not me though. Not again."

*   *   *   *

Later that day, groups of workers on break milled about debating the morning meeting. Dave and Bobby were in hot debate. "Maybe we didn't fully understand what we were told. But it will never work! The supervisors and managers had been to classes and read books on this new strategy before the big meeting. Even they're not so sure.

What makes you the expert?" That was Dave, as trusting as ever of management. Over the years, he was a leader of the anti-management crusade and worked hard to unionize the plant, although these efforts had just barely been unsuccessful.

Bobby responded, "Yeah, but this makes sense. We've been saying for a long time that we want to be heard. These Teams will give us a chance to tell the managers what needs to be done." Bobby and Dave often disagreed, argued, and made up. But this issue challenged that relationship, and some resentment lingered after these squabbles.

It almost seemed the meeting didn't give any answers, but created a very long list of new questions and concerns. The laundry list of questions centered on the impact these changes would have on the individual. People wanted to know if this meant that they would have to work harder, and whether or not they would be allowed to openly talk about the real problems. Who will be on the Teams? What happens to the authority of the supervisors? If productivity improves, will some workers lose their jobs? The older workers were concerned that they could lose their jobs or have to take pay cuts if they didn't do well on Teams and had trouble learning these new skills and ideas. There was an overriding fear that Teamwork would create more problems than it would solve.

Each of these questions deeply concerned the workers. They felt as though they were traveling into the unknown. Many had been with the company a long time, and although they were frustrated, some felt it might be better to leave things as they were and not try to make such radical changes.

As they anxiously anticipated the next step the work force gradually came to realize that it had to be done. Damned if you do, and damned if you don't. Their real choice was whether or not they would place their fates into the hands of this new leadership, and only time would tell if they chose well.

KEY POINTS FOR DISCUSSION

(1) The company selected three Improvement Project Teams to begin the Teamwork journey. Why do you think they selected only three projects? What specific improvement projects should your company select in the initial stages of the improvement effort?

(2) After the Big Meeting, the workers are deeply concerned and fearful of the proposed changes. Do you think this reaction is justified? Briefly assess the degree of trust between the work force and management at your company.

Chapter Five

The View from
the Top Down

"Who's running this place, you or me?"

R oger Honlinks stepped from the long black limousine
that chauffeured him to work each day and headed to
the specially designed entrance for the chief executives
who housed their corporations in this building. The structure rose over 70 stories, and was made of white concrete,
marble, and mirrored glass. It stood shoulder-to-shoulder,
proud and majestic, with the finest buildings in downtown
Chicago. On this cold and windy morning, Honlinks
strolled inside, and the mirrored chrome elevator sped him
to his perch on the 60th floor.

Honlinks had successfully guided this corporation for 10
years. It consisted of seven divisions, totaling over $500
million in sales. These divisions were in a wide variety of
businesses, from steel to plastics, products with both in-

dustrial and consumer markets. And Honlinks considered himself an expert in each. He was a demanding, hard-driven man who never took no for an answer. It had to be done his way, or you'd best get out of the way. He often thought to himself, "I'm here to make money, not friends," and ruled the company with the same stiff-necked military style that brought him great honors in Vietnam. He was a decorated marine sergeant, and reveled in recounting the military pomp and circumstance of his past.

Honlinks' administrative assistant was Janice, a feisty and self-confident woman of forty who served as a cushion between Honlinks and the rest of the world. She always seemed to know what he was going to do before he did it, and while not always in agreement, she often softened the blows to those who sought Honlinks' approval, support, or assistance.

That morning, as always, Honlinks burst through the door, tossed his heavy overcoat onto the black leather couch, and entered the inner sanctum of his office. Janice chirped, "Good morning," and scooped up his coat and grabbed for a hanger. He immediately made his requests and finalized his schedule for the day as she followed him to his desk. Janice was the only one privileged to enter his domain without prior approval or an appointment. His staff of vice presidents had to call ahead for a meeting, and Honlinks rarely made himself available for idle chit chat. He called them when he wanted.

As she scribbled notes, Janice held her breath because she knew a firestorm was approaching. And then she heard the words she had hoped wouldn't come. "And get that traitor Pat on the line at 10 A.M. I have a feeling he's not following through on our plans. If he's doing what I think he's doing, you'll be sending him plane tickets to Chicago for a visit here, with me." With that, Honlinks pointed Janice out of the office as he sat down to devour the papers she'd placed before him. She closed the door behind her and stood frozen momentarily in the middle of the reception area.

She pulled open a drawer and removed a file titled "Total Quality." There were several dozen articles sent to Honlinks from corporate staff and division general managers. Months ago she had passed articles to Honlinks for comment and review. There had been a lot of talk about the company needing to do a better job on Quality. Staff and managers often described the company as being old-line and in need of new, contemporary ideas and management techniques, like Employee Teamwork. There were a lot of success stories. She remembered asking him for a response. Honlinks had looked at her, and retorted, "Just what we need. More slick consultants and the inmates running the asylum. No thanks." He shoved the file with the articles back into her hands, and that ended discussion about TQM and Teamwork.

In meetings with staff and general managers, it had also come up, and Honlinks dismissed it as a phenomenon that didn't fit their company. "We need to stay focused on our business plan, capital investment, engineering, and new product design efforts. New products are the seeds for the future. Let's not veer off course and expend our energies on work force issues."

Honlinks let his staff believe he was uninformed on the topic. In fact, he was a voracious reader of a wide range of subjects, from military history and philosophy, to science and astronomy. He also read the weekly and monthly business journals, and as a result, was well educated on the subjects of Employee Participation and Total Quality Management. After all, there had been a continuous stream of success stories published in these magazines. And even though he played dumb, he could easily have been a speaker on the subject. He knew the buzzwords and the main ideas, and it all made logical sense. But he felt a gut reaction against it. It just didn't seem to fit his company, and he just couldn't envision the application and implementation of Employee Teamwork. Especially in a union environment, which several of his divisions had to endure.

Throughout his military and business career, he was rewarded for *his* decision-making. People had to do as he told them. Building consensus and waiting for everyone to buy in and agree to decisions would take too long. You couldn't be responsive.

Besides, Employee Involvement and Teambuilding was a bit too soft, too touchy-feely. He envisioned wishy-washy behavioral psychologists roaming his companies leading yoga and breathing exercises before each meeting. It all looked good on paper, and the reported results were impressive, but he didn't believe at face value everything he read. Beneath the surface it appeared costly and required too many years to achieve tangible results.

He thought back to Vietnam, when he led his marine outfit through treacherous fighting. They often dared the bullets and mortar fire overhead since they were determined to constantly move forward and attack the enemy. He simply couldn't imagine turning to his men and asking them what they thought they should do to solve this little fix they were in. Opinion polls under fire would mean sure death.

He had spent a year as an industrial engineer in a manufacturing plant during his rise up the corporate ladder. He experienced firsthand the traditional conflict, the cops-and-robbers mentality between labor and management. The application of Teambuilding on the shop floor meant both sides had to lay down their guns. It just didn't seem realistic to expect this to hold up as a long-term solution. The degree of trust required for success on both sides could not be achieved.

Employee Involvement and Teambuilding simply did not fit Roger Honlinks' vision of the world. There could be only one boss, and the job was already taken.

* * * *

Pat returned from the cafeteria and entered his office. He felt good about the response of the work force. Sure, they were frustrated and skeptical, but this was a typical response.

On his desk there was a stack of message slips from other general managers in the corporation that were several days old and intentionally ignored. His excuse would be that he was out of town and had some catching up to do before he took time to return phone calls. In reality, he wanted to delay their efforts for as long as possible.

The phone rang and Pat's secretary from the pool said, "It's Janice, from Chicago. Should I put her through? She says it's urgent."

Pat sat back and the phone rang. He looked out the window of his office at a group of teenagers hanging out on the street corner, the same bunch that seemed to be there every morning when he took his calls.

"Pat, Janice here. I'm calling for Roger. I just wanted to tell you there has been no progress in getting him to consider TQM and Teamwork. He seems very angry with you. Please handle yourself carefully. He's not in a very good mood this morning."

"Thanks for the warning, Jan. Put the old boy through." The kids on the street were playing a sort of monkey in the middle game with a smaller boy's hat. It seemed pretty pathetic for these teenagers to be killing time like that.

"Roger, good morning. Glad you called, I was just about to call you." Pat knew this wouldn't help.

"What's going on? You know why you were sent there. The only thing you've managed to do so far is frustrate and alienate every general manager we've got. I expected the consolidation plans to be complete by next week, and you've conveniently made yourself unavailable. Who's running this place, you or me?" Pat heard Honlinks pound his desk with his fist.

"Roger, you have my full cooperation. It seems a waste of time to figure out how to move several of our product lines to other plants when you don't have a buyer for the other product lines. Selling some of this equipment off will take time, and I think lining up these buyers should come first. Once we know we can sell that stuff, then let's plan how to consolidate the rest of manufacturing to your other locations." As Pat spoke, he thought, "It's a weekday. Those kids should be in school, learning. Instead they're goofing off, missing any opportunity to realize their potential."

Honlinks gained control of himself. "That's not what we agreed. That's not what the board of directors voted. I want that place closed, lock, stock, and barrel, lights out, within the next six months. Period. If you can't or won't do it, I'll get someone who will."

"I think this place has potential. We can turn it around and make it work if you give it a chance." This was the claim that Pat knew would push Honlinks to the edge.

"Oh. You think you can save it. That place hasn't turned a profit in seven years. The union just missed organizing the plant by a handful of votes last year. And you think you can save it." Honlinks spoke sarcastically, trying to keep himself calm. He crossed and uncrossed his custom made rattlesnake cowboy boots beneath his desk.

Pat knew he had an opening, and went for it. He saw the foolishness and frustration of the kids on the street corner, and somehow knew that they were part of this as well. He spoke with firmness and conviction, raising his voice to let his opponent know he was willing to lay his job on the line. "You and your simple solutions. Go ahead, quit here. You'll do some financial manipulations and you'll make this shutdown turn a profit. It will smell wonderful on the outside, but inside it's rotten. Short term, Roger, just short term." He continued, "Did you ever think that maybe these people are losing because it's *your* fault. Not theirs. *You* don't know how to manage them, to lead them, to motivate them. You might have been great on the battlefield, but these good people think you and your company stink. You're just lucky the competition is every bit as lousy. Look, it's a game of perceptions. And the people who are putting your products together are fed up with your arrogance. If you want to cut and run, go ahead. Count me out. But if you've got a shred of guts left, then let's put our heads together and figure out what to do to make this place the winner it can be." The small group of kids in the street was growing in numbers. They gave up taunting the little kid and turned their attention to something in the street beyond Pat's view.

Honlinks sat back. He knew this was insubordination, and it could not be tolerated. But there was a gutsiness to this kid Pat he liked. He had trouble remembering the last time someone stood up to him and told him he was wrong. It was somehow refreshing and admirable, and inside himself he applauded the performance.

Honlinks responded in a monotone, after a prolonged silence, "Two weeks from Friday I expect to see you in my office. That's the earliest possible day. Be prepared to explain yourself."

Pat heard the receiver on the other end click. He knew he had won round one.

KEY POINTS FOR DISCUSSION

(1) Pat is the originator and driving force behind Teamwork and Total Quality in this company, not the corporate office. Discuss the potential impact this could have on long term success. Why is your company pursuing Teamwork? Who is the driving force behind your effort, and how will this impact the long term outcome?

(2) The management styles of Pat and Honlinks appear quite different. Describe the management styles of the senior managers in your company. To what extent do you believe these styles are supportive of Teamwork? What are the perceived strengths and weaknesses of your senior management Team to build a Teamwork and Total Quality System?

Chapter Six
A Look in the Mirror

"Let the games begin."

N ow every single person in the company was facing change squarely in the face. The initial steps would be difficult ones for both managers and workers. Grasping this new way of working together, of communicating, of managing and leading, and of building new relationships, would challenge the traditions that had grown up over many decades. Some managers and supervisors initially felt that this meant the old ways were rejected and had failed, and that what they had put in place was fundamentally wrong. They did not want to believe this, and to avoid that negative feeling, they argued in their minds that Teamwork would not work, that it could not change the company's performance.

These people's only failure was in not recognizing change as a natural process, rather than some guilty verdict on the old ways. It simply meant that every individual had to seriously consider how he or she could be even better, to grow even stronger, by giving everyone in the company an opportunity to participate and be heard.

*　*　*　*

Pat and Clark huddled each morning before meeting with the Management Team. Pat's office looked very "unexecutive." There wasn't the traditional large mahogany desk and chair. Instead, he had a big, plain oval table in the middle of the room. The walls were plastered with chalkboards and large tablets, and several filing cabinets with constantly slamming drawers stood in the corner. A piece of lined paper torn from a spiral notebook was tacked to the wall next to the window. It was the only decoration that graced the walls. It read in Pat's own hurried handwriting, "The Customer is King," and had a doodle of a crown scribbled on it. This was a working office/ conference room, and it was in continual use by the Management Team.

This particular morning Pat and Clark spoke behind a closed door, and the novelty of that was noticed by everyone who passed.

Pat stood next to a board that had a heading "Improvement Project Team Status." He reviewed these notes one more time, and turned to Clark, "Well, today we finalize the member list of our first Improvement Project Teams. We need to go to a full court press to get these Teams moving."

Clark responded, "Right now, supervisors training as Team Coordinators are talking to potential Team members, inviting them to participate. We actually had quite a number of volunteers, the response has been excellent. I sense these people are ready for this."

"Have we explained the 'Ten Improvement Project Team Rules' to the company supervisors and managers? We've got to impress that all projects be conducted according to these rules and standards. Remember, *we* learned them the hard way," Pat chided Clark.

"Just so happens I have a stack of copies that we'll distribute to everyone and post on the bulletin boards throughout this place. If we carve them on stone tablets they'll be a little tough to handle." Clark handed a copy to Pat for approval. He read the page.

"I tell you Clark, just about every time we reach this point it feels like I'm right on the edge of the high diving board." Clark met his burning gaze. "I think the pool's plenty deep on this end."

"Right. Let's do it." Pat handed the papers back to Clark. "You know I've got to see Honlinks in two weeks and I want to report the status of these projects to him. Unfortunately, no way is two weeks enough time to show results and the impact these efforts can have." Pat put his hands together, elbows on the desk, chin resting on his fingertips and brooded. He reminded Clark of the altar boy he knew Pat had once been.

They both grunted halfheartedly from time to time as a silence descended on their discussion about the presentation strategy. Suddenly Clark interjected, "Whoa, remember that opinion survey we did several years ago at that other company, the one by the company employees? That hit the bigwigs like a ton of bricks."

That was the answer they were searching for. Why not let the people give Honlinks their evaluation of the company? Let them speak to the heart of the matter, and by doing so tell Honlinks the depth of the problem and the potential for improvement. They both knew what the survey results would show, and that Honlinks couldn't resist the direct challenge this would toss in his lap.

ILLUSTRATION 6–1

TEN IMPROVEMENT PROJECT TEAM RULES

1. Project objectives are measurable and can be achieved in the short term.

2. Coordinator has clout and is unbiased toward a solution.

3. Project workplan and implementation plan are clearly defined.

4. The problem is studied before a solution is created.

5. Meeting minutes are posted and feedback is requested.

6. Skeptics are involved on the Team.

7. Team members communicate frequently with supervisors.

8. Recommendations are presented to management for approval.

9. Participation is voluntary.

10. Project Team lives on and monitors the new system.

Pat looked up at Clark with a devilish grin, "Thank you, son, for an answered prayer!" Pat and Clark would set out to design the survey questionnaire that would paint an accurate picture of the workers' perceptions, and assess the potential for improvement.

* * * *

"Three A.M.? And I'm wide awake again. Man, I haven't had a solid night's sleep in how long? I was having a dream; I think Virginia was asking me a question. I must be losing it. Well, it's been a year next week since she's gone. It's weird, 'cause there's so much I wanted to ask her. I mean, I was supposed to be the withholding one, but I didn't really know what she was thinking. Even about me. I know what she said, but did she really love me? Am I a decent father? I guess I should ask Crystal that, but how could I? Her aunt tries to fill in the blank spots, but she's not Virginia. How could she be? What do I know about what a six-year-old girl needs anyway? I take her to the ballpark and I can tell she has to work up some enthusiasm just to make me feel good. Whoa, what am I doing to myself here? These are great thoughts to relax me.

"Let's see what's on the idiot box. That usually puts me to sleep. Heh, here's the answer for me. A little hair weave, give me that manly look, or how about 1-900-Luv-Line? Nah, I get enough abuse at work by my supervisors. I'll pass. No, thanks, preacherman, I know you can't buy miracles, although I know a company that might be interested. Here we go, a cool flick. It's from the '50s, a sci-fi story about this average guy who gets dusted by a radioactive cloud and starts to grow smaller and smaller. This is the scene where he fights off the family cat with a knitting needle and he's the size of a mouse. What's it called, *The Unbelievable Shrinking Guy*? Sounds like my life story.

"Everything started off bright and shiny. I wasn't a whiz in high school, but I had decent grades, a good shot at college, maybe even some scholarship bucks for athletics. And even when Dad got sick and family finances drove me to work I didn't feel too bummed out. I learned a skill, machining, and got pretty good at it and started pulling down a respectable salary by the time I was 21. I was able to move out, get a nice apartment, and even when Dad died I was lucky to meet Ginny. She helped me hold it all together. Shortly after, we married, and I got this job at the plant. I guess those were the glory days, especially when Crystal was born. Since then, somehow, things started to slip away. I felt like I was in a rut long before her illness. Then the funeral. It all knocked me down notch by notch, shrinking me down to next to nothing. Work became the dregs. I got so small that down started to look like up. You get used to the new scale of things at the bottom of the gutter. The curb looks 10 stories high, and you give up any hope of climbing out.

"Bright spots? My daughter. No, *our* daughter. No wonder I'm afraid of what she thinks of me. I've lost my pride. I've let myself slip too far down, and it'll take a hundred helping hands to pull this boy up. Ginny, what am I going to do now?"

*   *   *   *

Clark stood leaning against the wall by the cafeteria door and read his notes on the engineering change notice system. He was preparing for the kickoff meeting scheduled for tomorrow with the Project Team. The Team members would include Sandy from order entry, Fran from drafting, Steve from accounting, Billy from product engineering, and Keith, who was a machinist in the plant.

Keith, entering on his break, saw Clark and approached him. He wanted more information about the Team he had gotten himself wrapped up in. "Well, I guess I'm as ready as I'll ever be for our meeting tomorrow. So, what will we be doing?"

Clark was glad to see Keith. He knew he had the potential to be a positive force in the plant, that he was a significant influence on the opinion of the other workers. Clark could also see that Keith was carrying an unknown but very heavy weight on his shoulders. He had sincerely hoped Keith would come around and join in on the initial Teams. "All we'll do is talk about our project strategy. This is a challenging problem because it impacts almost all plant workers, *and* the solution will require the participation and cooperation of engineering."

Keith wanted to grab on to something more solid. He gazed out at his fellow workers hunched over their lunches. "In the old days, the managers and supervisors would have formed a committee to deal with the problem. This resulted in next to nothing getting done. There was always a lot of talk, but not much action. Who's going to make sure the Team's ideas are implemented?" Keith asked nonchalantly, trying not to seem too eager for answers, still hedging his emotional bets about getting in too deep.

Clark explained that he would facilitate and coordinate the initial Teams and that in the future managers from all areas of the company would be assigned to coordinate Improvement Project Teams. *They* are responsible to get things done. Also, the Teams will present their recommendations to senior management. This will also ensure that the right solutions would be selected and get followed up. This gives the Teams total visibility to the highest levels of the company. He concluded, "Improvement Project Teams are extremely effective at solving problems. Good ideas will get done, I promise."

"Yeah, promises, promises," Keith thought as he nodded at Clark and headed to lunch. Keith saw Fran, the draftsman, eating at a table with several other plant workers. He decided to join them. "Mind if I butt in?"

Predictably, the group was talking about the Teams, and Fran was answering a question. "After the big meeting the other day, my supervisor asks if I would like to be a

ILLUSTRATION 6–2

IMPROVEMENT PROJECT TEAM GOALS

1. Reduce rework due to late design change information by 70 percent.

2. Reduce time to approve product design changes by 50 percent.

3. Learn problem-solving techniques.

4. Establish continuous measurement and reporting system for product design changes.

---

member of the Improvement Project Team. I said fine, I'm glad to help out. So, my supervisor gives me this piece of paper that lists the four goals of the Team." Fran pulled out the sheet and placed it on the table for all to see. "This was written by Clark, the Project Coordinator. This goal statement explains what we will be trying to accomplish."

"Keith, I never thought I'd see the day when you would join up and do all this baloney." That was Jimmy, a maintenance worker, who was a close friend of Keith's. Jimmy had lobbied to get on a Team that improved the maintenance system in the plant. He thought management picked the wrong set of projects to get started.

"Jim, like I've always said, this place has given me a real taste for baloney." The group laughed as he pulled a bologna and swiss sandwich from his brown bag. Keith returned the discussion to the goal statement. "Anyhow, these performance improvements are going to be pretty tough to achieve on that project in such a short time period. I think you've got to set some measurable goals. Otherwise, you'd never know how you're doing."

Fran responded, "Sure, so long as all our efforts throughout the project are aimed at meeting these goals, we'll get the job done. Having clearly stated goals will keep us from getting off on a sidetrack."

Jimmy, from maintenance, barely looking up from his deviled eggs, laughed sardonically, "You've even got a bean counter on the Team? What good will that do?"

Keith, surprised by his own vehemence, said, "Look, I'm convinced that the selected Team members are the most qualified employees to develop the new system. Each of us has had a lot of experience with the problem and I think we all understand how things work, or don't work, around here. In fact, I bet Steve, the bean counter, will be a real asset."

"Who's the engineer on the project?," someone asked.

"Billy," said Fran quietly. There was a sudden hush, as a sense of doom crept over the group. Up until then, they were turned on by the thought of getting a chance to *do* something about the situation.

"Why would they let that goofball on the Team? Why he's the biggest offender in engineering we got. I've asked that guy for help and information over and over, and got nowhere. Good luck, Team. Hah," Jimmy sighed bitterly. "We always manage to screw ourselves up. Nobody has to beat us. We do it to ourselves."

Keith, feeling sore about Jimmy's badmouthing the Team and, by extension, his participation in it, saw the bright side to this. "Maybe, that's why he's on the Team. Heck, you can be sure that he's going to hear our side. Maybe he'll learn something. Let's face it, there's no point in preaching to the choir." Against his own gut Keith was defending the setup.

Fran sat back and thought for a moment, "Maybe it hasn't all been his fault, either."

Keith continued, "The Team members are also responsible for continually explaining our project to as many other people in the plant as possible so that we can get their ideas, too. After every Team meeting, a memo will be posted in the plant. These memos are a brief summary of everything the Team discussed and did. They'll keep everyone informed about our efforts and encourage others to share their opinions with the Project Team members. It's not as though we are the only ones working on the problem. We'll need your half-baked ideas, too, Jimbo."

Jimmy laughed, letting the gibe roll off him, "How often and where are these meetings going to be held? How about down at Flaherty's? A drink or two will stir the creative juices."

"Let's hope it doesn't come to that. I understand that during the project we'll meet one day each week for no more than one hour. These formal meetings are to review information gathered since the last meeting, to agree on recommendations, and to set tasks to be met before the next meeting. They refurbished the old tool room and made it into a conference room. Anybody seen it? It's real sharp."

Fran said, "Yup. We're not going to get any readier by talking about it. As the Romans used to say, let the games begin."

Jimmy winked at him. "Yeah, but are you one of the Christians or one of the lions?"

*   *   *   *

It was 6 A.M., and Pat had just arrived in his still-darkened office. He was expecting Clark and Terry and two plant workers to join him at 6:30 A.M. to help design the employee survey.

Terry was the operations manager, and had been with the company almost from the beginning. He was a survivor, a political gamesman who knew how to get what he wanted. Terry was always ready to bargain and negotiate patiently for his end. The organizational structure was such that the frontline supervisors in the plant reported directly to Terry. He was their boss, and he played the role to the hilt. He liked to intimidate, and throw his weight around just to see his people jump. He was, in all respects, the traditional manufacturing manager. The plant workers had watched him closely since Pat's arrival. They knew the two personalities would clash, that there would only be room enough for one of them in that particular town. In the past, when new general managers and their people came in, Terry would outwardly do everything possible to win their good graces. But behind the scenes, he was working overtime to derail any changes. He wanted to do things the old way, which was his way. He was smart, clever, and proved over time to be more streetwise than any of the other managers dispatched to run the company.

Terry knew that Pat and Clark would be his greatest challenge. He already knew they had him pegged, that there was nothing he could do to mask his motives. He also knew that he had to make the conversion to coach, and be what they wanted him to be, or lose the only job he'd had in the last 25 years. It wasn't that he didn't understand what they wanted. He could do it, probably as well as anyone. And it wasn't even that he particularly disagreed with their new ideas. It was his ego that got in the way. He was a power addict, and lived for the next chance to manipulate people and get his way. This was his turn on. He was like the self-acknowledged alcoholic who couldn't stay away from the juice.

Beneath the glow of the solitary light on the table in his office, sipping black coffee, Pat sat back and thought about Terry. He had met men like Terry before, and felt strongly that Terry would have to be removed from his position. He had decided to give him every opportunity though, and this morning he and Clark would put his future on the table for discussion along with several other topics.

Pat did not consider Terry and his seniority within the company sacred. He couldn't, although he did respect the part of Terry that had put the best interests of the company first in much of what he did. Pat knew, however, that he was misguided. Pat's priority was to be sure that everyone in the company considered his treatment of Terry fair and honest. He wasn't going to work sneakily behind the scenes to undermine him. That wasn't Pat's style. Up front and in your face was how Pat handled business matters, and the work force respected that. Pat looked out the window as the first rays of dawn brightened the early winter sky.

At 6:30 A.M., Robert and Dot, the two plant employees, gingerly knocked on the door. Right behind them Clark and Terry arrived. Pat looked at the chilly group, "Glad to see everyone could make it. Have some coffee if you'd like to warm up. We'll need to get this done quickly. We've got that Improvement Project Team meeting at 9 A.M."

With that, they began tossing around ideas about the survey. They all agreed it should be limited to no more than a dozen questions, yet cover all major company areas. For each question, the employee would rate the company with an A, B, C, D, or F. "Using a grade scale will be familiar. Just like in school, we'll end up with a report card for the Management Team." Clark continued, "And if we do the same survey every six months, we'll measure the effect of Teamwork and Total Quality on the perceptions of our employees. It may or may not be the truth, but it will tell us what people think."

"Let's face it, reality *is* what people think. And if our workforce is dissatisfied, frustrated, and doesn't rate us or our programs very highly, then how can we expect them to be motivated to do quality work?" Pat spoke directly to Terry. "This will also highlight the areas that are considered to be our strengths as well as our weaknesses."

Clark added, "What you're saying is that the survey results are directly related to company quality performance. If the workforce thinks there is room for improvement, then there *is* room for improvement. You guys agree?" He turned to Dot and Robert.

Both felt they needed to be cautious with their words. They gave each other a sheepish look, and Dot started to speak hesitantly. Before she could say two words, Pat cut in. "You've got to speak your mind. Don't hold back. Speak your piece. It's now or never."

Dot swallowed and began, "I think one benefit of the survey is goodwill. People always appreciate when you ask their opinion. They'll feel like they are being listened to."

"That all depends on what you do to follow up. You'll have to do something that lets everyone know that you read their answers." Robert looked directly at Pat.

The meeting continued for 90 minutes, and Clark wrote the questions on a chalkboard as they batted issues back and forth. By the end of that time, a workable survey had taken shape.

During this time, Terry said very little, chipping in an obligatory remark here and there. He felt left out from this group, put off by the intensity of their involvement in the meeting. He couldn't tell who was supposed to be in charge, and he felt Pat and Clark were demeaning themselves by being so casual and chummy with Dot and Robert.

"Let's wrap up. It's 8 A.M. We'll bounce it off the Management Team, post the survey and ask everyone for additional comments or suggestions. We'll give it two days, then hand deliver the survey to each employee. Terry, you and the supervisors will pitch in on that one." Pat continued, "Special thanks to Dot and Robert for your help. Couldn't have done it without you."

As they left, Dot turned to the three remaining in the room. "Good luck," she said, as though she somehow empathetically knew Terry would need some additional assistance during the next hour with Pat and Clark.

ILLUSTRATION 6–3

COMPANYWIDE OPINION SURVEY

Objective

The purpose of this survey is to provide you with an opportunity to voice your opinion and tell it like it is. This will serve as management's report card, and will be ongoing. It will tell us how well we are doing and identify areas of our company that need further improvement.

Survey Questions

Please indicate your response for each question in the blank according to the following grading scale:

A - Excellent	D - Poor
B - Good	F - Failure
C - Fair	NO - No Opinion

1. ____ The quality of the current training programs.

2. ____ The maintenance of the equipment.

3. ____ The fairness and worth of the current compensation system.

4. ____ Management's ability to communicate with company personnel.

5. ____ The overall attitude of company personnel.

6. ____ Satisfaction with your current job.

7. ____ The degree of Teamwork throughout the company.

8. ____ The quality of our products.

9. ____ The efficiency of our offices.

10. ____ The efficiency of our manufacturing facilities.

11. ____ The quality and efficiency of our computer system.

12. ____ Your overall opinion of your supervisor.

Please include additional comments/criticisms on the back of this form.

Dot and Robert went to the cafeteria and grabbed a coffee before the work day began. They were feeling good, if not a little giddy from what they'd just been through. Robert kidded Dot, "By the way, I'll be flying to Chicago for the board of directors' meeting tomorrow. Take my calls, will you?" He and Dot laughed out loud.

Robert continued, "Pat and Clark are serious. Dead serious. If I didn't know better, the dynamic duo there will turn this place around. I still can't believe they had us in there working with them."

Dot responded, "Yeah. And they actually acted like they were listening. Miracle of miracles."

KEY POINTS FOR DISCUSSION

(1) The Ten Improvement Project Team Rules are extremely important and help avoid some of the problems that can arise during improvement efforts. Be sure to review each rule, and evaluate how well Keith's Team has met each point so far. Is your Team organized to meet these guidelines?

(2) Keith tells his peers that he believes the Team members are the right people to solve their assigned problem. Briefly have each person on your Team explain the contribution they expect to make. Why is each person there?

Chapter Seven

The Pain of Change

"Don't let them get to you. They'll grow up."

I t was now 8:55 A.M., and the group of people huddled in
this new but makeshift conference room talked to each
other in low whispers. The employee Team members sat in
metal folding chairs at a lunchroom table that had been
damaged, but was repaired for this new purpose. Several
supervisors sat in the back rows, with sheets titled "Hot
List—Expedite Items" in their laps. They had just come from
the daily status meeting where production priorities are
determined for the morning. It was a tough way to start the
day. A similar meeting was scheduled following lunch.

The room had been straightened up and refurbished.
The aroma of fresh paint lingered in the air, and an open
window allowed in a fresh morning breeze and sunlight.
Clark sat at the side of the table between two Team mem-

bers. Coffee cup in hand, he spoke to the group about the news and their kids, waiting on Pat and Terry before starting the crucial first Team meeting. Clark passed copies of the kickoff meeting agenda to everyone in attendance. Pat and Terry entered the room. Pat and Clark's eyes met, and Pat signaled with a small nod that everything had gone well. Terry looked pretty grim, but Clark felt relieved. "Look's as though we're all here." Pat sat in the back, against the wall. He began the meeting, emphasizing the importance of these initial projects. "I have total confidence in the people here this morning. I expect this Team to present recommendations on this matter in six weeks. You will be expected to explain your findings and plans to me and the other managers. We may even have some people from the corporate office join us." He went on to explain why he wanted this presentation. "By having you present your ideas directly to senior management you'll be motivated to be thorough and do a quality job. I don't think too many of you want to stand up and look foolish presenting solutions that obviously won't fly. Second, we've just set a deadline for you to meet. Otherwise, project Teams tend to analyze forever and never come to definite recommendations. And finally, it gives us a chance to formally communicate with each other."

Keith spoke up, "We're going to be spending time on this project and not at our machines, producing product. Has anyone thought about that?"

"Look, your time solving these problems is the best investment the company can make, even though you'll have to shut down your machines. The guideline is that you shouldn't spend more than two to three hours per week on this effort. We won't lose productivity if we use Teams efficiently. You know as well as I do that you can easily make up the production during the same 40-hour week if you want to. And you'll want to so that Teamwork continues."

Fran, the draftsman, was fidgeting in his seat since the beginning of the meeting. He pointed his question directly at Pat and Clark, "What happens if we have ideas that are in conflict with how managers think it should be done?"

Billy, the engineer, added, "Yeah. Who wins? What do we do, arm wrestle and the winner gets his way?"

Keith chuckled and so did the others. There was an overall feeling of apprehension. They wanted to know what they had gotten themselves into, and were groping for the right questions and answers. Billy continued, "I guess that's what we *have* been doing."

"The answer to your question, and it's a good one, is sitting right next to you. Clark, here, is your Team Coordinator. He'll conduct the Team meetings and help keep you organized. The coordinator is not a decision maker on the Team, but is there to be sure you're getting all the information, support, and help you need from all company areas. He'll be talking to the managers to keep them informed and supportive. Conflicts will be resolved quickly."

Fran, the draftsman, heard this and it only made him more uneasy. He felt a pressure like a vice squeezing his head, tightening slowly a turn at a time.

Clark added, "We are going to have supervisors learn how to coordinate Teams under my guidance. The Team coordinator will be from an area least affected by the problem the Team is trying to solve. This means the coordinator is neutral and unbiased towards any possible solution."

"Well, we've completed the first agenda item. Terry and I are out of here. Good luck, Team. See ya in six weeks." With that, Pat and Terry left the room.

Clark gained the Team's attention. He held up the meeting agenda. "Let's move right down each agenda item. The next question is whether or not our goal statement is complete."

Steve, the accountant, spoke for the first time. He was a loner, and dressed the part. Large-collared shirts, bellbottoms, and polyester leisure suits with patent leather shoes were mainstays of his wardrobe, and a common source of jokes throughout the plant. He was a nerd. "We are all gathered here to define the Teamwork methodology that will inexorably define the cultural setting for the future of this company. We are setting the model and example."

Everyone smiled, and Steve didn't know why. Billy said, "Yeah, we're setting the example for Teams." And Clark added this to the goal statement. Everyone agreed.

A supervisor sitting in the back cut in, "Remember, Team, that everyone has an important role. Stick together." This served as a reminder not to alienate anyone, even Steve.

"Next, is there anyone else who should be included full-time on the Team? Did we miss anyone? Remember that we can also invite anyone in the company to attend any meeting for their help and expertise." Clark laid this out for discussion.

Keith looked at Clark, "We might need the help of a receiving dock person. Some of this stuff affects them. And we may need to know about some of their problems."

The Team set about to review the project workplan. Clark passed out copies to each person. This was a brief description of what was to be done each week during the project. Clark's objective was to give them an outline that served as a starting point, and then let them adjust the schedule as required. Clark said, "We will do everything possible to meet our agreed upon workplan. However, we will not compromise the quality of our project to complete on time. We can extend our effort if absolutely necessary."

The Team did not understand all of the tasks on the workplan, but agreed to live with it for now. Clark had to explain why they needed to spend two whole weeks describing the current procedures followed for engineering

ILLUSTRATION 7–1

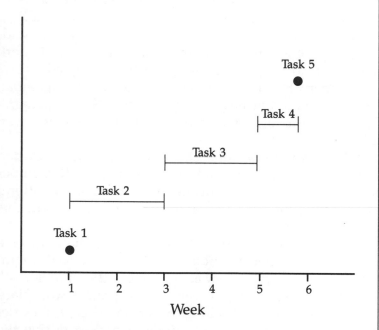

IMPROVEMENT PROJECT TEAM WORKPLAN

Product Design Change Notice System

Week

Task 1. Kickoff meeting.

Task 2. Review, evaluate, and document current system procedures.

Task 3. Create and document new system procedures.

Task 4. Prepare for management presentation.

Task 5. Management presentation.

design changes. He said, "I guarantee that while each of you may *think* you know how the current system works, or doesn't work, none of you has the total picture. In fact, you'll find that the current procedures are different from what you expect. To get an accurate description of what is going on today, we'll all need to share our experiences and understanding, and investigate what really goes on. We'll write it all down so that we're all talking the same language. Don't worry, you'll see."

Next on the agenda was a discussion about Teamwork and Total Quality. Clark handed out several articles and a small book on the subject that explained how Teamwork operates. Billy joked that he was glad he had built those new bookcases at home to hold all this new paperwork. Another supervisor followed Clark's comments, "If you haven't gotten it yet, *you* guys finally have the chance to put your heads together to attack our problems. Management now knows it cannot solve them themselves because *we* really do not understand the problems well enough. Only you do. We need your participation. In fact, we finally do understand that it is our responsibility to give you what you need to implement the solutions. And to make sure we stay the heck out of the way."

"Yeah, sometimes getting even simple stuff done was like going up against the Bears' front four," Fran said. "Management has bigger blockers than The Fridge on their Team," Keith added.

At this point each Team member cut loose on their frustrations with their work life during the last several years. Clark allowed it to flow. The supervisors in attendance had been prepared to respond to this type of discussion, which was fully anticipated. They listened sympathetically, and did not try to rewrite some pretty dismal history. They did emphasize, however, that everyone had now been given a chance to start fresh, with a clean slate, a new beginning. Even Steve proved to be a brother under the skin as he and Keith voiced the same opinions of management. Clark knew from experience that at the initial meetings, these feelings of anger and skepticism had to be vented and gotten out of the system so that they all could move on.

Clark also knew that he and the supervisors had to create an open environment in which the Team members felt comfortable enough to let their emotions go. After all, the issue of *trust* between management and labor was at the heart of their problems.

Clark said, "I expected each of you to let it all hang out at this meeting. In fact, to give you some focus you'll be receiving a plantwide survey that asks everyone to evaluate the company and the potential for improvement. It's a tool for helping to put the past behind us and redirect our energies away from destructive anger and to building a new and better future."

With that, the three supervisors stood and shook hands with each Team member. It was as though they had struck a pact which bound them together. They all sat back down with sighs of relief that the air had been cleared, and that the personal grievances they had held dear for so many years had begun to be cleansed from their consciences.

Clark forged ahead as the end of the hour drew near. The next subject was the education strategy for the Team. Clark spoke, "We are not going to put you through extensive, formal classroom training on problem-solving techniques. Many companies do this, but the return on this is often low. We don't want to bore you. Instead, we're going to spend our time on the problem at hand, and teach the techniques you'll need to know as you need to use them."

Clark had previously conducted several seminars for managers and supervisors on Teamwork and Total Quality. This prepared the Management Team for the Employee Team efforts. During these sessions he explained the methodology for structuring Teams, and taught the many problem-solving techniques available. He and Pat agreed that their experience had shown that conducting similar sessions for workers wasn't worthwhile. They needed a session that addressed their specific situation. It was best to teach the problem-solving techniques within the structure of the Teams at the meetings, and teach only the techniques that would be immediately applied.

Education had to be immediately linked to application in relevant situations, to immediate implementation of the techniques and ideas, otherwise the time and expense were lost. This was a pragmatic approach to Team education, arrived at from lessons learned the hard way.

At another company some years before, Clark had spent months designing a Total Quality education program for workers that lasted over 50 hours. That was how they decided to introduce these new concepts to the workforce, which consisted of a crew of streetwise steelworkers. By the end of the second session, the employees began finding excuses to not attend. It was turning into an enormous joke. The workers' perception was that *they* knew the problems, and all this fancy classroom and book stuff was a waste of time and too academic. They wanted to solve their problems, not learn statistics. Clark was nearly laughed out of the company. It was an experience he still recalled with a wince.

Now, Clark and the supervisors urged the Team members to read the articles and the book as soon as possible. They could stop by anytime during the week to have their questions answered and problems discussed.

Keith jumped in, "This makes some sense. I don't want to feel like I'm back in night school. Let's cut right to the heart of the matter. But I do suggest that you make this information available to everyone in the company. So if they want it, they got it." The whole Team agreed to this.

Clark eyed the clock and saw that time had expired. The meeting was ended, and Clark assigned tasks to be completed for the next go-round. He said, "The first step of problem solving is to create a complete description of the procedures, forms, and documents that make up the current system."

The Team members were assigned "To Do's." Some of them had to meet with selected persons to get a copy of a form or just to learn more about the current procedures. Others were asked to write down ideas about how the current system works and about the problems existing in the plant.

Clark set a time and place for the next meeting. The minutes of the kickoff meeting would be posted in the plant and office, and each Team member would get a copy. They were given binders to hold the paperwork of the project.

"So, Team," asked Billy, "did we score a touchdown off this kickoff?" Fran interjected, "I think we made it to the 50 yard line, at least."

Clark closed, "There is a lot of talent here, and much of it has been ignored over the years. If we all pull together, we can get this place humming again."

As they all stood to leave, they found themselves looking to Keith as if expecting some direction. Keith, sensing their need, looked carefully at Clark and the supervisors, and turned to his Team saying, "Okay. Let's go do it!" It was a rallying cry that would echo in their minds as they set out against the challenges ahead.

*   *   *   *

The next day, the meeting minutes of all three initial Teams were posted around the plant and office, as well as delivered to the work station of each Team member.

Employees throughout the company showed surprising interest, by carefully reading each of these memos. They became the subject of much debate within the company, inspiring a lot of speculation about the future of the company and the Teams, and the motives of management in all of this upheaval.

There was also a subtle resentment developing between the people on the Teams and a handful of others, who for various reasons, became either jealous or angry that they were not involved.

An older fellow, nicknamed Mule for a variety of reasons, some of them quite obvious, was the most anti-company, anti-management plant worker. He had been passed over for promotion to supervisor several times, and felt bitter about his fate. But Mule had the ears of many people at the plant, and Mule emphatically did not like the idea of Teamwork.

Mule, who was a machinist, Jimmy from maintenance, and Keith, often hung out together in the cafeteria. Others circulated around the group, but these three were especially tight.

One morning several days after the first round of Team meetings, Keith entered the cafeteria, and noted that the crowd surrounding Mule and Jimmy was unusually large. He could see Mule jawing to the group, and as he drew nearer he could sense the eyes of the group following him sideways.

"Gentlemen, good morning. So who saw the game last night?" Keith said a little insistently as though testing the waters. Normally, this would have elicited a round of wisecracks, but this time there was only silence. He didn't catch on right away. The group began to disperse in his presence, and no one said a word to him.

"Morning, Mule. Looks like we just had a huddle on the 50 yard line. What's the score?" Keith looked straight at Mule, trying to make eye contact to read the situation.

Mule turned towards Keith, and not looking at him said, "Goose eggs." He continued on past him. Keith stood silent as he watched him move deliberately across the cafeteria and out the door.

Dave, the Big Man, was standing nearby, and had witnessed the scene. He quietly said, "Keith, don't let them get to you. They'll grow up. Besides, we need you guys to hang tough and make it through."

"Yeah, right, right. We're *all* critics of management, but if the Teams win, then everyone, even Mule wins. That's why I decided to get into this Team garbage. And here's what I've got to put up with." Keith spun and stormed out of the lunchroom, his ears hot as he felt some shame mixed with his anger.

Keith walked back to his workstation, and he found the words *brown nose* spray painted in the appropriate color across his workbench. He quickly wirebrushed it off. "They'll have to kill me and drag me out of here first. We'll see what stubborn is, Mule, old buddy boy!" He wasn't going to be easily pushed around.

*   *   *   *

During the week, I plowed through the book and articles on Teamwork and wrote some notes on the current engineering change notice system. From what I've heard I'm not the only Team member who's getting the cold shoulder, but none of the others have become an outcast like me. I guess you find out who your friends are.

Tomorrow morning we attend our second meeting. Today, Pat and Clark stopped by to chat and to see how the Team was doing. "Wonderful," I said, "just wonderful," in a kind of snotty voice. What was I supposed to tell them in the middle of the plant with every eye in the place on me. I was embarrassed. I told them all was okay, and trying not to be too rude, I ignored them. They didn't seem to understand what was going on and the pressures I was under. I started this Teamwork with second thoughts, but now I'm getting close to the thirds, the fourths, and the finals.

*   *   *   *

The fax machine that sat outside Pat's office sprang suddenly to life. The high-pitched tone sent from afar switched the machine on, and it dutifully did its job printing the message. It was one paragraph, and as the call terminated and the word *complete* flashed across the monitor, the single page slowly dropped to its resting place in the basket below. It was the last fax sent that day.

The secretarial pool supported the many areas of the company. They were generally a trustworthy crew, but their human nature made them irresistibly curious, particularly in these days of uncertainty. The task of emptying the fax basket fell to Samantha, the most junior office worker. As she sorted the papers, she placed them in separate stacks based on destination.

There was something special about that last fax. It caught her eye, and while she rarely bothered to read other people's messages, she couldn't restrain her great interest. And anxiety.

> Pat, I've been trying to contact you and you refuse to return my call. Honlinks expects the consolidation plan in less than two weeks. I expect you will cooperate with the transfer of your main product lines to my plant. I also ran across potential buyers for your equipment. Germans who are expanding and need more capacity. You'll get a good price. Call me.

It was signed by the general manager of the division in Detroit.

After rereading it five times Samantha still wasn't sure of its meaning. She thought it must be some cruel joke, and tentatively placed it on Pat's desk. It was close to 5 o'clock, but before she left, she knew she had to investigate further. Looking side to side guiltily, she motioned to Mary to come with her to Pat's office. Mary obliged, looking slightly confused. They both read the fax, and as they looked at each other helplessly, there was no mistaking the meaning. Tears came to Mary's eyes.

There are few secrets kept in a company, regardless of size. Rumor mills churn mercilessly, often with deadly speed. By 9 A.M. the next day the fax had already begun to inflict the intended damage. Like a snake slowly squeezing life from its victim.

KEY POINTS FOR DISCUSSION

(1) The position of Team Coordinator is vital to a successful project. Why must this person be from an area least affected by the problem the Team is working to solve? Evaluate the neutrality and bias of your coordinator.

(2) The issue of trust was at the heart of the frustration and anger the workers felt. Briefly talk about trust in more detail, and explain what this means to you. What are some steps both management and the workforce can take to further strengthen the level of trust in your company?

(3) The education of the Team members in Teamwork and Total Quality is an important element for a successful project. Working with your Team Coordinator, briefly list each topic area on which you may require some additional education and information. This might include the subjects of workcell design, setup reduction, kanban and pull systems, production sequencing, statistical process control, or preventive maintenance. What books, magazines, videos, will your Team use to be sure you have a complete understanding of the Total Quality topic areas with which you will be involved?

(4) Unfortunately, peer pressure can be experienced by the initial Team members. Briefly discuss why Mule and the others rejected Keith and the Team members. What type of response do you expect from the others in your plant?

Chapter Eight
Understanding the Current System

"This is a discovery *process."*

I t was 8:45 A.M., and Keith and Fran were sitting tensely in the Team conference room, preparing for their second Team meeting to begin in 15 minutes. Of course, they too had been plugged into the rumor mill, and they knew that Clark would have to come clean with them. They were sure the rumor was true. But if so, then why all this fanfare about Teams, why this elaborate make-believe concerning their futures?

The other Team members and supervisors gathered gloomily. The latest rumor was only one of the uncomfortable concerns on their minds. Everyone described the experience of the last week in which they had been the target of criticism and peer pressure by a handful of vocal plant workers. Something had to be done to resolve this immediately. But of course, if the business were kaput, then all of that was irrelevant. The talk turned to finding new jobs, and the location of the nearest unemployment office.

Clark entered at 9 A.M. sharp. "Morning. Everyone set to go? Crack the windows. We'll need some fresh air. There are a few things to discuss, eh?" Clark was in control. As a leader in this time of crisis, he had to be. And he had to know the most intimate workings of the rumor mill.

"There are some people running around here like Chicken Little screaming, 'The sky is falling!' They're saying, 'How can we trust you? You lied. You didn't shoot straight.' And my answer to all of it is that this rumor that there's a plan to close us down is only partially true. What I mean is, there's still a chance to pull this out of the fire. What Pat said at the big meeting was absolutely dead on. We need to achieve real improvement, or else. The decision to pull the plug is *not*, I repeat, not yet final. And that's thanks to Pat." Clark lowered his voice and looked at each person. "The news shouldn't come as such a great big surprise. Be surprised that we have a leader who has faith in you and is willing to put his reputation on the line for his belief in all of us."

Keith, looking down at the still-unstained speckled carpeting at his feet, spoke for the group. There was an edge to his voice, the stress of the last several weeks obvious to everyone in the room. "There is a part of me that says just plain 'Quit.' Why go through all this agony? Go find another job. This company ain't worth it." He paused and caught his breath. "And then there's the part of me that wasn't built to quit. There's an emotional investment here, in this company, in the people, in the machinery. Don't let it go. But I tell you right now it's a dead heat." He paused as though waiting for the group to make the decision for him.

Steve, the accountant, broke the nerve-wracking silence. "Let's keep going. What's our agenda for this meeting?"

And Clark handed out the agenda to each person and began to read the minutes of the last meeting.

Keith sat quietly, staring at the paper in his hands. He suddenly became undone. "We can't just sit here and make believe nothing is happening." He looked piercingly at Clark and the supervisors. He fought to gain control of himself. "Let's tackle one problem at a time. What are we going to do with these pinheads that are harassing us? We are all under pressure by some workers in the plant to not cooperate. We need to solve *this* problem before we do anything else. Otherwise, I will leave the Team. It's not worth the hassle. Period."

The other Team members stared ahead blankly. They all agreed. There was silence.

Clark spoke, "You know, if life has taught me any one lesson, it's that there is always a positive side to difficult situations. The trick is to focus on the positive and use it to your advantage." Clark smiled faintly, realizing he sounded a little like Mary Poppins, although he had to let the group know he was not intimidated by the apparently overwhelming odds.

Clark continued, "Management has made a major blunder by not involving some anti-company leaders on the initial Teams, such as Mule, Jimmy, and the rest. There will always be some people who will resist by kicking and screaming even when you're not fighting. We wanted to involve only the people whom we thought could contribute the most to solving the problem. That was wrong."

Billy cut in with an idea, "Why don't we invite a handful of these negative buggers, like Mule, to evaluate our work. We could give them copies of our analysis and recommendations, ask them to attend a meeting and give us *their* big ideas. This will help get the best solution and get more people to buy into the final answer." He looked around the room and saw approval on all the faces.

Keith prodded, "This Teamwork stuff isn't an hour old, and you think you've become an international diplomat." He waited, then said, "And what's worse, you came up with a good idea that'll probably work."

The group agreed. By involving Mule and other anti-company people, perhaps they could see for themselves that management wanted to listen and to improve conditions for everyone. A sense of relief spread through the Team.

The next agenda task was to discuss the employee involvement articles. These were brief examples of successful companies using Teamwork. Everyone agreed that they, too, could achieve the same levels of success. Steve asked Clark to find other articles and books explaining Teamwork in detail that could be read by everyone in the plant. "This might help the others better understand this process and gain acceptance for it. Maybe they'll give us some insight into possible sticking points. Like the one with Mule."

Next, the Team began the task of creating a complete description of the current product design change notice system. Clark had a big board to write on and explained that they needed to spend the rest of this and another meeting to complete the description.

Keith spoke out, "This is a waste of time. We know how the system works or doesn't work. Let's talk solutions! Why do we have to make a list of the current procedures that are inefficient and we already know don't do us any good?" The others chimed in and supported this point.

Clark grew very serious, as he launched into an emphatic explanation of the problem-solving process. He said, "You *must* model and fully understand the current system and root cause of the problems before you can determine the solution. This is one of the most important rules we must follow. By writing it down, we'll be able to identify, specifically and categorically, what is wrong with what we are doing. Besides, I'd bet the ranch that there isn't any one person in the company who can explain the current system in total. We all have our own understanding, and each is different and somewhat incomplete."

Clark continued. This was an important part of teaching the Team problem-solving techniques that they would need immediately. "Once the current procedures and problems are fully understood, then a model of the new system can be created. A model is simply a written description of the procedures and forms used in the new system.

"Then we need to create detailed rulebooks. These are not like your traditional procedure manuals that were ignored and collected dust on the shelf. These will be the heart and soul of the company, and Teams will continually review these documents to find further improvements. Those enhancements will then be incorporated into these books.

"Only then, when the basic design and detailed procedures are written down, and all the participants have been thoroughly informed or trained, will we implement the new procedures."

Everyone listened intently. Clark had been down this road before, but he hammered home the message as though it were the first time. He sensed that they didn't want to screw things up. Everyone knew that too much was riding on the successful outcome of this project.

They began by listing the different steps at the top of the board that would create or initiate a product design change. They easily listed four, then another, then Steve thought of a sixth way, and surprisingly, Fran chipped in with a seventh. They began to list all the steps for each of these points in a flowchart, or diagram, that highlighted each step. Clark said, "We'll keep our flowcharts simple. A square indicates an activity, a diamond a decision, and an oval a document."

ILLUSTRATION 8–1

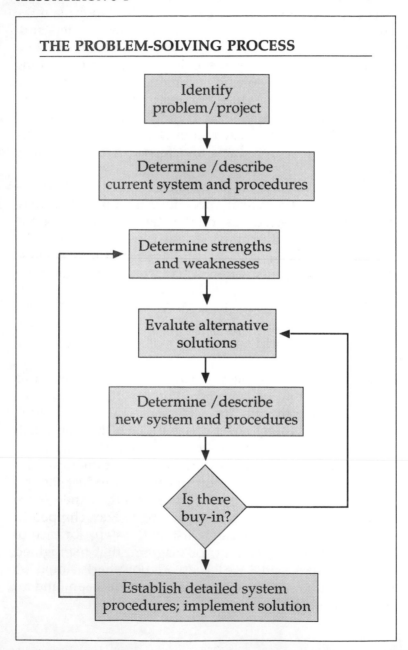

For the remainder of the meeting they flowcharted the steps of the current procedures. Clark kept asking, over and over again, "And then what happens?" And as a rhythm developed, each time another Team member would explain the next step in the engineering change notice process, Clark would depict the answers on the flowchart.

Clark's board quickly filled up until it was a mishmash of overlapping lines and shapes. As the group stared blankly at the maze before them, everyone realized that the problem they were trying to solve was not as simple as they had originally thought. And the description of the current procedures was not even complete yet.

As the meeting drew to its close, Keith shook his head saying, "I was totally caught up in this. We all learned a heck of a lot about the current procedures. I'm amazed at how much I didn't know, and I've been with this company a long time."

Clark added, "Well sure, this *is* a discovery process. We are *all* learning how to really do business. Today, there is nothing written down anywhere that explains our methods. There isn't any one person who understands how it all works. That's why we need Teamwork, because together, we can make all the pieces fit and create an accurate and complete picture."

Clark explained that the flowchart would be copied to paper and attached to the minutes. The To Do list was to review the chart during the week and note any changes. "I strongly suggest that you ask your peers to review this information and to provide their input and ideas. This is a companywide improvement project and you're here representing everyone in the company."

With that, the second meeting drew to a close. No one in that room was looking forward with great anticipation to the week ahead in the plant. They were just beginning to see the potential power of Teamwork, but they also knew

ILLUSTRATION 8–2

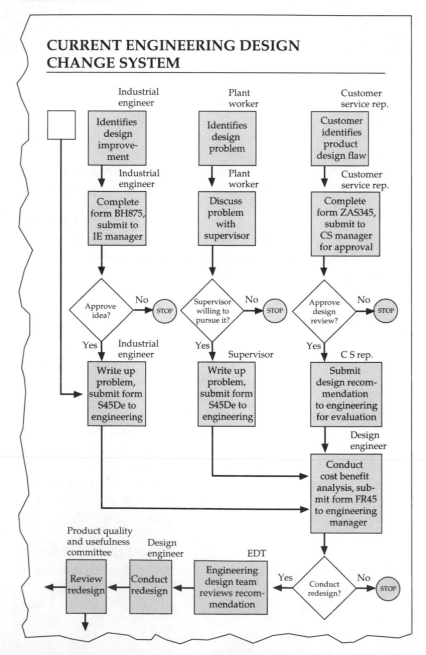

CURRENT ENGINEERING DESIGN CHANGE SYSTEM

that the latest rumors would further heighten the tensions that had already made their lives miserable.

KEY POINTS FOR DISCUSSION

(1) The Team begins their project by describing the current system procedures. Why was this more difficult than expected? Why do you think describing the current procedures is so important?

(2) Clark explains the need to create detailed rulebooks that remain up-to-date and describe the prevailing procedures. Why is this so important? How will your Team handle project documentation and written procedures?

Chapter Nine

Mr. Teamwork Makes the Pitch

"I don't see your magic wand and pixie dust."

T he stack of greasy, wrinkled, and worn papers sat on Pat's conference table, looking as though they had been collected from the slushy street gutters outside the plant. These tortured pages had received all-night attention from a handful of people working with the intensity of a laser scoring metal. By 7:30 A.M., they were both exhausted and satisfied with the results of their labors. Pat and Clark were left to deal with the results.

"You should have everything here you need to convince the old boy." Clark spoke in upbeat tones trying to convince both Pat and himself.

"I only wish we had more time. If only we had some tangible results from our Teamwork strategy. I can't point to any one thing and say "Here's a sample of what they can accomplish." Pat was bone tired and sounded it, too.

"You just get that hard-nosed son of a gun out here in four weeks and we'll put on a show for him. I know that if we can get him to attend a Team presentation, he'll be turned on." Clark grabbed Pat's shoulder and said this with such conviction that for a moment Pat almost forgot the complexity of the task that lay ahead. With a warm smile he clutched Clark's hand and nodded his thanks for the encouragement. As Clark left the office with a thumbs up sign, he thought to himself, "Thank God, I'm out of here. I can't wait to get home. Yeah, at least I can escape to my wife and the kids, but what about Pat? He never talks much about his private life. Does he have someone who can ease the pain?"

His bags were packed and he pulled on his parka, scanning his office for anything he might have missed. "Hmm," Pat thought ruefully to himself, "Did I remember the bullet proof vest?" He walked out the back door of the plant, heading to the waiting cab that would take him to the airport, and on to his rendezvous in Chicago.

* * * *

Roger Honlinks sat at his desk tapping his gold-tipped fountain pen on his water glass as he considered his meeting with Pat Forte. He would be in his usual position, on the giving end, in charge, the man who had all the answers.

But he was also smart enough to ask questions. Especially with someone as sharp as Forte. He wanted to know exactly what Pat intended to do. Not in general terms, but specifically, brass tacks, what he had in mind to turn the business around. He would have to explain himself down to the last detail. And only then must Pat agree to consolidate the business and shut it down.

Honlinks read the morning's *Wall Street Journal*, wrote a report, and waited like a cat hunkered down by a mouse hole, anticipating the chance to play happily with its prey.

*   *   *   *

Pat waited for the executive elevator to descend and whisk him to their meeting place. He felt an indignant pang of disbelief that he even had to do this, to be summoned like a schoolboy to the principal's office to explain himself when the solution seemed so obvious.

As he stepped into the mirrored chrome car, all he could think was, "what a waste of money." Pat left the elevator and walked down the muffled mahogany corridor to a door with gold lettering: Roger M. Honlinks, President. The door swung open automatically, and he saw Janice's friendly face as she sat behind her desk. Janice signaled that Honlinks was in his office, door closed, and Pat smiled and winked at her. She got up and approached him so that they could speak in some confidence. "Roger has been very different the past two days. Smiling. Happy. Almost in a cheerful mood. I've never seen him this way before. And I don't know what it is that is causing this reaction. As far as I know, there isn't a shred of good news in the business." She shrugged her shoulders.

Pat thought for a moment about this, and joked in a whisper, "Maybe his dog, that big Doberman, finally graduated from obedience school. He thinks his dog likes him." As he spoke, the intercom crackled on, "Janice, it's 10 A.M. Send Mr. Teamwork in." She dashed to her desk and acknowledged his command. Pat gave the thumbs up, and entered Honlinks' domain.

The spacious room was dark and quiet, except for the classical music that played unobtrusively on the stereo behind three potted bamboo trees. The walls were decorated with gloomy Italian Renaissance paintings in heavy brass frames along with the occasional modern abstracts that were the enthusiasm of his wife. The bookcases were crammed with antique volumes that looked unopened since their publication, and the bureaus were littered with the action-packed cowboy bronzes that Honlinks preferred. The burgundy carpet was at least two inches thick, and the couches against the wall were upholstered with the finest Italian leathers.

"Well, if it isn't Mr. Teamwork. When I grow up I want to be just like you." Pat knew he would be tested, that he had to pick his spots, and let that kind of taunt slide. He wanted Honlinks discussing the issues, not name-calling.

Honlinks kept on writing, not looking up from his desk. "Sit down. You'll be interested to know that I'm completing a report to our board of directors, explaining why our financials are so ugly this quarter. Recession, you know, recession. And in case you didn't know, your little plant out there is not helping matters at all. Not in the least." As he spoke, he turned and opened the venetian blinds on the huge window behind him, giving both men a panoramic view of the city.

"This city was not built by wimps. No sirree. Men with courage and determination made it, men with real guts, men willing to challenge and beat the odds. That spirit has made us the greatest and most powerful nation ever on the face of the earth. This view through my window is a tribute to those individual spirits." Honlinks turned and looked Pat square in the eye, and smiled the sweetest smile he knew. It was one of the most terrifying moments in Pat's life.

Pat didn't want to debate, at least not yet. "It's a tribute to the American spirit," he offered blandly. He paused and continued, "It's the same American spirit that exists in my plant, within the 450 or so people we employ. They are willing to quit, but would prefer the chance, a real chance, to be winners."

"Winners, eh? As opposed to losers? Well let's see. I can eliminate the overhead of that place, sell off most of the

ILLUSTRATION 9–1

unnecessary assets, consolidate the best product lines into our other plants, and get rid of a major annual loss." Honlinks looked straight through Pat. "Why shouldn't I do that?" He paused, as his eyes narrowed, and continued, "I don't see your magic wand and pixie dust. Leave it on the plane? You've got 20 minutes to explain yourself. I have other appointments." Honlinks grabbed for the *Journal*, as though he were preparing to leave.

Pat took a deep breath and reached into his briefcase. He pulled out the crumpled stack of surveys, and carefully placed these on Honlinks' desk. He placed on top of that pile summary sheets that tallied the results into nice, neat graphs.

Pat began, "We asked each person to complete a . . ." Honlinks cut him off, "I'm not blind. I can see what you've done. Just tell me what it means."

Pat decided it was time to grab hold of the meeting. He stood up, "It means the employees think you and your company are lousy managers. Looking at these results, they tell me that the fundamentals of sound manufacturing management aren't in place. Not even close. But read these carefully, and you'll see they haven't given up. They are willing to participate and solve the basic problems on the shop floor. And that is where the war is won or lost." Pat spoke emphatically, as he tossed out his first military reference. If nothing else, he would be the best spokesman for his cause. As long as Honlinks decided not to kill the messenger.

"Let's get to the bottom line. What are you suggesting we do, and how long will it take before we see results? Let's say maybe even break even." Honlinks spoke sarcastically.

"Teamwork and Total Quality, Roger, Teamwork and Total Quality." Pat said this as though he was talking to himself.

Honlinks looked at him as though he had just dumped a bag of fertilizer on his pristine pile carpet. Pat said, "We get the workers in the company organized into Teams. Motivated, totally motivated Teams, working to reduce the nonvalue adding activities throughout the plant. We make them feel, no, no, they actually become responsible for the performance of their assigned work areas. We give them the guidance and direction they need to build a high performance plant, and they give us quality in return."

Honlinks furrowed his brow as he expressed what seemed like genuine interest. "What does that mean? What are you saying, we turn the plant over to the employees?"

"Not exactly." And Pat proceeded to explain the Teamwork methodology. He explained the rules of the Improvement Project Teams and the Self-Directed Work Teams. He went on about the potential and power of this management technique. "The solutions lie with the workers. Traditional managers and supervisors don't listen to what they have to say. There usually isn't an organized and formal way for the workers to be heard, for their ideas to be considered. Read through the surveys, and you'll see exactly what I'm talking about."

Honlinks regarded the unkempt pile stacked on his desk with a sour look. Gingerly he began sifting through the stack.

"It is extremely important to all the Work Teams that they exercise the right amount of control over their areas, but management must establish standards and rules that the Teams must work within. You can't just turn the whole thing over to them. Their intentions are good, but let's face it, most don't have the manufacturing management expertise or the management experience to establish plantwide procedures and systems. For example, master planning, shop floor scheduling, performance appraisal and compensation, quality specifications and systems, even plant layouts, must all be determined with the guidance of the Management Team. But without the true participation and involvement of the workers, these systems will most likely be less than the best. That's because most managers just aren't close enough to the shop floor to know the details; we can't be familiar with the specific problems with the equipment or the products. We think we do, but we really don't. Managers in a business for 20 years find out how little about the shop floor they know when they take the time and listen to a Team solve problems. That's why a true problem solving partnership between management and the workforce is the only way to get the most from the manufacturing assets."

The intercom suddenly came alive. It was Janice. "Mr. Honlinks, I have an urgent call for you from Germany." Honlinks barked, "I'll take it." He turned back to Pat, "Please excuse me while I pick this up. In fact, this matter involves your little piece of the world."

Pat slowly stepped from Honlinks' office, closing the door behind him. He felt a great loss, for he knew time with Honlinks was short and precious, and this interruption could cripple his chance to win his case.

Honlinks sat there by himself, half laughing at Pat's predicament, and half mulling his words on this new Teamwork strategy. The fellow was obviously a card-carrying idealist but he did have an undeniable track record of success.

Honlinks turned to the phone on the credenza behind his desk. He handled the call, but felt disconnected from the conversation. It ended abruptly, and he turned back to the papers piled neatly on his desk.

He thumbed through the stack of surveys, and took note of the comments. These notes were short, but to the point.

> "Forget the above, no one will listen."
> "The quality of products needs vast improvement in most areas."
> "Employee ideas, don't worry about it, management will handle it."
> "According to some bosses, all employees are stupid."

Honlinks read on with growing interest. He considered himself to be a man of great courage and natural leadership. For some unexplainable reason the people in this plant didn't see it that way. Their reactions that sat before him hurt his pride. He cautioned himself against dismissing this evidence out of hand though his ego wanted him to. He knew that something very real was very wrong.

He decided to have his other divisions complete a similar survey that would also include a specific question about the corporate office.

As he continued flipping through the pile, he ran across a scrawled note at the bottom of a page. It read:

> "I was shot down behind enemy lines in 'Nam. An Air Force Rescue Team was sent to locate me. On their

92

mission, the leader was killed, yet the Team continued on, despite the risk to their own safety. They
found me after seven days in the jungle, and saved
my life. It can work if you want it to."

Honlinks sat transfixed, and read this over and over.
Finally, his voice could be heard in the main office, demanding Pat's return.

The office door opened, breaking the spell. Pat walked
straight to the empty chair and sat. Honlinks pushed the
stack of papers toward Pat, in a gesture that said he had
seen enough.

"So what do you want? Time? We don't have time. The
deal is in process." Honlinks sat back and waited with
nonchalance, but Pat could sense some subtle difference in
his demeanor, some nagging distraction that might make
him waver.

"We can get to break even in six months, and achieve 15
percent before tax within the next six. I need four weeks
and you to attend the first round of Team presentations.
The Improvement Project Teams will make their final recommendations." Pat knew that he had just gone to the
wall.

Honlinks pounded on the intercom. "Janice." He shut it
off and looked at Pat. "You better not be yanking my chain.
I'll fix it so that associate janitorial engineer is the only job
you'll ever get again." And as Honlinks vehemently spit
out those words, Pat knew he had won round two.

"Janice! Janice! Bring in my schedule." She burst
through the door. "Let me see. The morning of the 24th.
Three hours. That's it. The travel is on your budget, Mr.
Teamwork." Honlinks dismissed Janice. He stood up, and
threw the *Journal* into his briefcase. "Anything else?" he
said, not really paying Pat any attention.

"Just one more thing. I almost had a riot in the plant.
My good friend in Detroit sent this fax. He knows better.

This stuff has to be passed in confidence. Not very professional." Pat put a copy on the enormous cherry desk that sat in front of him.

Honlinks never turned around to look at him. "Now, now. You're a big boy. Fight your own battles." He paused, "And good day. Meeting adjourned."

Pat had already packed his briefcase. He headed for the office door, and said, "Thanks," in a low whisper.

The warm lights of the reception area were a relief to his stinging eyes. He looked at Janice gratefully, and they both knew that at that moment a glimmer of hope remained.

As Pat stepped into the corridor, he heard the intercom crackle on, "Janice. Get Mr. Wiseguy in Detroit on the line."

KEY POINTS FOR DISCUSSION

(1) The survey questionnaire was an important tool to understand the attitudes of the organization. What are some of the benefits of doing such a survey? What do you think is the relationship between attitude and performance? What would the results of a survey in your company show about the existing attitudes?

(2) Pat states that through Teamwork and Total Quality significant bottom line results can be achieved within 12 months. Do you think this is realistic? To what extent do you think Teamwork and Total Quality can affect the bottom line of your company?

Chapter Ten

A Solution Takes Shape

"It looked like a feeding frenzy of sharks."

Tom Glanahan was the day shift supervisor of the machine shop. He was a short, stout Irishman, who ran his shop with a cleverness that would make the local bookmaker proud. Tom was a wheeler-dealer, a bargainer, a traditional supervisor who found the right buttons in each person, and then punched them with gusto. The buttons that he leaned on sent an electrical shock through the victim, and his targets were just barely left alive and breathing.

He rose up through the ranks of the workforce. He was a talented, but not exceptional machinist who had been promoted to supervisor several years before, and the rumor mill had it that it was because he had some inside information about the extracurricular activities of the plant manager. Officially, he was promoted because he had demonstrated "management potential." The fact was that he *did* run an organized machine shop, and although there was much more than machining going on, he made sure his workers stayed ahead of their productivity goal. Whether or not they produced what was *needed*, was another matter.

Tom was a political animal, and he was certain that Pat, Clark, and this whole Teamwork thing weren't going away any time soon. At the very least, he knew he would have to learn the right words, and keep the big shots above him satisfied that he was doing his part and playing it their way. The notion of Teamwork didn't bother him, and the other departments really did need to get their acts together. It was just that he had a system, and his power was rooted in those traditions, like some political boss in a corrupt city hall. To change that would shake his authority over his people.

Keith was a machinist in Tom's department, and they had the perfect love-hate relationship. Keith was the most proficient and skilled operator, and was always willing to take the tough jobs, work the overtime, and take the extra money. And Tom was quite willing to oblige. But Keith despised the wheeling and dealing Tom used to influence people, and Keith made it clear that he wanted no part of the departmental politics. Keith had enough of his own problems, and didn't need to play head games on the job.

Keith's involvement on the Improvement Project Team was a thorn in Tom's side, and deep behind the scenes he applauded those who put pressure on Keith. Tom had attended both Clark's study sessions for managers and the Improvement Project Team meetings with Keith. He had received several personal visits from Pat and Clark, as had the other supervisors. They asked him a lot of questions about Teamwork and about its application in the department. It was as though they were not only trying to teach him but were also testing him to see if he could change his stripes.

Tom knew he had to become a coach, a helper, and not just a manipulator. He was willing to give it a shot, especially since it probably meant his job.

Shortly after the second Team meeting, Tom called Keith into his office. "Morning my good friend. How's my favorite Team member? Cup of coffee? Oh, that's right, you're a hot chocolate man." And Tom moved swiftly from behind his beat-up desk to grab the hot water kettle on the electric heater in the corner of his tiny room.

Keith had had a difficult evening with his daughter, who had just come down with the flu. "What do you want now, Tom, good friend?" Keith asked, mocking the tone in Tom's voice.

Tom put the kettle down, unable to find any cocoa mix. He picked up a book that Clark had written for the company titled "The Leader's Guidebook," and opened to a selected page.

"This Teamwork stuff *is* important, and I really want this to work." Tom stated in utmost seriousness, and for a moment, Keith believed him. He continued, "I know you don't like the way I do things, but it's the only way I know how." For the first time since they'd met, Keith heard him speak with a semblance of sincerity.

Tom motioned abjectly with his eyes and shoulders as if to admit to his vulnerability. "I'm going to do what I can to learn how to be a better supervisor, because what we're doing really isn't good enough." Keith sat and listened, awestruck.

"I called you in to be sure you understood what my role is on Improvement Project Teams." Tom placed the opened book on the desk for them both to see. Tom read each rule out loud. "So my role as your supervisor is to provide you with the support and encouragement you need to be successful. I know it's not easy to be a participant right

ILLUSTRATION 10–1

ROLE OF SUPERVISORS ON IMPROVEMENT PROJECT TEAMS

- Encourage participants to be creative.
- Encourage company members not on the Team to offer solutions.
- Provide input through Team members.
- Attend Team meetings and provide ideas in a friendly way.
- Formally and informally review analysis and recommendations.

---

now. And I haven't given you the support you should be getting." He paused, briefly recalling to himself how he had fueled the fires against Keith. He nearly bit his lower lip as he continued, "We are going to help the others in the plant accept this new way of working as quickly as possible."

Keith continued to listen with his jaw somewhat slack. "As your supervisor, my role is to provide input to the Teams through you, the Team member. I've got some ideas on how to make things better around here, too, you know. After each Team meeting, we'll get together once I have reviewed the minutes and other work, and we'll discuss the status of the project. You *do not* have to agree with my evaluation. However, you and the other Team members should carefully consider the ideas of the supervisory group. We'll participate in the final review and acceptance of the Team recommendations. Our job is to be sure all the pieces fit together. We may be able to provide you with

some additional insights. Heck, we work with departments throughout the company. We know what's going on
around here."

It dawned on Keith that he could influence how Tom
would accept Teamwork. Keith thought, "So by sharing
my participation on the Team with my supervisor, I give
him a chance to put in his ideas. That gives him a chance
to buy in. We work together, and he reviews my and the
other Team members' contribution to the solution. If I
freeze out Tom, and keep this to myself, then he, and the
others, are going to feel resentment. They'll resent me, the
project, and the Team."

They sat and reviewed the flowchart for another 15
minutes, and identified some additional steps that were
missing. Tom and Keith put together a brief list of weaknesses in the current system. Tom said, "This should be a
help at the next Team meeting."

Tom was visibly laboring during this process; he seemed
dazed and a little confused. He looked like a lost tourist,
unable to speak the language. Tom went to the window,
gazed at the shop floor, and said, "And I'm really gonna
need your help. This Teamwork stuff puts us supervisors
in a tight spot. I'm stuck right between top management's
desire to empower you and your desire to participate. It
wouldn't be so hard for me and the other supervisors to
feel left out. Keith, let's lay down our swords, and be sure
we communicate frequently, openly, and honestly."

Keith nodded and the two men stood a little awkwardly
facing one another, not knowing whether to shake hands
or to shake heads. Finally, Keith nodded again and turned
to leave. Now for the first time, he began to sense how
broad in scope the Teamwork journey was. It seemed
everyone had started to seriously question the roles they
had played for so many years. Even the wiseguys of the
world. Keith muttered to himself, "No place to hide," and
went back to work.

*   *   *   *

The third Improvement Project Team meeting was scheduled to begin at 9 A.M. as usual. Keith, Steve, and Billy, along with Tom, Keith's supervisor, sat and waited for the rest of the group a few minutes before the start time. The discussion briefly turned to work during the last week in the plant. There had been several major production orders that had to be reworked because the shop floor had not been made aware of recent product design changes.

"We can't get this bloody problem resolved quickly enough. We wasted too much time on those orders for the Crowster Company," Tom shook his head in disbelief.

"Yeah, and more than a handful of people spent most of that time just busting my chops over it. People laughed, and kept asking what we were doing about the problem, and Mule, the louse, kept teasing and saying 'Not much, huh?' all week." Keith shook his fist in mock anger.

But, they knew they were on the right track. Billy added, "We have to be patient and not run ahead and make changes without really understanding what the best *total* system should be. Otherwise, we'll solve some problems while creating others, and end up with no real improvement. And if we're not careful, we could make the thing a whole lot worse."

Everyone chimed in unison, "Can't be." They laughed.

Clark and the other Team members and supervisors arrived and the meeting commenced. Clark began by reading the minutes of the last meeting. There were no changes.

The discussion quickly turned to "peer pressure" problems. Clark explained that Mule and a handful of others had been called to the office right before this meeting. "I told them that this Improvement Project had become much more complicated than we had expected. I asked them if they would review the work of this Team and give us their ideas and criticisms each week." Clark was trying to reassure the group that he was working on the problem and a solution was in process.

Clark continued, "I explained that most Improvement Project Teams do not require as much participation in the design effort, but that I needed this favor. They have valuable expertise, and we need their thoughts."

Billy cut in, "So our coordinator is coordinating?" as Clark smiled knowingly. And the group joked about that. They felt much better that the problem was not being ignored.

Clark went on, "I'll stop by their workstations each week to talk about the project. I also invited Mule to attend the Team meeting in week five to present any suggestions that they may have. He and the others seemed quite willing to pitch in."

Steve was thinking hard, and said, "You know, that guy Mule doesn't look like much. In fact, his appearance reminds me of the winos downtown, but I can tell he's really quite intelligent."

Billy bit his tongue, but couldn't hold it in, "Yeah, he's a regular Albert Einstein. A real rogue's scholar." Clark had trouble getting the group back under control after that.

After a few minutes to settle down, Clark continued. "Okay, okay. Your part is to communicate with Mule and the others, ask them if they have any questions or new insights into the project. Go build a working relationship with them regarding the project. By doing so, they'll better understand that we, management, are really listening and that Teamwork can benefit *everyone*." It was understood.

Next, the Team continued their discussion about the current system procedures. Sandy, from order entry, was an attractive, petite, but aggressive woman in her late thirties. She had been quiet during the last several meetings, but she began this discussion. "Finally, it sounds like we're going to get this problem straightened out! Hallelujah! Order entry does a whole lot more than what you have on this flowchart. Here's the real world! These activities are not listed on the flowchart and are part of the system!" Sandy brought copies of revisions she had made in preparation for the meeting.

She continued, and the group wasn't sure if they had done the right thing by having her on the Team. Yes, they wanted to get the right answers, but they felt a touch of resentment that she was probably going to be right, and in being right make their task as a Team more complicated. Sandy continued, "The big problem, and you can see it in the chart, is that drafting takes three to four days to make the necessary entry to the database, and until this is done, we enter orders under the old design without the design changes. I've been saying this for years, and nobody listens."

Fran, the quiet draftsman, jumped up and forcefully disagreed, crying "No way!" Sandy and Fran argued for a few minutes back and forth. Clark let it go, satisfied with the exchange. He finally cut in, "OKay. Settle down. This is the type of passion we need! Obviously, there has been a conflict between these departments for some time. By the time we're through, these types of inefficiencies and tensions will be history. Let's look at the facts. It seems to me you're both partially right."

Clark got up and went to the flowchart of the current system on the easel, and sketched in a few more steps to the flowchart. "Now, is this it? Is this a complete description of what we are presently doing?"

The heads went up and down, and Sandy was followed by the rest of the group in cracking jokes about how incredibly inefficient it all was. Fran remarked, "How could we be so stupid? Look at how ludicrous this system is. And to make it even worse, we've been doing it this way for years!"

Keith pitched in, "And we would've kept doing it this way if we hadn't all sat down together and figured it out."

The flowchart of the current system was complete, and the next step in the standard problem solving process was to identify and list its strengths and weaknesses. Clark asked, "What problems must we ensure are solved with the new system?"

They listed the performance weaknesses of the current system. They noted the inefficiencies, the repeated steps, and the timing problems. Keith participated and used the list of problems he and Tom put together as a reference. Their list and the one the Team had just developed were not very different from each other. Clark, feeling satisfied, cleaned his eyeglasses and wrapped up the meeting by explaining that the Team would begin to design the procedures of the new system next week.

*   *   *   *

The fourth meeting of the Improvement Project Team was set to begin, but Steve and Billy had not yet arrived. Clark, looking a little distracted, decided to start the meeting without them. "Well I see some people aren't here yet. It's 9 A.M., and that's when we're scheduled to begin. We don't need them. Let's get started." He walked to the conference room door and shut it. He was really disturbed, but he tried not to let it show.

The completed flowchart of the current system was taped to the wall for everyone to see, and a blank sheet was taped next to that. It was titled "New & Improved System." The agenda for this meeting was to establish the procedures for the new system. The challenge was to determine the activities that would solve all the problems that were so carefully identified in the old system. Clark read the minutes of the last meeting.

Just as he finished reading the minutes, the door opened, and Billy and Steve waltzed in. Billy said, "Oh, excuse us. We got caught up on the way." They took their seats, as Clark leveled a steady eye at them.

"I think there must be some misunderstanding here. I assume you both know the start time. Everyone else was able to get here on time. Did you expect us to sit and wait for you? Do you think we need you that badly? If you don't have enough respect for us to get here on time, don't bother coming. How can you expect to help run the business and make important decisions if you can't even get to a meeting on time?" Clark was livid. Because of his proper image as a sort of college prof whose demeanor was always so measured this tongue-lashing really startled the group. But even here the effect was calculated as he knew full well they would not forget his words and they would be forced to approach the whole process with a greater seriousness.

Turning from the whipped-dog figures of Billy and Steve, Clark turned, pointing to the flowchart of the old system. "Now let's figure out what we want in the new system. Always begin at the beginning. Do we need to have eight different ways to start a product design change notice?"

With a renewed concentration, the Team dug in, deciding that order entry, sales, and machine operators should not redesign the product. Design engineers were moving their work areas closer to the shop floor. If there were any design problems, they would be easier to reach. They cut it down to five starting points. The Team then sketched the steps for each of the five. They eliminated forms, streamlined the remaining forms, quickened data entry, reduced approvals and signature requirements. They also set up a simple measurement and feedback system to measure how well the new system was performing. It looked like a feeding frenzy of sharks as they tore apart the carcass of the old system.

Keith emphasized the importance of measurement. "Listen. We've got to make sure we get accurate information for our measures. Every ECN has to be properly dated by the originator, and we in the plant have to also make sure we get

the right dates on the form." The Team had agreed to measure the time it takes to process the information. A large chart
showing the leadtime for each ECN was going to be posted
in front of the design engineering area in the plant for
everyone to see. "We can also average the data each week,
and see how much progress we're making on getting these
things through the system quickly."

With amazing speed, they had nearly completed the
flowchart of the new system. It had half the steps of the old
system. And as they reinvented the wheel they realized
how absolutely essential it was to have a complete description of the old system in place, serving as a basis for the
new. The Team members were continually referring back
while creating the new system, making sure it accomplished everything the old system had, only in a more
efficient and speedier manner.

This session wasn't without arguments, however. At one
point, Fran and a chastened Billy broke out in a loud
disagreement. Clark stepped in and quelled the debate
about alternative solutions. "Think about it; either way
would be okay. Remember, no matter what procedures we
create today, during implementation we'll have to make
both major and minor adjustments. It's not possible to be
smart enough to get it all right the first time."

"I'm just afraid that whatever we put in place today will
be there for the next 50 years." Fran had forgotten that the
Team would continue to meet at least monthly to continue
revising procedures. Steve was quick to remind him that
this wasn't like the old days when changes moved at a
glacial speed.

Clark continued, "At the very least, we'll have to fine
tune our new system. We are not using concrete. We'll just
create the best possible approach on paper, knowing that
we will have the chance to make changes and improvements. We can make the enhancements once we see how
this system works in real life. Think of the plant as a

laboratory where we can try out new ideas, and not have to get it 100 percent correct right out of the box." As though he was reading their minds, Clark said, "Hey, we have to do it safely. No disasters. But, that's why we've got a Team. If the right people are involved, it's pretty darn hard to really mess things up."

Keith jumped in, "Fine, so let's pick one of the options and go with it for now!" He knew that was the point Clark was trying to make.

Clark went around the table asking each of the Team members their opinion. After hearing their thoughts, he said, "It seems like the Team leans toward Fran's suggestion. Let's do it that way for now, and see what happens."

Clark turned to the supervisors in the room. "Chances are you'll never get everyone to agree on anything. As the coordinator, you just try to get all the ideas on the table, sift through, and get the Team to support the best one."

Fran spoke up, "Remember, we are a Team, and no matter how strongly you may disagree with the Team's decision, you've got to support it in every way and help make it work."

With some reluctance, they all agreed.

Clark asked Steve to copy the spanking new system onto paper. By day's end it was posted with the minutes in the usual locations in the plant and office.

The room cleared, and Tommy, Keith's supervisor, grabbed Clark's arm. "You know, Clark old man, it was hard for me and the other supervisors to sit quietly by. The final answer looks real good as far as it goes, but I think we all wanted to put our two cents in." He looked like he had been holding his breath for two minutes and finally let it out.

Clark responded, "Look. You can participate as an equal. Got it? As an equal. The minute I think you're throwing your weight around with this group and stifling their participation, well, that's when we'll take a break and have a private chat." Perhaps he was a little harsh, but Clark hadn't realized that the supervisors were feeling this confusion. "And let's talk about this during the week. I've got a meeting in five minutes, and I plan to be there on time." He hustled out of the room.

KEY POINTS FOR DISCUSSION

(1) The degree of support from company supervisors for your Team's success will have a great impact on how much you can accomplish. Discuss the five points for the role of the supervisor on Improvement Project Teams. Does the supervisor of each Team member understand what they need to do to help your Team efforts?

(2) Tom tells Keith that he feels lost, and stuck in the middle between his managers and his employees. Discuss why Tom feels this way, and what you can do to provide support your supervisor may need.

(3) Clark makes a strong point about being on time for meetings. Why do you think Clark emphasizes its importance? How well does your Team do starting on time?

(4) As the Team Coordinator, Clark helps them select a solution when there isn't unanimous agreement. Briefly discuss how well you think Clark handled this situation. How should your Team Coordinator handle differing opinions?

Chapter Eleven

The Destroyers Take Aim

"He could kick the ball as far as anyone."

I t was 4:45 P.M., and the second shift was preparing for work. Keith was different from most other workers in the plant in that he tried to remain productive until the closing minutes of the shift. Most others would shut down their machines 15 to 20 minutes early, gather up their personal belongings, and chit chat about the coming evening. Sometimes, second shifters would try to catch people on the first shift to check out production status, but usually they were left flat.

Keith had attended the Improvement Project Team meeting that morning, and he was particularly tired, due to his daughter's sleepless nights. His routine after 5 P.M. was to pick her up at her aunt's house, and then drive the three miles up the mountain to the modular home they had assembled several years ago when his wife Virginia was still alive.

The ride up the mountain was a time to unwind and enjoy the beautiful frozen landscape. Even though Crystal was only six, Keith spoke to her in a straightforward way. He wanted her to learn about life, people, and the world around her, and he didn't want to condescend. She had become the center of his life, and he would endure almost anything just to care for her.

It wasn't always that way. He and Virginia had had their big plans. They were both working and saving for the home they had set their hearts on. It was a three bedroom ranch-style house only miles from the modular unit. It was an ideal of comfort and would have fulfilled their desire to raise their family in the most respectable way. The white picket fence dream could have come true. They'd save for Crystal's college, and do everything possible to keep her on the straight and narrow. And maybe another child would be welcomed along the way.

It all came to an end last winter, when the cancer that the doctors were so sure was in remission suddenly erupted again in Ginny, this time fatally. Since then, Keith had been trying to put the pieces of his life together, striving for some focus in his own life even as he tried to provide the emotional security and stability his daughter desperately needed.

The Chevy Impala finally ground to a halt in the gravel driveway amid snowy patches. Crystal popped out, said hello to the dog, Jaws, and hurried toward the front door. Once inside, Keith pulled on his jeans and a T-shirt, set his work clothes by the washer, and went to the kitchen to prepare dinner.

Pasta a la Papa was the main dish, and it was Crystal's favorite, consisting as it did of cocktail franks tossed in with spaghetti and tomato sauce. "Soup's on," said Keith, calling her to the table. The dinner table was where they typically talked about school and work, and about their future together. Crystal liked school and first grade, and was a natural when it came to making friends.

"Well, we played kickball again today. It's fun, and our side always wins. That's because we know how to kick the ball in the empty spots." Crystal was slurping at a long string of spaghetti suspended between her mouth and the plate.

Keith always tried to engage her in creative conversation, especially about school. "That's the trick. So what did you learn today in class? And how's your friend, Paul? He's the one who stutters slightly?" Keith asked, testing her responses to people with obvious differences.

"Well he never plays kickball because everyone said that he didn't know how and would make their side lose." She took a sip of her milk. "But the teacher made us play with Paul on our side today. And you know what, he could kick the ball as far as anyone could." She hesitated, then laughing she said, "Even me."

"Cryssie, honey, remember that you should never think bad things about a person just because they're different or can't do something as well as you." Keith emphasized this point. He'd be sure to remind her again before bedtime.

With dinner over, it was time to help Crystal with her homework. This was the time he enjoyed most. He liked to teach, and to watch her eyes light up when she showed her work and was praised for doing a good job. Seeing her this way, sharing in her sense of wonder, gave him a feeling of rejuvenation, and a hopefulness about the future.

The evening drew to a close, and Keith sat back in his easy chair. It was his time now, as Crystal sat up reading in bed in her room. She would fall asleep shortly with the light still on.

Keith thought, "It's crazy, but when you're at work, you think about home. And when you're home, work's on your mind. Well anyway, there is a connection. The outcome of this Teamwork effort *will* affect my little girl. No job, no money, and no future.

"I think the Team is going pretty well so far. We've actually begun to solve some problems that have been around for a long time, ones that have been screwing us up for a long time.

"In two weeks we'll be in front of Pat and the Management Team. Pat's the man with an answer to everything. Maybe I'm too hard on him. He is getting results. Rumor has it that the big kahuna from corporate will be in, and we've got to do a show and tell for him. Worry? What, me worry? I wonder what I'm gonna do for that little session."

Keith reflected on his dinner talk with Crystal. "It's funny. Like Paul, the kid who finally got to play, Fran, our draftsman, was thought of as dead weight. Not literally handicapped, but I never heard anyone say anything positive about the guy. He's been pegged as a loser who just took up space and he could barely handle his own job.

"But now, at least on this Team, he's really taken on a leadership role. He constantly contributes great ideas. Without him, we wouldn't be nearly so far along. All this from a guy who lacked personality and just seemed to do the minimum to get by. And like Paul, Fran can kick the ball pretty far. Why the change? Was everybody wrong, or did the Team effort light a new spark? How many other Frans are there out there? Listen to me. I'm starting to sound like a convert. Well, sometimes it is better not to go it alone. I don't think we were made for solitude. Just like the monkeys, we need our tribes, we need our mates. Yeah, we weren't made to be alone, but you already knew that, didn't you, Ginny?"

Keith gently nodded off in his easy chair, as a silent snow began to fall outside the window, the flakes reflecting the blue light of the still-flickering TV.

* * * *

Later that week, Keith had finished the morning work, and headed to the lunchroom. He saw Fran sitting in the corner, eating from the lunchbox he brought from home. Fran looked like the old Fran, glum and downtrodden. Obviously there was a problem. Keith thought he'd head over and investigate.

Keith began, "Looking a little down in the mouth. Hey, I thought we had a great meeting the other day. What do you think?" Keith eyed Fran's project notebook on the table.

Fran chewed on his apple. "It was okay. Another meeting. Big deal."

Keith was perplexed. "I thought you were a big supporter of Teamwork and involvement. I have to admit that while we really never worked together before this, I've seen a different side of you during this Team project from what I expected. I mean, well, you've turned out to be a leader to us. You've really helped the Team get a lot done."

Fran looked at Keith, and acknowledged his kind words. "Let's face it, we've both been in this place for a while. This is the first time we've been given a chance to speak up. To put *our* ideas on the table."

"So what's the problem?" Keith probed. He sensed there was something beneath the surface here, a subtle shadow like the first signs of a virus. Was something insidious and deadly beginning to spread among the Team members, something Keith had thought he might have detected in the others but sloughed off as his own paranoia? Was Fran the first full-fledged victim of this virus? Would they all eventually look and feel this way?

Fran replied with disgust, "You would feel this lousy too if your supervisor had just pounded you into the ground the way mine just did. He said, 'I don't like this new system of yours, and you knew I wouldn't. You're responsible. You should have known better, Franny, but you blew it.'" Fran continued, slamdunking his garbage into a brown bag. "He said I shouldn't have tried to make so many outrageous changes. Basically, he promised to make my life miserable."

With that, Fran got up, and walked out. He fired his bag of garbage toward the large can by the door, and missed wide. He ignored it, and left the room.

Keith was stunned. He was unable to eat, and just sat and replayed in his head what Fran had said. "I can't believe that Fran, who's trying to do the right thing for all of us, and is doing so with the very best intentions, climbed out of his shell and then got hammered for it. I feel for the guy. It's like somebody reached into *my* body and pulled the heart out." Keith was numb and could only repeat to himself, "Now what?"

Keith muddled through the rest of the day, speaking to no one. He went home, and sat up all night thinking about what he had heard. "Now I understand why Fran seemed like a deadhead all these years. He was being held down, pinned to the mat by his boss. He was programmed to not make waves or to challenge the status quo. He was bound, tied, and gagged, with both hands and legs behind his back. And it had been that way for years. Just do what I say, and don't think. And if you dare you better not think any different from what I think. His boss was an intimidator, a real pro at it, and somehow Fran put up with it. But look at the cost.

"And all these years, everyone thought Fran had no talent. No brains. So along comes Teamwork. He finally gets a chance to perform. He does a great job, and gets thrashed.

"The company is trying to bring in this new culture and attitude. It's almost like what happened in the Soviet Union. It seems like we're going through some of the same challenges they did with perestroika and glasnost. Just like with Gorby, the big question is how will the company deal with the hardliners? How will they handle the managers and supervisors who resist change and do everything possible to preserve the old ways like the party hacks of communism? Does the company know who these people are? And what risk do we, the employees, take on by supporting change?"

Keith was deeply concerned. He knew that the company was doomed if Teamwork failed. Of course, rumor had it that they were goners anyway. But, rumor also had it that there was still a chance. Keith decided he would hold out hope and do what he must to get some answers.

The next day, Keith spotted Tom Glanahan in his office, and asked to speak with him. Keith began by chatting in general terms about the job he was working on, and then hinted at Fran's dilemma.

Glanahan saw the determination in Keith's eyes. He said, "Keith, good friend, I appreciate your bringing this to my attention. All I can tell you is that the Management Team is aware of the problem. Don't worry. Remember what Pat said at the kickoff meeting. *Nobody* will get in the way of this program. You and the other Team members have already convinced quite a few managers and supervisors that we need to make this Teamwork Journey a success."

Keith stood and listened. He still wasn't sure he believed that Tom could be sincere. He continued, "Look, we need to change our bad old ways. We're like a bunch of old drunks on the wagon for the first time. Some of us are struggling more than others. All I can tell you is that Pat is aware of how each of us is doing. That guy knows what's going on, and I have complete faith that the proper solution will come to pass. And soon." Not completely reassured, Keith left.

Several days went by, and Keith spoke to no one about this situation. It touched the very soul of what Teamwork stood for. He knew the destroyers were out there, and whether or not they would win the battle for survival would be determined very soon.

The day before the next Team meeting Keith ran into Fran in the parking lot. His Chevy Impala was parked next to Fran's weathered sedan. They had both stayed late. Fran called, "Hey, Keith buddy. Long day?"

Keith kidded, "Yeah. I love this place so much I just can't get enough of it. Like oxygen and food, you know?"

Fran grew serious. "Remember how I told you about my problem? I can't explain it, but my supervisor and I had this long talk. He apologized profusely, not just for our last disagreement, but also for the way he had been treating me all along. He said he was wrong and knew it, and would do everything possible to be open minded about change. He *thanked* me for my patience. Can you imagine?"

Keith was riveted. He imagined the battle of David and Goliath, the thrill of slaying the most terrifying monsters. Disease had been placed in check.

Fran continued, "He said that he had been taught to use fear to manage. Now, he had to learn new ways. He even asked me for my ideas about how our own department could be better. I can't put my finger on it, but someone, and I think I know who, stepped in and turned him around." Fran chose his words carefully, but Keith got the message.

Keith said nothing. He grabbed Fran's arm and squeezed. They both knew that, at least for now, the destroyers were backpedaling, thrown into reverse. You couldn't let your guard down, but they were in remission. Keith shuddered slightly as that word crossed his mind. He knew how disease, like rust, never really slept.

Later that evening, on his way up the mountain with Crystal beside him, he cracked his window to let in the crisp air smelling of pine needles and thought to himself, "I have a feeling I know who helped David load up his slingshot this time." He and Crystal both laughed all the way home.

KEY POINTS FOR DISCUSSION

(1) Fran has shown that he really is talented, but over the years he has not been given the opportunity to contribute. Are there people in your company who may be in a similar position? How can the company reach out to these people and involve them in the Teamwork program?

(2) Fran's boss was a hardliner, a destroyer of new ideas, an enemy of creativity. It seems Pat is working behind the scenes to remove the roadblocks and help turn them around. Discuss how your company should handle the supervisors and managers that resist these changes? How will your Team respond to resistance from above?

Chapter Twelve

Lessons Learned the Hard Way

"Coming together had given each individual a strong new voice."

A nd there, sitting across the table, in all his infinite glory, was Mule. Heinrich Mueller, the Mule himself, stared out the window as Clark called the fifth meeting to order.

Mule was the most unusual individual in the company. He was an assault on the senses, all five of them. He stood well over six feet, and appeared twice as large as the average man. His long scraggly beard covered his neck and collar, and his longish gray hair looked like it could be a nest for small birds and insects. His love of chewing tobacco had made a permanent pouch of his distended right cheek. His clothes were ragged, and ripely fragrant. Along the broad bridge of his nose the black-rimmed frames of his glasses were broken but rejoined with electrical tape. He looked like he had been on a long, long hike off in the wilds, and just returned to civilization.

Mule was, however, quite intelligent. It was rumored that he had gained significant wealth in the stock market. He understood business as well as anyone. And that was why he was the most outspoken critic of the company and past management. Because he had taken that position for so long, and had played it so hard, now, even though much of what he thought should be done was being done, by habit he could not refrain from attacking this new Management Team.

During the last several weeks he had backed off a bit on pressuring the Team members. And because he had, so did many of the others who looked to him for a lead. He was still as negative and skeptical as ever in the cafeteria and elsewhere, but since they were asking for his opinion and participation, he figured he'd give them a break. Play now, slay later.

The meeting agenda included a final review of the Team's recommendations, along with the presentation to the Management Team, which was now only one week away!

Each Team member had prepared notes containing additional recommendations for the new system. During the week there was much discussion in the lunchroom about the project and about the importance of the management presentation, and many people offered their ideas to the Team members. There was still criticism and skepticism that management would really do anything, but there was enough interest that people wanted to offer their suggestions.

It was difficult for the Team members to handle ideas from the other company members when they didn't fit in the solution. Some of the suggestions were excellent, and were going to be brought up and discussed at this meeting. But there were people who offered suggestions that didn't make sense, only because they hadn't been part of the entire discussion and hadn't read the minutes carefully.

Keith worked hard to be a good listener, and he always told people that he would try to mention their idea to his Team members. He didn't want to offend anyone, and of course, didn't want to shut anyone down from presenting an idea, because the next time that person offered a suggestion it might be a great one. Some of the other Team members weren't quite so diplomatic, and at one time during the week Billy entered into a near argument with another employee from order entry. Clark counseled Billy immediately after that episode. This was, after all, a learning experience for everyone. Rough spots were expected.

The Team conducted the final review of the flowchart for the new system. They reviewed in detail the new forms, and the basic rules and procedures of the new system. They carefully considered the suggestions and further improvements they had gathered during the week, and included those that bolstered some weak areas. The meeting proceeded without event, and they were all pretty satisfied that their new system would meet the performance goals of the project.

During this discussion Mule sat in silence and watched. He looked at them with disdain, especially Clark. The Team members were waiting to see how Clark would handle Mule and how Mule would handle the situation. Was he really the big tough guy, able to take on the top managers one-on-one, or would they show him up?

As the meeting wound down, Clark looked at Mule and prodded him for a response. "Mule, you and the others I asked for additional help have been tight-lipped. I stopped by to talk with you many times during the last several weeks, but neither you nor the others really had anything much to say. We're trying to get you involved, to get everyone involved. What's up?"

Mule let out a heavy breath, picked up a cup, and spat his chew into it. He was preparing to speak. He was aware of how hardnosed he appeared, and most of the managers were intimidated by him. He liked it that way.

Mule raised his huge hand and pointed at Clark. With his heavy German accent, he said, "*You* do not want my opinion. I know what is going on here. You think you can pick our brains. We shouldn't have to do this Teamwork thing. Why can't the managers do *their* own job, and fix the problems, instead of sitting in the office drinking coffee and writing memos, and making the workers do their work for them?"

Mule went on for several minutes. He had a lot to get off his chest. Clark held his patience, and the Team members and supervisors in the room watched him carefully to see how long he would put up with the tirade.

Mule then scanned the room pointing his finger at each of the Team members. He looked each dead in the eye. "You all think you're so smart. There is *no way* this new system will cut in half the rework due to late product design change information. It's nothing but a big joke, just like everything else around here."

Fran swallowed hard and jumped in. "Okay. If you're so smart, what's your bright idea?"

Mule reached in his pocket and took out a crumpled piece of paper. He unfolded it and tossed it on the table. It was full of scribbled writing.

Mule reached in his breast pocket and tucked a thumbful of chew in his cheek. "Fools. You didn't even think about the design changes that affect our vendors! We never give them the information they need. Heck, one third of our rework time is spent on rejected product from our vendors that is our fault because we did not communicate design changes to them properly. The project objectives didn't say just internal design changes, but included *all* of them."

He roared, "I'll send you my bill in the morning." He got up and walked over to Clark. He put his hand on

Clark's shoulder, and a smudge of grease marked his shirt. "Yes, Mr. Kent. We know who you really are. Don't worry, though, we won't tell a soul." He headed for the door, and, never looking back, took his leave.

Clark ignored the grease on his shoulder. "Let me tell you, he and I will have a private discussion about his performance here today. I'll put up with a lack of respect once, and that's it. Twice, and you're looking for a new job."

Clark changed his tone to one of conciliation. "The fact is, regrettably, that Mr. Mueller is right. Once again you find that you never know where the answers will come from."

He added philosophically, "That's why we need *everyone* in this place to support Teamwork. We'll schedule another meeting this afternoon with Mule and the others, and we'll address this new area in our recommendations."

The meeting continued to the next agenda topic, preparing for the presentation. Masks of total fear appeared on the face of every Team member. Clark tried to put his role on the Team into perspective. "Let's just stop for a moment, and briefly review the coordinator's role on the Improvement Project Team. This way you can see the mechanics and responsibility you have for presenting the Team's recommendations."

He referred the group to their Team manual, and they opened to the appropriate page. Clark read the six rules out loud, reviewing and amplifying each point. He wanted the Team members to understand that this was *their* project, and they were responsible for presenting the new system to management as well as for its implementation and continued maintenance.

"First, I made sure the project scope and objectives were clearly defined and were achievable. If not, I would have gone back to the Management Team to get the objectives properly aligned. In this case, there was not a problem.

ILLUSTRATION 12–1

ROLE OF COORDINATORS ON
IMPROVEMENT PROJECT TEAMS

- Ensure project scope and objectives are achievable.

- Ensure project management standards are followed.

- Ask the necessary questions, identify alternative solutions, and move the Team toward decision-making.

- Ensure Team recommendations are acceptable.

- Assist the Team in preparation for the management presentation.

- Coordinate implementation and continued Team reviews.

"Second, I've assisted you in meeting our Project Management Standards. I've ensured that the quality of what you've done here is superior. I made sure that we thoroughly understood the current system, that we evaluated the weaknesses, and so on. I've helped you complete the documentation Teamwork requires, such as flowcharts and written procedures. I've kept us on the path of our problem solving methods.

"Third, I've asked tons of questions and helped you identify alternative solutions. I pushed us to make a decision when it got to the point where you were stalemated and divided on which way to go. I broke the ties. Look, if your decision was wrong or would have obviously been in conflict with another area, I would've persuaded you to try another choice."

Billy was getting bored with the lesson. "Can't we move on? Okay, you've been a great leader. Let's get this presentation stuff out of the way."

"Billy, if you like, we can close the doors of this place right now and put the lights out. I want to make sure that the supervisors and you both understand how to proceed from here. I can't be on every Team. The best I can do is teach you how to carry on. We need to make progress in a very short period of time, and the number of Teams is going to expand very rapidly."

Keith jumped in to remind Billy. "We still have a lot to learn. Be cool."

Clark continued. "Fourth, I have continually communicated with the Management Team about the project. I've made sure that your recommendations are acceptable. There won't be any *surprises* for management or for you. In other words, I didn't let you spend six weeks coming up with a solution that isn't acceptable. I know that what we have done during this project is generally acceptable to the Management Team, although you may have to make some minimal changes.

"Next, I will help you prepare for your presentation. This is *your* presentation, not mine, but I am here to help you. And let me tell you that, even though you may have great recommendations, if you don't present your ideas convincingly and with determination, management *will* reject your solution. *You* have to sell your ideas.

"Finally, this Team will meet at least monthly in the beginning to monitor the performance of the new system. We'll still need to adjust and make improvements. So the Team will live on indefinitely and be responsible for the new system. You'll be its guardians."

Steve broke in. He really liked that idea. "What happened in the past was that some manager would be assigned to implement a new system and procedures. It might finally get done, and he or she would then be applauded by the boss. The flag was hoisted up the pole and everyone saluted. Bravo, job well done. But the people who didn't like it worked hard to undermine it. And if it survived the short-term pounding, it would eventually revert to the old way because there wasn't anyone who had *continued* responsibility for the new system."

Fran joked, "I seem to remember a few of those little earth-shaking developments. At least this way there are people always assigned to be the guardians of the system."

Clark handed out an agenda for the presentation and a sheet listing management presentation guidelines. Each member had a different aspect of the project to explain. Clark spoke slowly and clearly, really trying to make his words sink in. "I know you are not professional presenters. That's okay. When we have the meeting, I want each of you to look at one person in the audience, either me, Pat, or someone else, and talk just to that one person. Don't let the others in the room distract you. You'll be more nervous if you're trying to reach all 25 managers."

"Oh yes, and we expect that Roger Honlinks will be joining us." That sent an electrical shock down the spine of each person in the room. They all knew what that meant, and no further discussion was necessary.

"Remember that you understand the problems and solutions *better than anyone* in this company. Just get up and tell 'em what you know." Clark saw that they were all thinking hard on this one. He went around the room asking each Team member to summarize their key points.

"If we have any questions during the week, we can stop by and see you?" Fran needed reassurance that support was around the corner. Clark nodded. Fran paused a moment, then said, "If you all agree, I think we may want to invite Mule and have him explain the vendor recommendations."

The Team members all agreed *that* was a brilliant idea. At that moment they all shared a feeling of empowerment, the sense that this coming together had given each indi-

ILLUSTRATION 12–2

MANAGEMENT PRESENTATION GUIDELINES

- Present yourself in a professional manner.

- Always give a candid and honest answer.

- Be persuasive and demonstrate your knowledge.

- If you don't know, say you'll get an answer.

- Don't lay blame: be upbeat and positive.

- Sell your recommendations based on the facts about the current system.

- Present an implementation plan.

- Be humble and thankful for the opportunity to express yourself.

---

vidual a strong new voice. And they realized too, that they had, indeed, become a Team and that they were all in this together, sink or swim.

*   *   *   *

The next morning the cafeteria was buzzing about the latest Teamwork events. For the first time in many weeks Keith was anxious to get to work and to meet his peers. There was an unmistakable momentum now in place, and he and the other Team members found themselves right in the center of the storm.

Dead center in the lunchroom Mule and the usual gang were finishing their morning coffee as they busted on the Teams. The talk was at a fever pitch. The 50 or so people in the cafeteria were animated, like a high-strung herd of horses preparing to cross a swift and deep river.

Keith, Fran, and Billy started discussing the coming presentation. "This Honlinks fellow is going to be there. I wonder what in the world he expects." Steve was searching to see what the others knew about him.

"From what I've heard, Honlinks is military. Real military. With all the years I've been here, he's only stopped through once. But the word is he's a pure bottom-line man. Nothing else. And tough as nails. Hates unions, and would get rid of every employee tomorrow if there was even a chance the place could be run by robots. He's got the compassion of a slug." Billy spoke as though he were suppressing the urge to spit. Keith too, had heard the Honlinks stories over the years, and knew this description wasn't too far off the mark.

"That's what he gets paid the big bucks for. To make the tough decisions. Only thing is, tough doesn't mean smart." Mule overheard them, and shared some pearls of his wisdom. "It'd be nice to have a corporate officer that knew which way was up." Mule laughed, and rambled out of the cafeteria to his workstation.

Waiting for him was a brief note, directing him to meet with Clark in his office immediately. Mule knew what this was about, and he grimaced. He knew he was to be taken to task. He tucked another wad of tobacco into his cheek, and prepared for the worst.

Clark, Pat, and Terry were gathered in the office predictably discussing the Teams, and Mule knocked on the open door to get their attention. "Heard you wanted to talk." Mule tried to look as nonchalant as he could but a quiver in his voice betrayed his nervousness.

"Yeah. We're going to talk, and you're going to listen. Have a seat." Clark staked out his ground. Mule knew he had pushed the envelope past bursting.

The three managers, including Terry, set about explaining in no uncertain terms that open disrespect to anyone, manager or worker, would result in his immediate dismissal.

Clark took the lead. "If we do nothing else, we will have people treating each other with decency and respect. Teamwork means that there are definite standards for behavior. It doesn't mean that I or anyone else has to put up with badmouthing. I'm willing to listen, but only if I'm treated as an equal, another human being who has the same right to be treated civilly."

Pat picked the ball up. "You only get two strikes here. Next time you're out."

"Very well. You're right. So what's the deal? What do you want from me?" Mule had expected worse and now searched for what he felt must be their hidden agenda.

"We expect the same from you as from everybody else. Or don't you get it? Be the best you can be. Quality, productivity, and a positive attitude. Mule, if we could get you to spend half the energy you put into the negative stuff into *solving* the problems, well, a whole lot more would get done around here." Clark's objective was to recruit Mule, not to alienate him.

Terry added, "The old ways are dead. Me, the old man, is history. Put your gun down and help make it work." That struck Mule, for Terry represented everything wrong from the past, everything that Mule despised. Perhaps that war really had been won, and the question Mule needed to answer now was how to go on once your motivating force, the enemy, has been beaten.

"We want you to be part of the presentation next week. Just tell it like you see it. Talk to the other Team members, and get their opinions about the future. But remember to pay everybody the same respect you think you deserve." Not waiting for an answer, Pat ended the session, and Mule trudged back to his workstation.

"So they finally want to hear from the horse's mouth," Mule mused as he returned. On the way, he decided he might even wear a new shirt for the occasion.

KEY POINTS FOR DISCUSSION

(1) Keith and the Team members do an excellent job of getting ideas from other workers not on the Team. They accomplished this by posting their meeting minutes and by talking up their project. How will your Team communicate progress to other company personnel?

(2) Review the six points that comprise the role of coordinator on Improvement Project Teams. Discuss each of these with your Team Coordinator and be sure each rule is clearly understood. What are the most significant challenges the Team Coordinator faces?

(3) The Improvement Project Team lives on forever, and even though over time the Team members may change, the Team remains the guardian of the ECN system. How often will your Team meet to review the performance of the new system and to determine further improvements?

(4) Clark presents the management presentation guidelines to assist the Team members who have little experience at making formal presentations. Briefly discuss each of these points, and be sure to review this checklist with your Teammates before your pitch.

Chapter Thirteen

The Team Is Center Stage

"Send some kneepads out here."

T he silver 757 made its final approach onto the runway. Its enormous outstretched wings suspended the plane over the mile-long strip of concrete. As it swooped low to the ground, black puffs of burned tire rubber exploded from the pavement, billowing like an Indian smoke signal, warning of the arrival of Roger Honlinks.

The black stretch limousine was waiting for him, and the driver moved with the grace of a ballet master to carry his bags, open the door, and prepare Honlinks for his ride through the city. Janice, his secretary, had called ahead to the plant to alert them of his approach and to order his lunch. Throughout the plant, people were scurrying to put the final touches on the cleanup effort. The freshly painted lines on the shop floor were still tacky to the touch.

Pat had made it clear to his Team that they should conduct the meeting as though Honlinks weren't even there. No choreography. This was not to be a scripted show for Honlinks, no cue cards, no laugh track. This was as he said, "an opportunity to *listen* to the Team members, the workers, who had endured a lot during the last six weeks and who have some excellent solutions to present. Remember this isn't the Pope who's arriving, just another boss." The managers and supervisors were to challenge the recommendations, to explore the logic and thinking behind the work the Teams had done. They had a responsibility to make sure the new systems were right and would solve the problems. But it was also a chance to bring out the best in the people, to recognize hard work and dedicated effort, and to further the sense of everyone, management and workers, together striving to improve the performance of the plant floor and the office. Teamwork and Total Quality was the theme that would be hit home.

Keith's Team had been selected to present their recommendations to Honlinks in a meeting that was expected to last 60 to 90 minutes. Honlinks was scheduled to then spend another hour with Pat and whomever else, before heading back.

The Team members decided to take a break together, if for no other reason than to offer moral support to one another. They were all too uptight to really eat, so they just sat, huddled together, responding to the reassurances of their fellow workers. Keith, Billy, Fran, Steve, and Sandy reviewed and practiced their presentations over and over in their minds and to one another, each fighting the inevitable stage fright.

The only person missing was Mule.

* * * *

The cafeteria was the site of the presentation. The "cheery" green walls were gone. A group of workers volunteered several days earlier to paint the walls bright white. The floors were scrubbed, and the table tops cleaned to a bright shine. It looked like a whole new room. The cafeteria became a symbol for change.

The overhead projector and screen sat at the end cleared out of the old picnic tables, and 30 or so folding chairs faced the screen to accommodate the 20 managers and supervisors, and the presenting Team members. Also invited was a Team member from each of the other two Improvement Project Teams and several volunteers from the work force who wished to sit in. Pat saw this as an educational experience for as many people as possible.

As 1 P.M. neared, the managers and supervisors slowly filed in and filled the waiting seats. There was an air of caution and apprehension, a feeling that they were coming to watch some odd and uncomfortable spectacle, a show of and about themselves like some particularly intimate home movies, and none wished to sit too close. The back rows filled first.

An information packet, including an agenda for the meeting, a summary of current system weaknesses, and a listing of recommendations for improvement, was placed on each seat. The four foot square flowcharts of the current and new systems were propped on easels facing the audience.

The supervisors and employees dressed casually. Keith and his Team members wore jackets with open neck shirts. They all had agreed that this would be better than work clothes and help convey the message that they wished to be taken seriously.

The executive entourage entered the cafeteria. The directors of marketing and engineering, Pat, Clark, and Terry moved into the room chatting among themselves. In the middle of the pack was Roger Honlinks, like a prizefighter being led to the ring.

Pat took Roger around and introduced him to the supervisors in nearest proximity. Keith and the others were standing uneasily by the easels, and he escorted Honlinks in their direction. The group stared hard at him, trying to bring this outsized figure into focus.

"Ladies and Gentlemen, please welcome Roger Honlinks. Roger, these are the Team members that you'll be hearing from in a few moments." Pat introduced them with the pride of a father for his new child.

Honlinks responded, "Men, ma'am, looking forward to it. We need people who are willing to challenge traditions. That's the only way anything gets done. I know it's not easy." Though dubious, Honlinks sincerely appreciated what these workers were trying to do, and he knew what they needed to hear. He didn't want this to be any more painful than it needed to be.

Pat took Honlinks over to the flowcharts, and the two men spent several minutes discussing these documents. Pat explained that attention to detailed procedures was the only way to improve operations, and that the only way to get the details was through the participation of the workers. Only they knew how things were and how things should be. Honlinks seemed to understand.

Keith sat down and eyed the people around him, thinking, "We've never before been given an opportunity to *earn* the respect of company management. Even if we do earn it, will they give it to us?"

Pat and Honlinks sat in the back of the room. Clark was with them, and came up front to start the meeting. He introduced each of the Team members and briefly explained the project. "Well, the rest is up to the Team. Take it away."

Fighting back a wave of nausea, Fran started off, rising to explain the project's scope and objectives. Though his mouth felt full of cotton, he continued on about how the current system worked or didn't work, and took the group through the flowcharted steps. At the end of his talk there were a few puzzled faces. The director of engineering began questions. "I can't believe we really do all that! I really can't! Where'd you get that information? And if it is true, how did we get into such a mess?" The director of engineering was totally supportive of the Team's work, but he wanted to test their resolve and determination.

Fran was exasperated. He couldn't believe a director could be so detached from the very process that was his responsibility. "The people who *do* this every day were the source of this information. This really happens. Maybe you should speak with them and learn more about what happens in this company." Fran immediately knew that his words were too emotional, too angry. That was not the way to handle the question.

Clark cut in to help both Fran and the director out. "Fran, hold on. I'm going to give you another chance to answer that question. Take it from the top. Try adding a pinch of professionalism." A trickle of laughter rippled through the room.

Fran tried again. "The Team members, we, are the ones who work with this every day. That's how we know." He paused for a moment and looked at Honlinks. "We found it incredible and unbelievable also. We needed *everyone's* input to help figure out what it was we were doing. That was the toughest part of this project."

Then Billy, the product design engineer, stood to summarize the weaknesses. Throughout the project, the other Team members considered Billy to be a lukewarm supporter of change. It was essential that engineering accept the recommendations and adhere to these new rules if the new system were to meet performance goals.

Billy ticked off his points with poise and when he was done the audience was clearly in agreement. The director of engineering responded, "I'm embarrassed. Are you suggesting that our engineers are responsible for these problems?"

Billy turned and said, "No. The point is that the *system* is inefficient. Just look at it! But, engineering will be at fault if we don't follow the new procedures and rules."

The director snapped back, "What can I do to help make it work?"

Suddenly Billy became extremely passionate. He demanded the full attention of the audience, and Honlinks particularly liked to see this. "Your job is to *enforce* these new standards of performance. If anyone, especially engineers, knows that they can break the rules and not be disciplined, then we'll circle right back to the current mess. There can be no exceptions!" Billy made that last point with a fist raised above him like an old-time preacher.

Pat jumped in. "I want every manager in here to make a note of what Billy just said. Remember, *no exceptions to the rules.*"

Next up was Steve, the accountant, in all his leisure-suited splendor. His appearance created a few chuckles, but the audience came to listen. His task was to explain the new system and why these recommendations would achieve the performance goals of the project. During this presentation the managers had numerous questions, and Steve handled these extremely well. Although, at one point, Pat asked Steve a question about a specific procedure, and why the new system did not include that possibility as it should. Steve became unsettled, and tried to wing an answer, going on aimlessly about "potential potentialities."

Clark jumped in this time. "I'm not so sure we really have an answer on that one. Right Steve? But we'll get back to you as quickly as possible. Right Steve?"

Steve was grinning from ear to ear. "Right, Clark."

Keith turned to Billy, and kidded in a hushed tone, "The second cardinal rule of presentation is to never try to fake an answer. If you don't know, tell 'em you will *get* the answer. By the time I go, I'll have it all down pat. I hope!"

The audience of executives, managers, and supervisors began to understand the improvement process. They began to envision what it would be like to evaluate and redesign other areas, the ones that were their own private bugaboos. You could hear people say to each other, "Imagine if we did this to the maintenance system, or to the scheduling system."

Keith's turn was up, and he stood as tall as he could. He presented an explanation of the measurement procedures. He explained how information and data that measures how well this new system performs would be collected and how it would be used to further improve the system.

Keith continued "After implementation, our Improvement Team will meet monthly or as frequently as necessary to monitor the performance of the system. We will continue to be responsible for managing these procedures, reporting on performance, and making recommendations for improvement. We will continue accepting recommendations from other company members, and we will guard against violations of the procedures. We also will update the procedures manual when there are changes. As time goes by, we may find that we need to meet only every quarter. But, there will *always* be a Team that monitors this system in the company."

This answered the question that was on many minds. They had all seen improvements put in place, but they always seemed to fade over time. This made sense to everyone, because it assigned continued responsibility, which would guard against the backsliding that had always happened in the past.

And then, much to everyone's surprise, Fran's supervisor, the mystery man who was so dead set against change and workers' participation, spoke up. "How will *everyone* in the company know how well the system is working? Perhaps we should make this information *visible* to everyone?"

Keith responded, "How's about we post a large chart by the engineering department so that everyone can see how well it is going?"

This produced a pensive silence in the room. Pat recognized the concern that tugged at the crowd. "We have to make our performance visible by putting our cards on the table. When we do well, then we know we're doing something right. This gives the leaders an opportunity to recognize good work. Now, if the chart shows decline, then we've got to put our heads together again and come up with solutions to the problem. It's not a situation to fear." He emphasized his next point. "The information is *not* going to be used against anyone."

He went on, "And while we're on the subject let me say this. If *ever* anyone is found intentionally falsifying the performance numbers, that person will be fired on the spot. There's no room here for cheats! We need honest numbers to get better."

It was time for a quick 15 minute break. The Team members remained the focal point as managers and supervisors huddled around each one to ask questions and talk about the project.

Honlinks excused himself from the executive group. He said he needed to make a few calls, and would find his own way back to the front office. Pat had no choice but to let him go.

Honlinks thought of this excursion as intelligence gathering, a most important fact-finding mission. The survey results remained emblazoned in his mind, and he had to find out more, to understand why and how his leadership had apparently failed here, and perhaps, elsewhere.

He went on a solo tour to meet and talk with his soldiers.

He headed for the deepest recesses of the operation. His path would take him through the warehouse, maintenance, and into the machine shop and assembly areas. While all the employees knew the corporate boss was in, few knew him by sight, and nobody expected him to be hobnobbing. And he had no plans of telling who he was.

He first encountered two people in the warehouse whom he found getting off the hi-lo lift. They were stock pickers, and were responsible for moving items from the stockroom racks to the plant in the quantities the computer sheets stated.

They were muttering to themselves, and didn't notice Honlinks approaching. He leaned in behind a stack of cartons and overheard them speaking to one another.

One said, "So what's the chance this one will be there? We're having a pretty rough day here." The other responded. "The computer system is so screwed up, the info is so inaccurate, I don't know why we even use it at all. Better to count off on our hands and feet."

Honlinks stepped in and interrupted. "Afternoon. How's it going?" He gave them a big, happy grin. "I came by to follow up on the survey everyone completed. Just wanted to chat with you guys about that, you know."

They kept working. "What do you want to know? Ain't nobody gonna do nothing no how." They joked that way to each other.

Honlinks asked, "How's the computer system? It wasn't rated too high." Pretending to read notes from his pocket planner, he continued, "It's all new equipment, isn't it?" He didn't want to tip his hand and appear too uninformed.

They both turned and looked at him as though he had been beamed down from another planet. "If we could get info that was even half right, we could fly at least at half speed."

"How fast are you going now?" Honlinks probed.

"Brother, we're just barely crawling, and our knees are worn out. Send some kneepads out here, will you?" They turned back to their work.

He forged ahead toward maintenance. He felt like he was behind enemy lines, and the verbal bombs were bursting all around him. For the first time his snakeskin cowboy boots made him feel self-conscious.

As he entered the maintenance area, he saw three figures with glass masks, illuminated by the white hot welding sparks shooting high into the air. He continued on, to where a fellow was operating a drill press. Honlinks interrupted him, again using the ruse that he was looking for information concerning the survey.

"Help me understand why the maintenance system was rated so low. You guys got what you needed to fix the problems out there and keep this place going, didn't you?" Honlinks tried to penetrate this fellow's obvious suspiciousness.

"You don't see anybody sleeping here, do you? Yeah, we got what we needed. But we're always fighting the fires. Never enough time to do things right. Priorities are always changing. And the operators out there don't care. They run the equipment till it drops, then expect us to fix it within five minutes. It don't work that way." Honlinks cut in before the worker could ask him any questions.

"If this was your place, what would you do?" Honlinks really wanted an answer on that one.

"It's simple. If you boil it right down, this place would be a thousand times more efficient if we could get cooperation. If we could get cooperation from the machine operators, and, well, even from each other. Then we could get organized." The guy stopped and looked up, and Honlinks was almost gone. He heard him say "Thanks. See 'ya again."

He forged onto the machine shop. He knew he had to hurry, otherwise Pat would send a search party out for him. He heard the hum of heavy equipment, and knew that operators must be near. He saw a man and two women operating a computer controlled machining center. Off in the distance they looked a little ghostly in the glow of their CRT's. It was only a few weeks past Christmas, holiday decorations still hung about the shop here and there, and just for an instant Honlinks felt like a character from his favorite story as a child, Ebenezer Scrooge on patrol.

Two workers were moving parts and the other woman was reviewing some sort of computer printout. Again, he explained his reason for being there. He focused their attention on the low survey rating of plant layout and product quality.

He first spoke with the woman reading the report. She responded, "Do you know how far I have to walk every day in this place? I clocked it once with one of those hip counters. I put in over seven miles. That's the average day. You know why? I have to get tools and materials. Let me change that. I have to look for tools and materials, and if I'm lucky, I find them. If there's a maintenance problem, I've got to go find a supervisor. And when I run out of work, I've got to figure out what to run next. Don't forget, I'm the machine operator. We're not making any parts while I'm out running around. My daughter bought me a gym membership last year. She thinks I want to go there and get on the treadmill. No thanks! I don't need to go because by the time I get out of here, I'm pooped."

The fellow with them finally turned around, and Honlinks felt a tingling at the nape of his neck when he looked at him. He was of medium build, had a mangy crew cut, and walked with the recognizable strut of a soldier. Honlinks froze, because that was what he'd truly come seeking, the Vietnam vet who had written that note on the survey. When he saw the squadron patch stitched to his shirt sleeve he was quite sure, but he realized at that instant that he could not face this man. Though he fought it, he felt ashamed, like going home a failure, like having his wife, sons, and daughters know that he had let them down in the biggest way. He felt torn, wanting to beat a hasty retreat, but also wanting to make a stand and confirm his worst fears.

He stammered for words as he "checked" his notes, speaking to all three. "Just stopping by to get more info on the, er, survey results. We were just talking about plant layout and quality. Not real good, huh?"

The other woman spoke. "We do the best we can, but we need help that we're not getting. Engineering, maintenance, and the other workers in the plant need to come together, but we know that's not going to happen for a while. Maybe never."

Honlinks struggled to keep his eyes open, to keep from screaming out as the fellow spoke. "We follow the orders *they* give us, and that's all we can do." The word "they" ignited his deepest and most profound fears, for it was the final judgment of his leadership skills.

He had gotten as close to the fire as he could stand. He thanked them and left. Though he strode as confidently as ever, he felt like he was running, dashing for his life from a nightmare that wouldn't end when he awoke. Even in the cool winter air of the plant he was sweating, and it seemed like hours before he found the cafeteria door, the place where he had begun this journey. The meeting was just getting underway, and he saw a look of relief on Pat's face as he approached. He sat down beside Pat with a sigh of relief and would stay put for the rest of his time in the plant.

Clark called the meeting to order. "Where's Mule? I know he had a few recommendations that he wished to share with the group." He had been sitting in the first row since the very beginning, but had escaped the notice of everyone there.

"I'm right here. And you're right. I do have a few things to say." The voice was familiar to everyone, but the man that stood up was not the Mule that everyone knew. As he stood and turned to face the audience, those who knew him were startled by his new appearance. He looked, well, human.

His new denim shirt and black pants were clean and sharp. His hair was cut and parted on the side. His beard had been trimmed neatly, and his glasses, while still broken on the bridge, were reattached with a fresh strip of tape.

Keith decided at that moment that he would do the introduction. He did it very formally, with just a hint of irony in his voice. "Mr. Henry Mueller would like to discuss some of the management issues that are on everyone's mind. Henry, it's all yours."

Keith was one of the few who had known of Henry's makeover. He applauded him for his efforts, but reminded him to handle himself cautiously. Pat and Clark looked at each other and cheered quietly. They tried to explain this transformation to Honlinks, but he couldn't appreciate the full scope of what was taking place.

Henry began, and jokingly said, "Well, everyone here knows how I feel about all this. We, the workers, have enough to do, and shouldn't have to do all this extra work. You, the Bigshots, should do something for all your money!"

By now, there was a sense of camaraderie in the room. This included Henry. Everyone laughed good-naturedly at what he said. One supervisor shot back, "Mule, I mean Henry, we have to spend most of our time keeping an eye on you." More laughter.

Then Henry became serious, and said, "I was not invited on this Team from the beginning, but got caught in the draft. I guess I helped by pointing out the problems our vendors have with getting product design change information." Henry proceeded to explain the old way and the new. He was very persuasive.

When he finished he said, "Well, all this looks great on paper." And looking directly at Pat and Clark, said, "But I'm not sure we'll *do* any of it. It's lots of big, big talk and promises. But will anything really change?" Henry sat down.

The ball was in Pat's court. Pat said in a low tone, "If I were you, I would feel the same way. But I don't see an implementation plan here. You must tell us when and what you need to implement change."

The Team members looked at each other and collectively shrugged their shoulders. They didn't *have* an Implementation Plan. They didn't know they needed one. Clark said, "My mistake, but the Team hasn't yet devised a plan. It would be best if the Team met during lunch, put it together, and then presented it to this group right after lunch."

It was 11:45 A.M. Pat said, "Fine. We'll continue at 1 P.M. No time like the present. During lunch, the Management Team will stay together and we'll discuss these recommendations. We've got to decide to reject or accept the proposal and go ahead with implementation. We'll tell you our decision after lunch."

It was Keith's turn again, and his task was to wrap up and summarize the project, and highlight any potential major roadblocks. He concluded, "The biggest potential obstacle we face is *ourselves*. We have learned that solving efficiency, quality, and procedural problems is simple stuff. The tough part will be to get everyone in the company to take on a new, positive attitude, and to follow the new procedures."

Everyone waited for Roger Honlinks to respond. His body language, his manner throughout the session, were closely observed and would be debated upon later. "I've got to catch a plane, otherwise I'd stay for the rest of this. I'm extremely impressed with the quality of your work. It's been very illuminating. I believe we could use this type of effort throughout this place, and, undoubtedly, throughout our other companies. Cooperation is the key watchword, and if we all keep our minds open to new ideas, then together this corporation will make progress. Thank you for having me here today." He went up and shook the hands of each Team member.

The meeting ended, and the Team headed for a conference room to work on their implementation plan. Honlinks motioned to Pat that he wanted to meet with him and Clark immediately. "Let's go to my office," Pat directed them.

As the group filed out Keith stood in the now empty room for a few final moments. He replayed the meeting in his mind, recalling the smiles and handshakes that gave him the sense of accomplishment that he now felt. He wanted to hold on to that feeling for as long as he possibly could.

*   *   *   *

"All that is wonderful, just plain wonderful. But it's a drop in the ocean. You haven't done anything yet." Honlinks spoke sarcastically, pacing back and forth as Pat and Clark sat and watched.

He continued, "I can't, and won't, promise anything. There's a lot in progress already, the wheels are in motion. In fact, I'm supposed to go to Germany next month and begin formal negotiations for the sale." He was talking as though to himself, out loud.

"I want to know what the next six month plan is. Where from here? Specifics, too. How many people will be involved? What are the improvement projects? The whole nine yards. But you've got to show tangible results, and soon." He finally turned toward Pat and Clark.

"Our next steps are to form Self-Directed Work Teams, as well as create more Improvement Project Teams. The Self-Directed Work Teams are permanent Teams on the shop floor, and they become responsible for performance." Pat began to give a detailed explanation of his attack plan, but was cut off.

"I know that. I want specifics. On my desk by week's end, or I'll find someone who can." Honlinks slammed his Coke bottle to the table. He grabbed his briefcase and coat, and headed out the office toward the front door. The chauffeur met him by the door, expecting to carry his belongings.

"I'm not lame. Get in and drive," Honlinks ordered him. The black stretch limo dashed off, and smiling eyes peered out of every window, watching this spectacle.

*   *   *   *

"Our Team was extremely productive in their lunch meeting. It was amazing how much we accomplished when we were in a situation where we *had to* produce and agree upon results."

At 1 P.M. the meeting reconvened. Pat says, "The Management Team discussed your work during lunch, and we all believe that we should move ahead and implement your recommendations. You have convinced us that you have carefully designed the new system, and that you are dedicated and will stick with this to make it work." Thanks Pat, mighty big of you.

"We presented our implementation plan, but one supervisor isn't satisfied. 'If getting people in our company to change their attitudes and behavior is so important, what are you doing to solve that problem? When do all the other people in the company get a chance to buy in to and voice their opinions about these recommendations?'

"I say, We've posted all the information each week about our work, and have talked with as many people as possible to get their ideas. Everyone is well informed."

The director of marketing, who had been quiet throughout the meeting, says, "Let me make one suggestion. After you write the detailed procedures, personally give each person a copy and again ask for their ideas. The personal touch always creates a positive response." These marketing guys do understand the basics of human nature.

The meeting is drawing to a close. Pat says, "You've all done a great job, and by being one of the first Teams, have set a shining example showing how Teamwork can work. I want to thank each of you for your dedication and courage. Mr. Roger Honlinks was very impressed, and I believe we've got his support. I want you to know that."

"That's what everyone in the room was waiting to hear. I hope it's true."

ILLUSTRATION 13-1

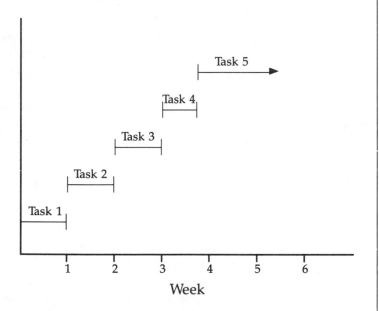

IMPROVEMENT PROJECT TEAM

Product Design Change Notice System Implementation Plan

Task 1. Create, review, and finalize detailed procedures manual.

Task 2. Distribute manuals and train users.

Task 3. Review and update new forms.

Task 4. Implementation; convert to new procedures.

Task 5. Measure and report performance.

* * * *

The implementation of the new system required a great deal of participation by the Management Team. While the employee Team determined the procedures of the new system, the *implementation* had to be coordinated and guided by the manager of each department.

Clark, as coordinator, wrote a brief but thorough procedures manual that reflected the steps on the new flowchart. All necessary information was contained in less than 10 typewritten pages. He scheduled a Team meeting to review the manual and to be sure it was complete.

Each Team member hand-delivered a copy to each person in the company. This was easier than it may sound. Supervisors let each Team member take one half hour each day during the week to complete this task.

Keith returned to his workstation, having completed his rounds for the day. Tom Glanahan stopped by to see how it had gone. Keith explained, "Everyone I've spoken with so far has been totally impressed with the results. In fact, they're complaining that other areas of the company need fixing, and suggested that Teams attack these problems. People are willing to volunteer and help."

Tom was a realist. "I think you've begun to show how this just might be a way to patch up some of our weak spots. But, let's face it, management hasn't gained much more respect. The overall attitude is still 'show me.' And rightfully so."

During the next four weeks the new system proved itself and showed significant measurable results. The time it took to process design change information was reduced by 70 percent and the amount of scrap resulting from late information to the shop floor was reduced to almost zero, saving some $2,000 each week.

The large posted charts and graphs near the engineering area showed these results. The Team was very proud of this accomplishment. They continued to meet every quarter to review the results. In fact, every time they met thereafter they further improved procedures and reissued the manual.

Several days after the management presentation, Pat stopped by to see Keith. "The objectives of your project were too easy. Next time, we'll get you on a tough project that will really be challenging." Pat gave Keith a warm smile, a look of deep appreciation and respect. "Okay?"

"Okay," Keith nodded with his own smile. This was the man he had pegged as smug and full of himself. Now Keith recognized that Pat deserved respect. They'd come through the battle together, side by side on the frontline and helped set the stage for the future of Teamwork in the company.

KEY POINTS FOR DISCUSSION

(1) An important activity for Keith's Team was to present their recommendations to management for approval. What are the benefits of doing this? Is your Team scheduled to present recommendations to the Management Team? When will this occur?

(2) Pat emphasized the importance of visible, honest performance measurement as a way to monitor how well the system is working. How will your Team measure its impact on performance? How will you make this information visible to everyone?

(3) Clark, as Team Coordinator, helps write detailed procedures, and these are hand-delivered to company personnel. Discuss how your Team intends to document new procedures and to train the users of the new system.

(4) The presentation by the Team was considered a success by both management and the Team members. What were the key components that ensured a beneficial outcome? What steps must your coordinator and supervisor take to ensure your presentation achieves the desired result?

Chapter Fourteen

A Brave New World Order

"If we don't make changes, then nothing will change."

N ow that they had successfully established a beach-head by introducing the concept of Teamwork through Improvement Project Teams, Pat and Clark were prepared to take the next step in their battle plan and begin the process of building Self-Directed Work Teams on the shop floor and in the office. The pair worked tirelessly during the next two weeks to establish an agenda for the next six months. They met continually with managers and supervisors, day in and day out, to get their ideas on how to proceed. They wanted to build a consensus within the Management Team, to go forward with as much support as possible from the men and women who were on the frontlines.

ILLUSTRATION 14–1

THE INITIAL SELF-DIRECTED WORK TEAMS

- Winding department.
- Power supply manufacturing.
- Office and administrative support for power supplies.

They settled immediately on forming three Self-Directed Work Teams. Each would represent a different area for improvement, and each would serve as a model for the balance of the Teams. Of course, this was in addition to several new Improvement Project Teams that would begin their work right away.

The first Work Team was assigned the task of reorganizing all aspects of the current way the winding machine was staffed and managed. There were four winding machines, and each was a 250-foot-long mechanical monster that required five employees to operate. The workers had to continually load and unload bobbins of wire that were wound together onto an enormous high speed takeup reel. The wire was later used in another area of the plant in the manufacture of motor coils. One of the four machines was selected to model the Teamwork approach.

The second Work Team was challenged to create a workcell that pulled together the necessary equipment for the exclusive manufacture of power supplies. Currently, the plant was organized by process, and this was the traditional way to lay out a plant. The existing departments included the machine shop, motor winding, electrical assembly, mechanical assembly, and final inspection and test. All of the major products moved through each of these departments. The long-term plan was to establish small mini-plants throughout the factory, with each dedicated to the total manufacture of a product line. This Work Team would include the people and equipment from each of the departments, and would be dedicated to produce only the power supply product line.

The third Work Team would be established in the office and administrative area. Processing customer orders had become a paper jungle, and the time it took to internally process the order from order placement to receipt by the planning department ranged from five to six weeks. Often, there were mistakes, and the poor quality of the paperwork caused scrap and rejects in the plant and at the customer site. A Work Team would be formed to create a workcell dedicated to processing customer orders for power supplies only. As in the plant, the traditional departments of customer service, credit, data entry, order editing, and filing existed, and processed all customer orders for all product lines. The objective, too, was to create small mini-offices dedicated to each product line.

The ability of the supervisors to provide positive leadership and support would make or break each Team. Whereas supervisors were not directly involved in the Improvement Project Teams, these Work Teams reported directly to the supervisor and were under his or her complete authority. The supervisor for each Work Team would be a key player, called upon to be responsible for areas of the process that they had never before been involved with.

Of course, the real burden was on each of the Team members individually, who would have to go beyond their own individual needs and goals, and pitch in for the benefit of their Team to get the job done.

The winding machine Team would be supervised by Ruth Mummer, a seasoned and savvy woman in her early

forties. She had overseen the winding machine department since she joined the company five years earlier. She
was as tough as any supervisor in the company, and was
well respected by her subordinates. She had always been
able to make the best of the existing timeworn approaches
to the shop floor. The tool and die system, scheduling, pay
system, and maintenance, were daily hurdles that she had
learned to surmount. The Team would consist of five
employees, who would be selected from the 20 people
who presently ran all of the equipment. Their task was to
redesign the procedures in each of these support areas and
to define the rules for Teamwork in the winding machine
department.

The power supply workcell would be placed under the
supervision of Tom Glanahan. He had learned a great deal
about Teamwork during the last two months, sometimes
reluctantly, and he still had a long way to go. Clark was
prepared to work very closely with Tom to shepherd him
through the transition. The Team members would include
an employee from his machine shop and workers he was
not familiar with from the other areas of the plant.

The office workcell was assigned to Bob Walner, a 52-
year-old, 20-year employee, who was one of three supervisors in the customer service department. Clark knew he
was an excellent choice because of his strong orientation
toward serving the customer. His frustrations with the
current way of doing business would energize him to bring
new ideas to the Work Team and make him receptive to the
creative solutions from others. He was, however, a bit of a
crank, and he would have to significantly improve his
attitude and leadership skills if he were to be successful.
Not to mention amending his habit of reporting late night
Elvis sightings to the authorities.

These three supervisors had been directly selected by their
peers. The choices had been openly discussed in exhaustive
meetings with managers and supervisors, and Clark was

ever present to help that group make these decisions. All three were proud to have the assignment, although each had his or her own private reservations and concerns.

By this time, all company supervisors had been trained in Total Quality Management techniques. Clark led the classes, and taught workcell design, production sequencing, kanban, preventive maintenance, and SPC techniques. This was essential to these three supervisors, as their initial task was to meet with Pat and Clark to define the guidelines for the design of each area and the definition of Work Teams. Pat and Clark would provide the guidance they needed to establish a clear vision of how these areas should function using Teamwork and Total Quality. This ideal vision would serve as a starting point for the Teams, and the challenge was to define the detailed rules and procedures of Teamwork and Total Quality to reflect that high standard.

*   *   *   *

Clark and the three Work Team supervisors gathered in the Team conference room. They had met four times previously during a two week period to strategize. They agreed to meet at least weekly as each Work Team formed and got its bearings. Clark's main objective was to be sure these supervisors shared their weekly experiences with each other, and discussed and debated solutions to problems as they arose. This coming together would serve as a support group for each supervisor, a refuge and shelter to help build Teamwork and esprit de corps among these frontline leaders.

The agenda for this particular one-hour session included a final review of the strategies and guidelines for each Team. Supervisors were scheduled to launch the kickoff meetings for their various Work Teams next week.

"I think we've covered the key areas and techniques that each of you will be dealing with. Obviously, we're not just going to slap the 'Team' label on our people, and make believe we have Teamwork and Total Quality. We need much more than window dressing and flashy public relations. We need improved performance. Remember, if *we* don't make changes, then *nothing* will change." Clark continued to hammer home the fact that *they* had to promote change. And they had to make sure the changes were for the better.

Tom was sitting there and listening, feeling a bit under the weather. "I was at Flaherty's bar last night, and was talking to some of the boys working over at Burdle Industrial. They were telling me that they had done a lot of Teamwork over the last year, but it didn't sound like it's working out too well. They said it was totally implemented in under two weeks. Every employee was assigned to a Team and made responsible for their work areas. Meanwhile, the supervisors were pushed aside, and senior management worked directly with the employee Teams." Tom said this hesitantly, checking Clark's reaction as he spoke.

"I was wondering why you looked a little worn out and rough around the edges. So it wasn't just Flaherty's chili! So how are they doing over at Burdle?" Ruth questioned him gently, but with great interest. The two had always gotten along well, and could speak candidly to one another.

"Well, it sounds like now they're trying to undo the damage. Trying to pick up the pieces. I couldn't imagine turning over the plant to the workers in one fell swoop without an organized way to manage the changes. They said the Teams were sent to conference rooms to brainstorm the problems without objectives and goals from management. Just go for it. Whatever 'it' is. Apparently it ended up with each Team setting up their own little methodology. No plantwide standards. No uniform way to document rules. They even set up their own work area schedules. The Teams actually began to work against each other because there wasn't anybody or anything keeping them together." Tommy shook his head miserably. "I think that's why they were all down at Flaherty's last night."

"A sad tale, Tommy, but *that* won't be our problem." Bob added, "Let's get through our meeting, here, I've got customers screaming for my head." He jerked them all back to the business reality that they were facing.

Clark had assigned each Work Team different areas of Teamwork and Total Quality to address. The objective was that the three Teams combined would set the guidelines for Teamwork and Total Quality throughout the company.

Ruth took the lead and began explaining the objectives of her Work Team. "Let me summarize the Total Quality issues and then I'll get into the Teamwork hurdles.

"Our Team will focus their efforts in four Total Quality areas. We'll establish new procedures for maintenance system management, and working closely with Frank, the maintenance manager, we'll decide how production and maintenance can best work *together*. The Team will also work with the tool and die room to create new procedures to better manage those resources. Third, the Team will be trained in simple statistics to evaluate the quality variation of the product, and put in place simple process measures and controls."

Tom cut in. "I think that's real important. We struggle all the time in the coil department because the quality of what comes off those winding machines is different every day. I think it's different every hour."

Ruth and Tom had a longstanding argument about this. Ruth came back with, "I bet we find that there isn't hardly a whit of variation on the winders. The problem is in the coil department."

Clark could see that they were preparing for their one millionth debate on the subject. "The point is that we *don't know* for sure what the source of the quality problem is. So maybe we should go find out." Clark was preparing a most persuasive monologue on this subject, but both Ruth and Tom motioned that they already gotten his point.

Ruth continued, "And last, the Work Team will create a playbook. This is the document that describes all Team rules, from machine setup procedures and scheduling, to maintenance and Team Leader responsibilities. And we'll keep the playbook simple; it won't exceed 12 pages. Otherwise, no one will read it." She said these last words with emphasis, mimicking, goodnaturedly, Clark's oft-repeated words.

"Now, for the people issues. The Team members have had problems working together over the years because of personality conflicts. My challenge is to help them get past these differences and work together. The old job classification system has a dozen different levels, and each person on the winder is in a different class and receives a different hourly wage. The real challenge is to help them and motivate them to be willing to *pitch in and help each other*, despite their present assignments on the machine."

Clark, Bob, and Tom sat and listened intently, running Ruth's words through their minds, each imagining how these tasks might be accomplished. Ruth finished up, "And of course, our first task after some TQM training is to define Team performance measures. How well are we doing? We'll go and measure it and post it." She said this grudgingly. She didn't think making performance information visible was a good idea. She felt this would create too much competition and a lack of cooperation between Teams on the three winding machines. Yet she knew that along with the playbook and thorough documentation, this was another *standard* senior management had set. There *would* be visible performance measurement on the shop floor, and it simply wasn't open for further debate.

It was then that Tom began to explain the issues that affected his Work Team. He wasn't nearly as prepared as Ruth, and he was visibly uncomfortable during his pre-

ILLUSTRATION 14–2

PLANTWIDE MANAGEMENT STANDARDS

1. Establish a playbook of rules for each team.

2. Establish visible performance measurement.

3. Establish a pull system on the shop floor.

4. Establish a job certification program to promote crosstraining.

5. Establish peer performance appraisals tied to compensation.

---

sentation. "My Work Team is of a very different nature from Ruth's. While Ruth is establishing Team rules on a single large machine, our Team is going to create a *workcell* for power supplies. These Team members have never even worked together before, and each works in an entirely different department. We'll design the workcell with the equipment we need to specifically manufacture complete power supplies." Tom stopped, and looked to Clark to hint at the other elements of his Team.

"Think of the Work Team as comprised of two components, Total Quality and Teamwork issues." Clark prompted him.

"Oh yeah. The TQM issue is the scheduling system. We get to play with this baby." Tom shook his head helplessly from side to side, totally overwhelmed by the task, as though he had been assigned to climb Mount Everest. "We have to figure out how to use a pull system to link our workcell with the supplying departments. Long term, we'll use the pull system throughout the entire plant, linking every workcell and department. Production sequencing looks like a viable answer."

Tom, Clark, and Ruth all understood the generic concept of a pull system. Instead of every department working to its own schedule and pushing material ahead as it's completed, each department would somehow signal that it was ready for more material, and the supplying department would send it ahead only when that "pull" signal is received. The problem was that they couldn't imagine how this and many of the other Total Quality techniques would be applied in *real life*. How would these new ideas actually *work* in the plant with which they had become so familiar. This was the nuts and bolts of *change*, and their discomfort was in that they couldn't clearly envision how this new world order would function. At the root of this skepticism was the question of what role *they* would play. How would this affect them?

The third standard senior management had set was the implementation of such a pull system plantwide. It was yet another requirement and constraint within which the supervisors and the Teams had to work.

"Now, the people issues. My Work Team will be challenged to deal with the need to have its members cross-trained, so that each member can work at each operation in the workcell."

"Is that an important point for my Work Team, too?" Ruth questioned Clark, looking for further explanation.

"That's right. We'll let Tom's Team set up the methodology and system to accomplish this, then your Team and the others can participate." Clark was willing to continue, but he saw that they understood.

"So we have to develop a training program that teaches the participants how to do the job, and then challenges them to pass both a written test and a hands-on test. This creates a certification program that recognizes each worker as qualified to do a job or be a member of a Team." Tom said this as though he were repeating verbatim what he had been told.

The group was quietly considering and trying to absorb everything that had been said thus far. Bob broke the silence. "This place is going to be a whole lot different, if we get even half of this stuff in place."

Clark again emphasized his number one point. "And it will *perform* a whole lot differently. We're not doing these things to be cool, to follow some fad. They work, and they will get us the improved level of performance the company and everyone who is a part of it needs to compete and be profitable." Clark signaled Bob to present next.

Bob was the most polished supervisor in the company. He had to be to diplomatically handle the crush of problems customers bombarded him with daily. "My Work Team will pursue many of the same techniques as Tom's Team. We're going to create a workcell that includes the office operations to process customer orders and billing for the power supply product line. One of our major Total Quality tasks is to measure the impact of Teamwork and Total Quality on customer satisfaction. So the Team has to come up with a way to do this measurement and share this information with Tom's Team."

Tom grimaced, because he knew what was coming next. Bob spoke more emphatically, "And I've been saying this for years, but we will get both plant and office workers to better understand the customer. We're all going to get closer to the customer, and really understand their needs and consider their opinions of our products."

Bob and Tom had been battling each other for a very long time. They argued continually, and over the years had lost even the minimum respect required to deal with one another on either a business or professional level.

Simply put, Bob accused Tom of ignoring the customer. He believed Tom ran a very efficient department, but only at the expense of customer satisfaction. Although productivity was high, at least by their own internal standards, deliveries were always late. It seemed to Bob that Tom's priorities were on being cost-effective, and that he didn't care about delivery and the promises made to the customer. Bob felt he had been continually hung out to dry. He'd commit the company to doing something, but got no support from manufacturing to meet these customer commitments. Tom's view was that Bob wasn't bottom-line oriented. He'd promise the customer anything, make all kinds of pledges that couldn't possibly be kept, and then expect the plant to jump through hoops to meet them. It was a great scam to pressure the supervisors to do things his way, and Tom would have none of it. Tom didn't believe Bob's claim that the competition could and would beat Bob's commitments. Quality, delivery, and price were all Tom ever heard, and Bob had no idea how to run a cost-efficient operation.

This ongoing conflict created some very uncomfortable situations for the employees of both supervisors. It was like belonging to the camp of one or the other of two opposing armies, and you had better not give the enemy *any* information that could be used against your side for fear of trial for treason. The gap between the office and the plant workers was broad, and the two supervisors worked tirelessly widening it.

Bob continued, "Our Team challenge is to streamline the paperwork and develop a fail-safe system for quality management in the office. We've got to reduce errors in the paperwork to the customer and out to the plant and warehouse." He spoke like a convicted burglar in front of the judge for sentencing.

Tom couldn't hold back. "That sounds awfully familiar; *I've* been saying it for years." Clark gave them both a look of grave impatience.

"Now, regarding Teamwork, my Work Team is going to tackle the performance appraisal and compensation issue. The standard set by senior management is that there *will* be

performance appraisals done every six months and they will
be tied to pay increases. For workers, the appraisal will be
done by other Team members and the supervisor. For the
supervisor, the appraisal will be done by his or her Work
Team members, peer supervisors, and by the manager."

Both Tom and Bob quietly gloated that they would have
an opportunity to evaluate one another. Revenge would be
so sweet.

"So my Work Team needs to figure out just how all this
works." Bob made it clear that he was finished. "Now can
I go back to work?" He began to stand up as though to
leave.

"Sit down. You know better. You *are* at work, and your
job is not only in running the business, but also in improving the business. You've *got* to wear both hats at all times."
Clark proceeded to hand out a sheet of paper titled "Ten
Self-Directed Work Team Rules."

"I'll post this on the boards. Be sure to include a review
of these rules with your kickoff meeting agenda and subsequent education. I'll be the coordinator for these initial
Work Teams, and will attend most of the meetings. But
remember, unlike the Improvement Project Teams, and
each of you participated on those, the coordinator will sit
in the background. You, the supervisor, will lead our
Teams through the setup meetings. And here's a summary
of my role as coordinator on your Work Teams." Clark
paused for a reaction, waiting for a question, then began
again, "OKay. That's all I have. I think you're ready for next
week. Good job."

They all rose to leave. Bob suddenly remembered that
he desperately needed to speak with Ruth and Tom about
a pending disaster. "Listen, we really screwed up the order
for Dukester Company. We need to expedite three more
units through right away. They lit a fire under us and we
had to promise delivery next week." As Bob spoke, both
Ruth and Tom's faces froze into masks of exasperation.

ILLUSTRATION 14–3

TEN SELF-DIRECTED WORK TEAM RULES

1. TQM education is focused and continuous.
2. Self-management means members decide day-to-day issues.
3. Team is under authority of supervisor.
4. Team is responsible for performance, which is measured and visible.
5. Team meets weekly to review performance and improvement efforts.
6. Team receives customer satisfaction information.
7. Team designs their work area, and rules and procedures are written.
8. Team must meet plantwide standards.
9. Team may appoint a member as Team Leader.
10. Team Members determine who will join and leave the team.

Clark listened fleetingly to this exchange as he stepped out into the plant. He closed his eyes as he imagined the chaos that expediting the order would create on the shop floor. As he headed for the aspirin in his office medicine chest he realized that none of them could afford too many more hot jobs.

* * * *

Pat stretched and sat back in his chair at the conference table in his office. The workday had finally drawn to a

ILLUSTRATION 14–4

ROLE OF COORDINATORS ON SELF-DIRECTED WORK TEAMS

- Serve as advisor to the supervisor.
- Facilitate the supervisor's transition to leader.
- Provide access to company personnel and resources.
- Assist the Team in preparing documentation.
- Serve as counselor and supporter to each Team member.
- Review and evaluate proposed new systems.
- Inspire the Team to be creative and to challenge existing traditions.

---

close, and he waited for the phone to ring. He was more anxious than usual to get home, shower, and escort Loren Johnson, his close friend and confidante for the last two months, to a late-night dinner.

He had been a bachelor all his life. He thought he might have met the right woman several years back, but a sudden job change forced him to another distant city, and she had to stay behind to pursue her career. The pulling in two different directions tore apart the relationship, and it slowly and painfully faded into Pat's past. His career had put such enormous demands on his time and his thoughts, that he couldn't imagine settling down and sharing his time with a wife and family. Sure, he'd figured someday he'd take on the traditional family life, but for now he was satisfied with apartment living, to coming home to his own space, tired enough not to notice its emptiness.

He would work hard on business matters well into the late evening. The financials and customer communications consumed most of this time. More than anything, Pat took great pride in building personal relationships with customers and suppliers. It served as a way to compete, to better understand these business partners, and to develop a bond of commitment between his business and theirs. This was especially crucial when the business was in a turnaround position and fighting for its life.

Finally the last caller of the day rang and was answered, and Pat bolted for the door hungry for a lungful of the cold and crisp evening air.

Pat and Loren went to their favorite Italian restaurant, planning to spend a few hours over dinner and drinks. This served as the perfect way for them to unwind and share the events of the day, to vent the frustrations the world had laid on their shoulders. They enjoyed each other's company immensely and took pleasure in probing and exploring each other's minds. They both relished the intellectual challenge and spontaneity of their time together.

Loren was tall and willowy, with long light hair, a beauty who could have pursued high fashion modeling as easily as she had become a top-flight attorney. Her career had soared, and she was currently a top trial attorney, a senior prosecutor in the district attorney's office. She volunteered for the toughest and most dangerous cases. It was her way of fighting back against those who would doubt her. She wasn't so much a crusader, for she was convinced that with or without her, the world would go on in much the same way. But she did relish the challenge of each trial, putting the pieces together and solving the puzzle, and proving her case in front of a jury. Unlike much of her life, it was cut and dried; there was closure. Despite the moral complexities involved, you either won or lost, and you knew it.

"So how's it going, Mr. Teamwork? Keeping it floating?" Loren knew this was the nickname Honlinks had used, and she liked to tease him.

"Well, we're fighting the war on a dozen fronts. So far the good guys, with the white hats, are winning, but the casualty rate is high. There are some brave soldiers out there." He sipped his drink, enjoying the banter, sounding like a Honlinks-style tough guy. "It's a high-tech war."

"Just don't let yourself become a casualty. You get too emotionally involved. I think the last several weeks have put a few chinks in your armor. You're looking a little beat. Take care of yourself, Pat." She warned him, but knew that he would pay no attention to this and would put his every last bit of energy into winning. He always told her that he did *everything* with "reckless abandon."

"Honlinks called today. He had a million questions about our Teamwork and Total Quality implementation plan. I sent it to him only last week. The guy is sharp. I have to admit, every time I talk to him, I learn something new. He's one of the few execs I've worked for that cares about details. High-level baloney won't fly and pass inspection. He wants to know *exactly* what we're going to do." Pat relaxed as he spoke, venting the pressure of his job. It was a release, a way to step back and take the long view.

"Sounds like you've got his support?" She knew this was the key to his longevity with the company. It was a selfish question.

"I guess so. He said he's going to do his part. But we've got to show results, or else." He became quiet. "He did say he wants to set up a corporate awards program, where his office recognizes employees for outstanding effort in leadership, Team spirit, and other key behaviors. He's willing to fund an annual awards dinner for our plant, and provide educational scholarship money to the children of the winners." Pat said this triumphantly.

At that moment she saw in him a childlike spirit, a face totally unencumbered with stress or strain. It was a look of accomplishment, of celebration. It made her smile softly as she delighted in his victory.

"How's that guy Keith you've talked about?" She knew he was important to Pat.

"He's been one of the employees who's led the way. Keith has put up with a lot of static, and he's stuck his neck out. He deserves a lot of credit for what's been accomplished so far. I hope he can continue to carry the torch. But he's already been a great example. As time goes by, others will join in. We've seen it already. He's a member of one of the Work Teams starting up in a few days." Pat crossed the fingers of both his hands as he held them before him.

"The employees respect him. I was out in the plant today and he and a group of workers put me under the hot lamps. They wanted to know why, if they are going to be 'self-managed, self-directed, empowered,' did I set standards that the Teams have to meet? Isn't it the same old baloney, management telling them what to do?" Pat smiled.

"Sounds like they're learning the system. Keeps you on your toes. And if they won't, I will," Loren responded vigorously, pointing at herself with her index finger. Pat could see her clenched teeth framed by her smiling red lips.

"I explained that there has to be uniformity among all the Teams. We'd have total chaos in the plant if we had forty Teams each doing their very own thing. There are certain functions, like maintenance, scheduling, and documentation, that have to be done uniformly plantwide." He shrugged his shoulders, gesturing that this was plain as day.

"And did they accept your answer?" Loren continued to explore, seeing how it was unburdening Pat.

"Sure. They began to understand that the specifics of each of these areas would be defined by the Team members, not management. Although we are there to make sure they are heading in the right direction. They are ecstatic that they have the opportunity to make recommendations, and to be heard. Let's face it, that's all anybody wants. When I left they were talking about new procedures for the maintenance system." As the waiter arrived, they stopped the shop talk for a moment, and turned to the menu to order.

"It looks like we even found a position for Terry, the old plant manager. He'll be joining my dear friend at the Detroit plant. He'll be in good company, he likes the progressive thinkers." Pat stopped short. He didn't like negative talk, and stopped himself from indulging his pettiness. "It's just that Terry and I both came to the conclusion that he wasn't about to lead the plant in this direction. He wasn't going to make the conversion from dictator to leader any time this century. Clark has picked up his responsibilities." Pat sat back and thought about Terry as he sipped his red wine. He knew their paths would cross again.

"How is that change viewed by the supervisors? I would think he was their fearless leader?" Even as their food arrived they continued the question and answer session.

"Most of the supervisors have told me privately that they are scared to death. They hear the workers talking about self-management, and they can't envision the role they need to play. They think they're going to be left out or pushed out like Terry. Most don't understand that they can manage and lead the Teams without being a dictator. It really gets down to the fact that they don't think the workers can assume the responsibilities that Work Teams will place on them. They are betting the plant will go haywire. One supervisor told me it would look like the circus had come to town and set up the tent on our shop floor." They both chuckled. It was a metaphor they had often used to describe absurd situations in their own lives. Loren hummed the melody of "Send in the Clowns."

Pat continued, totally involved in explaining the work environment to Loren. "The fact that Terry is on the sidelines has severed their umbilical cord. Clark is training them, working closely with them, and trying to build Team spirit among the supervisors. There are a lot of old battles between the players.

"And I know one supervisor who probably won't make it. Tom Glanahan is going to have a heck of time. He's real political, and that won't fly in a Team-oriented work place. But he's worth the time investment, and with Keith on his Work Team, he should get all the help we can provide. If we need to cut him loose, we will." Pat took another swig of his drink as he contemplated the part of his job that he hated most. But he knew he could make the tough decisions for the sake of the company.

"So what makes you so sure you can pull this one out of the fire?" Loren was trying to imagine what the future held for Pat. If the situation fell apart, how long would this man who enlivened her existence be near her?

"The reality is that *any* shop floor can perform at a higher level. The objective isn't to be 'World Class,' whatever that term really means. I doubt many people who use the term could define it. The objective is to be your very best. To get the utmost from the resources you have. The combination of Teams, quality, and if necessary, new players will improve any situation in a company that hasn't pursued these strategies. A lot of companies *think* they are doing it, but they know they're only kidding themselves. A lot of hand-wringing and talk, but no real change. Signs, symbols, buttons, key chains, but not much else. *We* are really doing it. And it will bring significant improvement in financial performance and customer service. Our question is whether or not Honlinks can hold

on and give us the time we need." Pat spoke as a man
begging mercy from the court. It was out of his control,
and that mere fact brought the greatest frustration. "If only
they hadn't waited so long." Pat looked up at Loren and
saw a warm light in her eyes, of compassion and fondness.
He flinched a little to think how lucky he was to be with
her.

They slowly consumed their meal, enjoying every moment together, feeling the comfort and safety that a sense
of belonging lends, of being a part of a larger whole.

It was a clear, crisp, and still winter's evening. The snow
fall during the early evening hours continued, and had
already left a two-inch white blanket. The snow turned the
ground clean and untarnished.

Pat's apartment was atop one of the many renovated row
homes in this newly gentrified part of the city. Each house
looked the same, and each had a perfectly manicured small,
square front yard, just barely large enough to hold a snow-
man and a child's sleigh. The homes were neatly decorated
for the holiday season. As they walked the block or so from
their parked car, the beauty of this simple scene captivated
them. At 2 a.m., they were the only ones on the streets, and
the walk was quiet and peaceful. They could feel the wet
flakes gently touching their faces.

"Why do you do what you do? Why take on the destroyers?" Loren sought an answer, not just to understand Pat,
but to quell the yearning she had to better comprehend
human nature.

Pat heard her, and images of his father toiling in a
sweatshop floated through his mind. The silence gathered
for several long minutes. And finally, he responded, "I
don't know. I don't think about that."

They trudged up the front steps, and he held the large
oak door open for her to enter the hallway. He turned to
close and lock up, and as he did, he saw the trail of their
footprints in the snow. It was all that marked the pristine

ILLUSTRATION 14–5

carpet of white. He noticed the footprints slowly disappearing under the dancing flakes, and knew they would be gone in a very short time.

That frozen moment jolted Pat. It held the answer to Loren's question.

KEY POINTS FOR DISCUSSION

(1) Three Self-Directed Work Teams, each in a different manufacturing environment, were se-

lected to serve as initial implementation points. This included the winding machine, power supply workcell, and office workcell Teams. Why were each of these selected? Identify three areas in your plant that would be appropriate to initiate Self-Directed Work Teams and would cover a broad range of manufacturing environments.

(2) Clark assigned each of the three Work Teams different aspects of Teamwork and Total Quality to address. For example, Keith's Team was responsible for designing the scheduling system. In this way, the combined Teams would set guidelines for the plantwide manufacturing system. How does your company plan involve Work Teams in the design, development, and implementation of plantwide systems such as scheduling, quality measurement, inventory management, performance appraisal and compensation?

(3) Ruth Mummer's Team was assigned the initial task of creating a playbook, although all Work Teams are responsible to do so. This documents the rules and procedures of the Work Teams and the role of each Team member. Why is this so important? How will your Team document the rules?

(4) Senior Management defined plantwide standards that the Work Teams had to meet, such as using a pull system. Why is it so important that these standards be established? What standards have been established in your company? What areas still require additional standards to insure uniformity throughout the plant?

Chapter Fifteen

A Dream
Inspires the
Team

"When one of you bozos goofs up, you'll be passing it right away to a Team member."

It had been a long day at work, and Keith was glad that Crystal was tucked into bed and asleep. She was his angel, and the legacy of his wife Ginny. Crystal looked so much like her mother, that at times Keith saw too clearly his wife's reflection in her smile and her eyes. Keith hadn't yet completed mourning her loss, and still needed quiet time to allow the wounds to heal. He sat downstairs, as usual, in the big comfy chair in front of the silent television, looking out over the mountain view, and silently wept. He could never let Crystal see or hear him like this.

The Teamwork papers were scattered over the dining room table and chairs. Keith had spent time in the late afternoon reviewing this pile of information. He was preparing for the Power Supply Work Team kickoff meeting in the morning. Tom had provided each Team member a proposed workplan for designing the workcell, several articles that explained the workcell technique, and a kick-off meeting agenda. Also included was a brief description of the Team members, including both work and personal background information. Of course, Keith had already met each of the Team members over the course of the years, usually during a friendly and brief chat in the cafeteria. He brought his machinist skills to the Team, and he had worked on power supply parts as well as on the other products machined in the company. But the power supply products were particularly difficult, with a high frequency of quality problems due to the extreme degree of precision and accuracy necessary from the machining standpoint.

Keith had planned to spend a bit more time preparing for the morning meeting. He slowly lifted himself from his chair and moved to the dining room. He felt better, as he shifted his focus to the project that lay ahead.

"The idea of bringing together all of the equipment needed to build a complete power supply makes a ton of sense. Looks real good on paper. The key to success will be if the Team members can get along. Today, the parts I make go off to another department, and most of the time I don't even know *who* will be using what I've manufactured. But in the workcell, the parts move directly to the next Team member. And if we don't get along, for any reason, there'll be a continuing headache. We'll be working this way every single day, all day, side by side. The conflicts between departments that exist today can't be carried on by the Team members. No way!"

Keith read through the Team member list. "Let's see. There's Bob, Suzanne, Dave, Sally, and myself, and Tom is the supervisor. Quite the diverse group of people."

Keith skimmed the background information on each Team member. "Bobby has been with the company longer

ILLUSTRATION 15-1

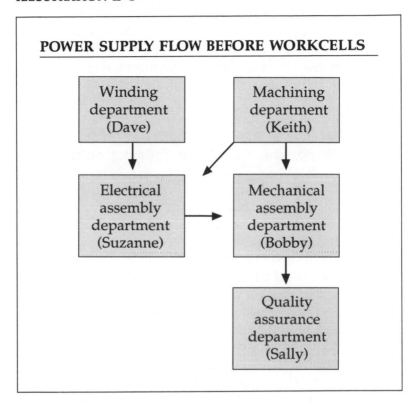

POWER SUPPLY FLOW BEFORE WORKCELLS

Winding department (Dave)

Machining department (Keith)

Electrical assembly department (Suzanne)

Mechanical assembly department (Bobby)

Quality assurance department (Sally)

than anyone on the Team, even me. He's a mechanical assembler, married 22 years, and has two daughters, both of whom are attending college. What I know of Bob is that he's a real gentleman, and very well-spoken. He'll be a good, leveling influence on the group.

"Suzanne is coming from the electrical assembly department. She's a mother of three young children, and very involved in church and community affairs. I really don't know her. I know that everyone points at electrical assembly as a source of real problems in product quality. That department looks like a tornado hit it. Inventory everywhere, and I can't imagine how they can find *anything*, let alone the right thing, in the mess. I'll be interested to hear her side of the story.

"Dave is the mountain man. I think they even call him 'Big Man.' Seems like a heck of a nice guy. Engaged to be married at 29, he's from the motor winding department. A sportsman who likes hunting, fishing, and mountain climbing. Historically, there's been major conflict between motor winding and electrical assembly. We'll see how Dave and Suzanne get along.

"Sally is the scrapper and street fighter on the Team. She won't let us fall asleep, that's for sure. And she's usually screaming about quality and every other problem she thinks she finds. Nothing is ever right for her. She's married, 34 years old, and has a son. Her husband is a concert pianist. I guess he plays and she sings. Final inspection and test gets pounded from everyone. The old management would beat them up whenever orders were late, which was most of the time. And you couldn't go near the place at the end of the month, which was when everything down there was shipped anyway. And in turn, they would do battle with engineering and the other plant departments because of quality problems. With Sally, we'll need our seatbelts strapped on.

"Our meeting tomorrow is supposed to be just an introduction of the Team members, and Clark and Tom will explain the workcell technique, pull systems, and Work Team rules. I wonder what a 'pull' system is? Do we get our chain yanked?"

Keith thumbed through the articles he had been given, and read about scheduling techniques using a pull system approach. "I'm sure they'll explain this in detail. The one thing I know for sure is that whatever we do, we'll need to bring some sanity and organization to the production schedule. Today, the priorities change just about hourly, at least in the machine shop, and *everything* is a rush job."

Next, Keith read through the "Ten Rules for Work Teams" in a effort to get a clearer fix on the scope and responsibilities of the Work Team. "My understanding is that we will spend about six weeks to plan and design the Team procedures and the physical layout of the work area. When the design is complete, we'll present our recommendations to management, and *then* we'll physically rearrange the plant and begin working as a Team. In the meantime, we stay in our departments and meet weekly or as required to get the design complete.

" 'The Ten Rules for Work Teams' suggest that the workers *make decisions*. This is different from the Improvement Project Team. We decide the day-to-day approaches to problems that arise, and the supervisors consider the more global and far-reaching problems. This makes sense because today supervisors decide just about everything, and they can't keep up with their workload. What's worse, they're not close enough to the process to make all the decisions *right*." His eyelids were growing heavy and he realized it was time to turn in.

Keith gathered the Team paperwork and put it in the refrigerator so he'd remember to take it with his lunch in the morning. He checked on Crystal and headed to bed. He set the alarm for 6:15 and cracked the window next to his bed. Only the stars and a faint, cloud-covered moon provided the light he needed to check the alarm setting. He lay down, and put his head on the soft, thick pillow. Instinctively, his hand reached out to where Ginny should have been. Sleep came quickly.

* * * *

"I'm entering the cafeteria at work and both my arms and legs seem like they're injured. I don't know why, they don't hurt, but my limbs are bandaged. I've got this limp, but my arms and hands seem fine.

"This is weird. The cafeteria is a dirty, filthy mess, much worse than usual. What's that green stuff oozing from the walls? Instead of the guys having a relaxed lunch or on break, at the far end there are two dozen or so company managers and supervisors. No other workers are in the room. I recognize several faces, but they're all dressed differently than usual, in blood-red three piece suits. What's that music? Some sort of German beer drinking tune playing over and over. It seems like this is supposed to be a party, a big celebration.

"What's he saying? Several supervisors are gathered around Terry. They're congratulating him. 'I told you if we just did it my way long enough, we'd win. All the jerks they sent here, new managers, consultants, the whole lot of 'em. We showed them.' The crowd's growing around Terry and he's bragging about his promotion to general manager.

" 'We stonewalled them the way you said we should. They weren't going to show us up.' This guy's doing a little dance as he's clapping for Terry. They're all drinking from beer kegs along the wall. What's going on here?

"Let me look out the window, into the parking lot. Only a third of the usual number of cars are there. Where's Pat's car, where's Clark's? I don't see them anywhere. What are these two directors saying? I can't see their faces. 'Yeah. We sure bagged that Teamwork stuff. Just like bowling pins, tough to set up, but easy to knock down.' Terry's going over to them. 'Now we'll run this place the way we want to. And if anybody squawks, just let me know.' A veiled threat, and the execs are gladhanding him. But, they're loving it. One is saying, 'We've been waiting a long time for this. We always knew you were the right man.' Terry, red-faced and grinning, is bursting at the seams.

"The whole crowd is getting more and more intoxicated, from both the alcohol and their backslapping.

"I've got to get out of here, check out the plant, but it's really hard to move with these splints on my legs. Oh no, the Work Teams and cells are gone, and the plant looks the way it used to. Over by the shipping dock, I can see some familiar items sticking up from the trash. I recognize all this stuff, the large corkboards that held the charts for the Teams, they're broken and swimming in filth. Poking through the rubbish, I see the wet and rotten remnants of the Teamwork manuals, the paperwork, all the books we had used. My stomach feels like it's doing somersaults. I think I'm going to be sick.

"This is horrible. The old days and the old ways are back. I want to scream out, but I can't. I'm afraid to even think. And I know those others know that I've found out what they've done. I'll try to straighten out the garbage so it looks undisturbed.

"I better go back to the cafeteria, try and mix in with the crowd. Maybe they don't realize I've been gone. I hear a supervisor saying, 'It's really too bad we had to fire over 100 people today, but this economy is simply dreadful. If only there were something we could have done, but we had to roll with the punches and accept our fate.' He's slogging down that beer, not looking too sorry at all.

" 'It's all the government's fault. They keep letting those foreign companies ship their products halfway around the world, and with such cheap, unskilled labor, how are we supposed to compete?' another was crying as his eyeglasses dropped into his oversize mug.

"Terry's swinging a huge gavel, thumping the picnic table, calling the group to order. 'Okay. As you know, we've got to get better. I've hired several topnotch people with real expertise in the use of stop watches, and they will teach us all to timestudy the workers. We're finally going to get that piecework system we've all wanted for so long. And we'll keep track to the millisecond how much break time these shiftless workers are taking.' Oh no, Terry's looking straight at me. He knows I don't belong, that I'm an outsider, a spy. He's lifting that gavel, as big as a sledgehammer and screaming, 'A traitor in our midst. Seize him! Seize that man!' "

Keith jumped up, unsure of where he was. It was his bed, but how did he get there? Was Crystal all right? He ran in to check on her, and then tested the locks on the front and back doors. He was in a cold sweat, and needed to take several deep breaths trying to regain his composure.

He stared at his alarm clock, reassured by its familiarity. It was 4 A.M., and he was wide awake. He went to the kitchen and prepared himself a hot chocolate. Opening the refrigerator to add milk, he spotted the Teamwork papers, and felt great relief. He took them along with his cup to the big chair, and sat, sipping his warm drink. He stayed there in a sleepless blank state, watching the sun rise. By 6 A.M. he was showered, shaved, and ready for work.

*   *   *   *

The meeting was scheduled to begin at 8 A.M., at the very start of the shift. Keith pulled into the parking lot a few minutes earlier than usual. He drove around the lot, and rather than parking in the first available space, cruised slowly along, still trying to dispel his private fears, looking for tangible evidence that all was okay.

Finally, he saw the light blue sedan that he knew was Pat's. He stopped behind the vehicle, and got out of his car. He stepped nonchalantly, as though he was going about his usual business, and placed his hand on the rear bumper of Pat's car. It was like a hard pinch, like cold water in the face, and it finally broke the nightmare's spell. He parked his car as close to that spot as possible, and hurried inside.

He avoided the cafeteria, and with 20 or so minutes remaining until the meeting, he went straight to his work area. He saw Tom, whom he was looking for, and cried out, "Hey Tommy, ready for our meeting? Ready to move some mountains?" Tom gave him two thumbs up.

Keith felt like a kid. There was a newfound joy, an enthusiasm that came over him that was evident to everyone he met. He just seemed happy. As he walked through the plant he called, "Good morning," to the familiar faces as though he'd been appointed goodwill ambassador.

He was the first to the conference room, and clutching his Teamwork papers, he reserved his seat at the opposite end of the table from where Tom would lead the meeting. As the Team members entered the room one by one, Keith introduced himself and welcomed them. It broke the ice, and made them immediately feel comfortable in the presence of this relative stranger. The waiting time passed quickly as some sort of natural chemistry clicked in among the five of them. Even the simple chit chat was unforced and comfortable. As the group sat and waited, Keith half-jokingly described his late-night dream to his new Teammates. It had a bigger impact on the attitude of each person than Keith imagined, and would never be forgotten by any of them.

Tom and Clark entered together, and even though they knew all the players, they each personally welcomed the Team members. Tom sat at the head of the table, and Clark pulled up a chair in the second row, behind and between Suzanne and Sally who sat together on one side of the table. Bob and Dave sat beside each other, directly across from the women. These were the positions that they would assume by habit each time they would huddle together in this room.

Tom was extremely nervous about this session, for it was the first time he had to run a formal meeting in the presence of management. He was deathly afraid of awkward silences, and he struggled to keep the discussion moving. Clark was there as the Team Coordinator, and his job was to teach and train Tom to handle this effort.

Tom handed out the meeting agenda. After the introductions, the Team got down to business. Sally was never bashful about speaking up. "I think the key question on everyone's mind is 'What the heck is a Self-Directed Work Team'? I mean, that's what we're supposed to become, right? I read through the Work Team rules, and I guess it's not very clear." The others chimed in agreement.

Tom responded, "So let's go through the Work Team rules together. You've all got a copy." As he spoke, he looked to Clark for reassurance. Clark nodded approval.

Tom began a halting explanation of the rules himself, but Clark cut him off. "Instead of us giving you the answers, maybe each Team member can give the group his or her interpretations." He looked at Tom and mouthed the words, "Ask questions."

The light bulb went off in Tom's head, remembering what Clark had told him. "Ask questions, and get the group to talk to each other. Build open discussions. Nobody wants to go to a meeting and just be told facts. The objective is to get everyone involved."

"Sally, why don't you take us through the list and we'll see how much *you* know." Tom thought he had done well.

Clark bowed his head and rubbed his eyes with his left hand. Tom was no diplomat, and he was proving it. Sally grimaced, but proceeded. "To start, we design our own work areas. So the first thing we have to do is figure out what this workcell thing looks like."

Dave picked up on that. "Can we lay it out any way we want?"

Suzanne spoke, "Not any way. I'm sure there's a right way and a wrong way. We'll have to meet the standards of a workcell. Why does it have to be a workcell?" The question was aimed at Clark.

"Management has set a standard that all new plant designs must meet the definition of workcells. We believe this is the absolute best way to design a plant, and we've mandated that the Teams *must* apply these concepts. This has been proven by hundreds, maybe thousands of companies. It works and can get us the performance advantages we need. Exactly how you do that is up to you." Clark said this with his usual confidence.

Clark continued, "Your design objective is to move the product from operation to operation in as small a lot size and in as short a distance as possible. You'll position your equipment to meet both of these objectives."

Bob caught a glimmer of light. "Sort of like a little self-contained factory for power supplies within the big factory. This Team will focus all of our attention on this product line, and we'll become experts in building the little buggers."

Suzanne enjoyed the role of devil's advocate. "Okay. So we set that up. Big deal. What have we really accomplished? What's the big benefit?" She thought she knew the answer, but wanted to hear the others verify her hunch.

Dave, the Big Man, took his time with such matters, but understood the implications as well as anyone. "Well, I know that today, Suzanne will sometimes bring to our department defective motors several weeks after they were produced. It's tough to figure out what went wrong. We need to know if there are problems a lot sooner."

Sally liked that one. "Yeah. When one of you bozos goofs up, you'll be passing it right away to a Team member two feet away, and we'll find the problem *right there*. This way we won't make two billion of 'em with the same dumb little problem. Catch the screwup right away."

Bob saw another point. "You know, it takes weeks from the time the customer places an order to the time we ship it. It seems like workcells will reduce the leadtime to days. Or am I not seeing this straight?"

Keith finally spoke up. "Straight as an arrow. The potential improvement here is awesome." Keith had been sitting back, observing the group's interaction, basking in the feeling of being a part of a creative and positive change. He *knew* they were going to be extremely successful, he could feel it in his bones.

"So that's why we measure and post performance. To prove that we're better than in the old days." Sally hesitated, thinking, and then continued, "And to show we keep getting better." She knew Clark would approve of that one. "So we get together weekly and evaluate ourselves. Talk about how well we're doing, about problems, and about why engineering still isn't getting anything done." Everyone grumbled under their breath about that.

"Yeah. If that doesn't change, then we're still dead in the water. We'll be hurrying up to wait." Keith hit Clark directly, and waited for a response.

"How soon we forget. It was based on employee suggestions that engineering physically move onto the plant floor. I know they only arrived last week, but at least you know they've got their marching orders." Clark knew that would give them some hope.

"Yup. You're right. He's right, isn't he!" The Big Man became visibly excited about all of this, and it keyed up the others as the rush of adrenaline gave them all a slight high. Dave continued, "What does it mean that we'll be deciding the day-to-day issues?" The question brought a look of uncertainty and concern from all the Team members. Tom was hoping to avoid that one.

"Well, it means that you, instead of me, will have to decide how to solve some of the problems that arise each day. For example, you'll have an organized and structured way to communicate directly with maintenance. Another Work Team is developing those procedures. And today, I am the only one who talks with them." Tom knew he would get clobbered on that point.

Keith shot in, "Yeah, and we tell you about maintenance problems, and too often it doesn't even get to maintenance. I mean, it's not your fault, cause you've got 40 other balls up in the air. But important stuff like that often falls through the cracks out there."

"That's why we need a system that *you* can make work. The task of this Team is to design the scheduling system with simple procedures that the Teams can use and make decisions with. That's where I spend 90 percent of my time today, juggling schedules, and if we can get that straightened out, we'll all be golden. But that's another area that you'll assume daily responsibility for." Tom kept glancing at Clark to make sure he was getting it right.

Suzanne added, "Well today, we only do what the supervisors tell us to do. And we waste a lot of time waiting for you to come by and give directions. I always said that we could make decisions, at least the simple ones. And if there's going to be set procedures and rules, then it's even simpler."

Clark liked everything he heard. It seemed the Team members were getting it. But, he wanted to be sure that they didn't think that they would be running the show without supervision. It was a fine line, and difficult to explain. "I think you'll have to give it time and let the relationship between you and your supervisor develop. Every Team will have a slightly different relationship, and that's okay. You'll need the time to build confidence in each other. But rather than have supervisors dictate what everyone will do, we think it's better to have them in a position where they can help *you* cut through some of the bureaucracy and get you quick answers to the questions that come up."

The Big Man smiled. "I'm holding up three dozen motors because my supervisor doesn't have time to get an answer from engineering. In fact, half the time, he's out there working equipment with us because we're behind schedule."

Sally cut it short. "We're going to run our own show, and Tom here will get us the resources we need to keep going." It was clear in her mind. "We'll sweat the little stuff, and he'll take on the bigger items."

"In fact, I've been told that this Team has a budget of $3,000 to spend on any equipment or tooling that you think is necessary. It's yours to use however you wish." Tom knew that would help clarify the meaning of self-management. "You're going to help make decisions."

Bob still was not satisfied on this point. "Like what? It's still not clear to me what Tom is responsible for. I mean, what is he going to be doing if we're 'self-directed'?"

Tom looked right at Bob. "I'm still responsible for the performance of the Team. You are under my authority and management will be looking at me regarding our performance. I still make the final decisions about our area. I'm still involved in manhours and overtime budgets, and I'll have to approve major changes to production schedules and delivery commitments. But I'm here to evaluate and help on *how* we do things. I'll make sure that we apply the new techniques and ideas correctly, and that we are meeting the plantwide standards set by management. More than anything, I'm here to continually *challenge* you to be your best and even better. I'm the coach and leader of this Team, and I'll conduct our weekly meetings and discussions and keep us organized. And I've got to keep a steady stream of educational material flowing to you people. Articles, books, videos, and so forth, and I'll make sure you absorb the stuff too." Tom said this as though he had done it all a thousand times before. Everyone seemed satisfied with the answer. Clark felt relief and a twinge of pride.

Keith kicked in, "The next thing on this list is that we're going to get customer satisfaction information. So all of the complaints are going to come directly to us?"

Sally couldn't hold back. "We'll put a phone booth in the plant, and you'll be there full time answering the calls. You can tell them why we keep messing up and can't get it right." Her tone was sarcastic, and she directed her gibes at the whole group.

Tom took control. "Listen. I'm realizing that we've got to stay positive. So let's get rid of the old baggage, right now, and focus on what we're going to do to fix it." It was the first display of leadership from Tom, and every Team member's respect for him climbed a notch at that moment. Even Sally's.

Suzanne had the answer for Keith. "Maybe we hook up with the customer service people in the office, and they tell us what kind of problems the customers are having. And we get the info daily. One of their people should be at our meetings, too."

Everyone recognized that as a brilliant idea. Tom turned to Clark, "I'll talk to Bob, the power supply office supervisor, and see what we can work out."

Everyone, even Clark, sat there dazzled by Tom's apparent willingness to work with Bob. Tom immediately realized why everyone grew silent, as if holding back some wiseguy remarks.

"Okay, okay. He and I will never be best buddies, but we'll have to work together a lot better than we have. I'm equally guilty. Anyway, they're setting up the same work-cell system and Team in the office for power supplies. And that should finally, after all these years, get them squared away. Maybe when it's all done, they'll actually be somewhat useful." He said this last line with a smirk, and everyone burst out laughing.

"I knew you couldn't resist busting on them." Sally scolded him, laughing, knowing it took one to know one.

Suzanne quietly read the list of Work Team Rules as the others continued the banter. "Hmm. What's the Team Leader do? How does that work?" She pointed to this line on the paper and showed it to Sally sitting next to her.

This rule was still fuzzy in Tom's mind, and he motioned to Clark for help. Clark responded, "It's a position on the Team that everyone gets a chance to hold. You may rotate through that slot every two months, or however often you wish. You'll set that up once the Team is in place and the feet are firmly planted." Everyone liked to hear that, for the concern was that it would create just another permanent boss or supervisor.

Clark continued, "You'll all define the day-to-day responsibilities and tasks of the Team Leader later on. But it's usually more efficient to assign a person on the Team to serve as a sort of central point for communication between the Team, the supervisor, and other Teams. This person also helps keep the Team organized, and may do all the peripheral jobs, like measuring and posting performance, running the scheduling pull system, communicating with maintenance, and so forth. Remember, though, that the Team Leader is also a worker, and must also man assigned manufacturing operations. You'll see."

Dave spoke up. "Yeah. I can see how we'll always need someone who does all that stuff while the rest of us keep producing. Not a bad idea."

Keith was reading the list of rules, and was preparing to raise what seemed to be the question everyone was avoiding. "How about the rule that says Team members determine who will join and leave the Team? What does that mean?" Keith crossed his arms and sat back, waiting for an answer.

Tom was at a loss. He understood the basic premise that the Team had to police itself, but he wasn't yet able to explain how this would work. Clark saw that he had to explain. "Initially, management will assign members to Work Teams. And we'll do so to find compatible groups of people, those who we think will work well together and cooperate. However, once the Team is established, you will be responsible to interview and approve any new member joining the Team. We're not going to put people on your Team without your assessment and approval."

"Let's face it. If we don't think someone fits in, then they probably won't. And forcing them on the Team could hurt our performance. So what you're saying makes sense." Suzanne said this slowly and deliberately, reflecting on her own words as she spoke.

Clark let the silence hang, and this notion of self-direction sunk in. He finally continued, "Now, on the flip side, let's say that a Team member, for some reason, starts to not work out. Maybe the person just isn't cut out for Teamwork, and begins to slack off and not pull their weight. What do you think should happen?"

"Usually we can't say anything. We'd have to do so individually, and then you get the reputation for 'ratting' on another fellow worker. All you can do is wait for the supervisor to provide some discipline. Usually, that doesn't happen, and then you wonder why you're working hard and the other person isn't, and nobody cares. So eventually everybody slows down because it's acceptable." The group could tell Dave was speaking from the experience of several frustrating years.

Clark could see Tom was ready to defend himself, but cut him off. "So how *should* it be?" They all just sat quietly, and no one wanted to speak, afraid they would be tagged as the culprit of new rules.

"Okay. We both know the answer. If someone isn't pulling their weight, then the *Team* will have an opportunity to voice their concern. You must talk to your supervisor, who wants to know. Bring it to their attention. They'll confirm the problem and discuss it with the Team member, and try to work out a solution. I've always found this is easier to solve than you might think. You'll usually find the lagging Team member doesn't *want* to be on the Team. So your recommendation to remove the member doesn't come as a wild surprise, and the adjustment can be done without lasting hard feelings. Of course, you all should try to work the problems out before you take this step." Clark took pains to give a clear explanation on this sensitive point. "You see, the supervisor plays a critical leadership role."

The Team members were each beginning to feel the potential power and authority this new system would give them. They would no longer be spectators in the bleachers, watching the game played from afar. The Ten Rules put them smack in the middle of the playing field, and recognizing the significance of their new involvement was both frightening and seductive.

"You see, there will be very few jobs on the shop floor that aren't part of a Team. And so if no one is willing to have you on their Team, then employment opportunities in *this* company are scarce, and you'd probably be better off seeking employment somewhere else." Clark said this matter-of-factly, not meaning to threaten or intimidate in any way.

"In other words, Team players make the cut, and lone rangers hit the trail." Sally summarized in her "dead-on" style.

Tom regained control. "So that's a Work Team. Those are the rules we'll meet. Make sense?" He watched the heads nod. "Next week we'll continue education, and discuss articles and books. We'll also begin to document the routings, equipment, and operations power supplies require for manufacture. This is the starting point to designing the workcells themselves."

They all agreed, and animatedly discussed their future for the next several minutes. The hour had expired, and Tom completed the usual closing administrative tasks. They all began to recognize the concepts and techniques they were planning to put in place as plain simple. Almost too simple, and that thought made them all a little uneasy.

They all knew that success relied on each person's ability to adjust their attitudes and behaviors, and to work and cooperate as a true Team. This was a "people thing," and each individual felt pretty confident that he or she could do it. But what about the person across the table, could *they* do what had to be done? This was the foremost concern in their minds and hearts. And it was a question that could only be answered in the doing of it over the course of time.

KEY POINTS FOR DISCUSSION

(1) Review the Ten Rules for Work Teams, and discuss each among your Team members. To what extent is your Team presently meeting each of these rules?

(2) Organize the Ten Rules For Work Teams in a descending list, from the easiest to the most difficult to achieve in your company. What company traditions stand in the way of making each rule a reality?

(3) The Team has been charged to adopt a workcell plant layout. Briefly describe how this compares with the traditional process-oriented departments. Why should you expect significant improvements in quality and leadtime to result?

(4) The Work Teams will communicate directly with maintenance, and will be empowered to request their assistance. A set of procedures will be established to make this part and parcel of the shop floor. What are the strengths and weaknesses of this approach? Suggest ways to improve the relationship between Work Teams and maintenance in your company.

(5) A pet peeve of most workers is feeling that discipline is not fairly applied by supervisors, and that some workers don't pull their fair share of the load. This Work Team will be empowered to hire and fire Team members. Why is this such an important component of Teamwork? How will your company handle this issue?

Chapter Sixteen

Fire and Brimstone

"It doesn't sound as though they did it the right way."

It was late afternoon several days after the kickoff meeting, and Keith was running the last batch of parts for the day. Tom was on his typical rounds through the department when he spied Keith from across the shop floor. A devilish gleam flashed in Tom's eye as he saw an opportunity to get some inside information. Tom schemed to himself, "Keith and I used to put 'em away pretty good years back. I wonder if he'd join me down at Flaherty's for a few. Loosen up the old boy a bit, and see what he might know about my future here. Somebody's saying I may not be long for this place. Keith is pretty chummy with the big guns, and he just might know the scoop." Tom smiled wide as he approached Keith.

Keith had seen that smile all too often, and was ready to duck from whatever was heading his way. Tom was as subtle as a freight train with a full head of steam. First would come the cheap compliment, immediately followed by the roundabout request for whatever he wanted. Usually Keith would get testy, they'd argue, and Tom would stomp off and not talk to him for a week.

But not this time.

"Hey Keith, I think you outproduced the entire plant today. Yup. Looks like you really smoked the equipment." Tom studied his board, as though he had conclusive evidence there to prove his assertion.

Keith thought, "Check. Cheap compliment duly noted and recorded." He laughed out loud, unable to hold it in. He'd play along this time. After all, he was feeling pretty good this week. "Okay, Tom. What can I do for you?" Keith said this indicating he was sincerely prepared to assist.

"Well, I was remembering the times when you, me, and the others used to stop by Flaherty's after work and hoist a few. *Those* were the good old days. We really did *feel* like a Team back then." Tom knew that last line might sway Keith.

It was several years ago, when Ginny was still alive, and Keith would spend a night out with the boys every once in a while. Back then, Flaherty's was the booming night spot for the blue-collar crowd. Darts, shuffleboard, and pool were the mainstays for entertainment. Keith recalled the smell of the greasy chicken wings that would go down so easily with a mug or two of beer serving as dinner on those woozy evenings.

Keith thought, "Those days are long gone. Going back would be some cruel trip down memory lane." He responded unenthusiastically, "Almost all of the boys that would go are gone. No, maybe one or two are still here. So, who's going?"

"Just me and you." Tom said this in a tone that could be interpreted as an order.

"Okay. Alright, let's go. But I can only stay for a few hours. We'll leave by 6:30. I'll call Crystal's aunt and tell her I'll be a bit late. And why don't I be the designated driver." Keith knew Tom would down more than a few.

Flaherty's was located in the heart of the industrial center of the city. It was a two-story brick building shoehorned between two ten-story brick warehouses. These two stood like silent sentinels, now vacant, having shut down operations several years ago. The largest and most powerful industrial businesses had once resided within this 10-block radius.

As Keith chugged his Impala down the beat-up street pavement, he was wide-eyed at the vast degradation and deterioration of the buildings. It had been years since he last passed through, and while he knew from his route to work how the city had sickened, he hadn't imagined that the blight had infected this once thriving locale.

"Keith, stop! You're going right past Flaherty's!" Tom called out as the car flew past the storefront. Keith hadn't recognized the spot. The black metal bars that covered the glass picture window were unfamiliar. And the neon light that always welcomed patrons was unlit. They parked down the block by a big green dumpster, and walked back to the bar.

As they entered Keith expected to see the usual large crowd and hear the booming jukebox playing Springsteen tunes. Instead, he only heard the faint crackling sound of a small television behind the bar and the hum of a space heater. Tom bellied up and exchanged greetings with the barkeep. Old man Flaherty, who had been in this spot for 30 years, had finally retired to Florida, and his son-in-law, Butch, grudgingly manned the post. Keith ignored the two and took a walk around the place.

Red lights replaced the usual bright white lights, and the fans ceased to turn. It gave the place an eerie glow, even as twilight descended outside. The wood floors had lost their luster, and the old jukebox stood in the same position, unplugged, and empty of disks. Keith walked past a group of three sitting at a table in the eating area munching on packaged nuts, moving towards the pool table nestled in the back of the room. The felt was worn and ripped in places, and Keith looked for his lucky cue stick. It was missing, and the ones that remained were bowed like divining rods.

The colorless walls were dingier than ever, still plastered with the familiar photographs of sports heroes and legends. "I hope I never look that lonely," Keith thought, as he came across the yellowed picture of a young Joe DiMaggio sitting on the bench by himself. It was taken by Old Man Flaherty himself, and was the pride of the place.

Amidst a few well-worn holiday decorations, their cheeriness ironic in this setting, there hung a faint, acrid odor in the air, as though the garbage needed taking out. It penetrated everything although there was no identifiable source. Keith had seen enough, and joined Tom at the bar.

"Keith, meet Butch Flaherty." Tom left them abruptly, and headed to the lavatory. They exchanged courtesies, and Keith ordered a diet soda. As Keith waited for Tom's return, Butch tried to make small talk.

"Tom was saying you used to be a regular. Back in the good old days." Butch tried to laugh, but it wasn't real, and it wasn't convincing.

"Well, not really. I'd come down, maybe once a month. Hardly a regular, but it was a good time. About 10 of us would come down after work." Keith sipped his soda. "This place has changed a lot. I mean a *real* lot." Keith looked at Butch for a response, and the barkeep tightened his lips and shook his head side to side.

"One by one, the businesses are going. You remember what this place used to be. Heck, 15 of the 20 big companies right around here are either shut down or running at quarter speed. They're moving to Mexico, sending the jobs overseas, or just plain going out of business. I don't know just what's causing this to happen, but something stinks in Denmark." Butch turned to get a drink for the other patron, who sat two bar stools away. He continued, "And when the neighborhood loses the jobs and the money leaves, well, tough times move right in. It's just a progressive downward spiral. We've been broken into and vandalized here four times, just this year!"

Keith could empathize with this man's sense of loss, recognizing the bitter truth in his words. Butch wiped the bar under Keith's drink. "When the good times were here, we never thought how much we depended and needed those businesses to be successful."

The other patron sat on the stool, slouched over his drink, elbows on the bar. "I do now. I used to be a production manager at one of those big companies, and I can tell you, everyone is at fault. It just seemed like it could never happen to us."

Tom returned and began chatting until he saw how carefully Butch and Keith were listening to the other fellow. The ex-production manager continued, recalling the past, "The workers were all unionized. And I remember spending more time during the day dealing with grievances than I did on production issues. Or we'd meet to figure out strategy to get back at the union for their latest 'get back'. I'd spend 80 percent of my day on this stuff. And of course, the employees and union leaders were spending an awful lot of time trying to get right back at us." He took another swig of his drink and swallowed hard. "It stopped working, and as our competition grew, their quality simply exceeded ours. We couldn't break the cycle of animosity. We shut down last year, and now we import product from overseas and just distribute for another manufacturer."

Keith turned to Butch to add a translation to what they just heard. "The cause isn't any single, grandiose government policy decision. The answer lies on the shop floor of every company. Teamwork and quality is the solution."

Tom spoke next, "Maybe, maybe not. Keith, some of my friends are on the way down, and I think you'll see that they are doing this Teamwork stuff and haven't had too much success. Maybe there just isn't a solution." He nudged Keith's elbow, and pointed to a table by the window. "Let's sit down and chat a bit, you and I.

"So how's your daughter, Keith? Er, uh, Kristen?" Tom groped for her name. Discussing personal matters with his employees didn't come easy.

"*Crystal* is just fine. She looks more and more like her mother each day." Keith had the gleam of a proud parent mingled with a certain sadness in his eyes. As they talked, Keith sat watching the street outside through the streaked window, and paid close attention to the shadows of the buildings growing denser and longer as the sunlight faded and dusk set in.

Keith saw that Tommy was becoming very relaxed; perhaps it was the ambience, perhaps it was the drink in his glass. Keith wanted to understand the motivations of this man who had served as his boss for so many years. He had always viewed Tom as close-minded. He was rarely willing to listen to new ideas from his people, and always behaved self-importantly.

"Tommy, over the last several months, we've all been introduced to a lot of new information. Books, articles, videos have explained so many new ways to manage our plant. It's as though this entire body of knowledge about manufacturing management has been in existence, but we as a company either didn't know it was there or decided to ignore it. There *are* definite ways to lay out equipment, to plan and schedule the plant, to measure quality, and so on, and we haven't been doing it that way. How could we have missed this?" Keith meant how could "you" have missed it, but, either way, the question really nagged at him.

Tommy sensed Keith's need for an answer. "I must tell you that quite a few of the books, and well, even the basic ideas, that Pat and Clark have introduced aren't so new to the Management Team. We've *seen* most of this before." Tom stopped, hoping Keith would be satisfied.

But Keith needed to understand. "So why didn't we *do* something?"

Tom took another gulp of his drink. He muttered in a low voice, "Arrogance, arrogance. We were too arrogant to acknowledge we needed help." He continued, "We said we were doing it, but knew we weren't. We said it wouldn't fit us, but knew it would. We said we didn't have the time, but knew we could've made it. We all thought we already had the answers, but deep down we knew we were kidding ourselves."

Both men sat in silence in respect to the truth that had just been spoken. Keith needed to hear this confession. He needed Tom to acknowledge the past and not deny it, so that each day henceforth could proceed framed by the truth.

"Hey Tommy, you old dog! For once, you're here before me!" The booming voice across the room belonged to Manuel Ortiz, a heavy-set man in his mid-forties. Mustachioed and slightly gray, Manuel was a close friend and confidant of Tom's, and they often met with the other regulars at Flaherty's after hours.

Tom stood up. "Speaking of old dogs! Come on over Manny!" Looking towards Keith, he said, "This fellow here has already been through the famous Teamwork and Total Quality. The stories he could tell!"

Manuel was a production supervisor at another major manufacturer in the city. They too, had been hard-pressed to improve business performance, and the Management Team turned to Teamwork and Total Quality several years ago. The negative impact of the changes left a bad taste with company personnel, especially the supervisors and middle managers. It was gradually abandoned and left to die a quiet death.

After polite introductions and some small talk, Tom explained how the improvement effort at Manuel's company was conducted. "They formed Teams on the shop floor and redesigned the plant to workcells, just like we're doing." Manuel nodded approval.

"That's right, every employee was assigned a Team. We had over 70 Teams started at one time. We, the supervisors, couldn't keep up." Manuel shook his head, recalling the chaos. "I was lucky, though, because I only had four Teams to watch over."

"How long did it take for the Teams to design the new workcells?" Keith was eager to learn from the experience of this fellow.

Manuel hesitated. "Well, they didn't do much design work. Maybe a day or so. Our company strategy was to just go do it, and not think too much about what to do. Everyone thought they knew how the equipment should be placed. We didn't take the time to study and consider the routings of each product." Manuel turned to Tom, "I know you guys are doing that. Looking back, we should have done that too, especially given that each Team produced at least 50 different end items, and the routings were often quite complex for each product."

Tom didn't like what he was hearing. He cut in, "What he's saying, Keith, is that they tried workcells, and they didn't work worth spit!"

"Yeah, but it doesn't sound as though they did it the *right* way." Keith turned to Manuel, "So how did it end up?"

"Well, after the first few months, the Teams finally settled on the position and location of the equipment, and the responsibilities of each Team member. But production and quality never even reached the old levels." Manuel shrugged his shoulders. "We had to return to the old plant layout within six months because we couldn't keep missing deliveries."

"But that doesn't make sense. Workcells brought the needed equipment closer together, didn't it? What was the real problem?" Keith probed him for a response.

"The workcells did do that. But we forgot a very important part of the workcell strategy. We didn't set up a *scheduling system* that was compatible with the new plant layout."

Tom was listening intently. When he'd first heard this tale he thought the essential concept was flawed, but now he began to realize that the failure Manuel spoke of was due to a lack of consideration of all aspects of the manufacturing system. "In other words, all you did was move the furniture around, and thought everything else would work itself out?" Tom questioned him. Manuel again nodded agreement.

Manuel continued to explain, "In the old system, the supervisor's primary function was to expedite the work through the plant. We all had a way, although maybe each a different way, to prioritize the orders and determine which job should be produced at each operation. Even though it wasn't computerized and was pretty informal, it worked well enough to get the product through and effectively compete." Manuel paused. "But when the Team physically reorganized the plant, it was like joining a whole new company and on the first day struggling to just find your way back to your desk. It became an unfamiliar maze, and our old way of scheduling *couldn't* be used."

Keith cut in and turned to Tom, "That must be why our Team is responsible for designing a scheduling system for the workcells. We'll avoid the pitfall your company fell into."

"I hope you do, because we still haven't fully recovered," Manuel replied. The three men continued to talk about their Teamwork experiences, and as Keith listened to the struggles Manuel endured, he became more confident that

Pat and Clark were leading them on the right path. He also realized how disappointed Tommy was because he obviously thought Manuel would serve as a witness testifying against the evils of the new system and in the process convince Keith to soften his support.

Manuel finally excused himself, and left Keith and Tom at the table. As they finished their drinks, Tom said, "Oh yeah. You know, I've heard that Pat may not have full confidence in me. Do you know anything about this, old pal?"

As they prepared to step out into the cold night air from that dimly lit red room full of stale memories, Keith responded, "I can't speak for him. Ask him yourself. Before you do, take a close look in the mirror. Otherwise, you won't understand his answer, Doubting Thomas."

And Tommy shook his tired head in acknowledgment.

KEY POINTS FOR DISCUSSION

(1) At Manuel's company, the Work Teams ignored the need to design a scheduling system compatible with the new plant layout and workcell strategy. Explain why this is such an important component of the shop floor. How effectively does your scheduling system presently function? List the strengths and weaknesses of the current scheduling methods.

(2) Another mistake at Manuel's company was to just "go do it," and not take adequate time to plan and design the new layouts and procedures. What conditions might push a company to take this approach? How much time will your Team require to properly design the new systems? What pressures will be experienced by the Team to complete this task as quickly as possible?

(3) Discuss with your Teammates the economic conditions of your city. To what extent do you believe that improved management of the shop floors of the industrial companies in your area can further strengthen the local economy?

Chapter Seventeen
Organizing for Quality

"It looks good on paper."

K eith's Team met each week over the next several weeks to design their workcells and to establish the rules and procedures of the Team. There was an electricity in the air, a contagious sense of excitement in the group. This sensation began to spread throughout the rest of the workforce. A joyous feeling of renewal could be felt by everyone. The cafeteria was continually abuzz with Teamwork banter, and people were genuinely banding together.

Of course, people still felt a bit uneasy with the uncertainty of change. But as time went on, it was becoming less and less cool to be negative, and positivity was in. Everyone was focusing their attention on real solutions. Gripers were becoming an extinct breed. New ideas, from the sublime to the ridiculous were everywhere, and this heady stew was proving habit-forming.

*   *   *   *

Keith's Team gathered to hone the design of their new worklife. They had spent much time working on the layout of their "plant," and were preparing to finalize their recommendations.

It was a clear and crisp late winter's morning. The Team members had all voluntarily hustled to work an hour early to spend extra time on their brainstorming. Tom struggled to bring the drowsy group to order. "Okay. Let's get going. This morning the task is to finalize the layout and get on to the other areas of the workcell. Let's see, we also need to cover inventory management, pull system rules, maintenance system, quality system, performance measurement, and the responsibilities of each Team member." He read in an authoritarian tone from a prepared list.

Bobby spoke first, "I think the best way to double-check the strength of our new layout is to follow each product through the process and see how each one moves and flows. Overall, I think we've got it right, but the handful of products that are highly customized and unique worry me. The *exceptions* always cause havoc."

"Yeah. Let's just walk each product through and double-check to make sure the flow is consistent and in one direction." As Keith spoke, he opened the blueprint of the floor space assigned to the Power Supply Team. They had cut paper to scale, representing each piece of equipment. This would accurately reflect the impact on space and distance of the proposed layout.

The Team worked through the entire product list, and tracked the path of each product through the Power Supply mini-factory. They followed the routing of each product, and found that a small drill press was needed in the Mechanical Assembly and Final Test workcell. "We've got the equipment and the layout to efficiently produce any power supply. We'll beat the pants off anyone." Dave spoke proudly. The other Team members also knew they had hit on strong solutions to many of the old problems.

"We'll be able to produce a power supply in one one-billionth of the time we used to. The leadtime will be cut from weeks to days, maybe even less." Suzanne sat back and crossed her arms triumphantly.

Sally added, "Well maybe, one-millionth. It does *look* good on paper. I'll pass judgment after we spend our first week in there. If we make it out alive." The group laughed and prodded each other.

"The biggest potential problem is that we'll argue with each other about the *quality* of the work. So far, we've all avoided this discussion, but maybe it's worth touching on." Keith wanted to put the tough issues on the table and get them resolved *before* they blew up in real life situations.

Clark saw an opening to clarify a key point. "You're on the right path. And I agree you need to resolve the historical conflicts now, before they get in the way of your success in the plant. But keep in mind that quality is your primary objective. Meeting the product specifications as defined by engineering, is your goal." Clark knew that the members would debate the quality of the work done in the past, and the center of the disagreement would be the issue of acceptability. Everyone had different standards as to what was acceptable.

"Well, everyone knows how I feel about the quality of the work from the winders. Even though you use the small mobile winding equipment, the quality of the product you send to electrical assembly varies so greatly that a large percentage of product just isn't good enough." She paused trying to contain her rising excitement. "So, we've moved the winder into the workcell, but I'll still have to deal with the same pathetic problems." Suzanne closed her eyes in exasperation.

"It's funny, but over the years no one has ever come to me and personally explained the problems. I've heard about the problems second- and third-hand. You know how we work around here, or used to work around here. You tell your supervisor, who tells the manager, who tells another manager, who tells the janitor, who leaves me a note in German. And I don't read German! By the time I get the message, it sounds like I'm wanted in five states for armed robbery." Dave looked sorrowful as he shared *his* perspective, and his Teammates could see he was sincere in his desire to solve problems. Suzanne was dumbstruck, because she had always considered the winders as her biggest enemies, the vilest and most despicable slugs on earth. But before her sat a perfectly nice fellow, a likable guy, who had obviously been doing his level best over the years just as she had.

"I bet that if you two head out to the plant and talk, one-on-one, about the quality requirements, you'll solve it in a heartbeat." Keith addressed them both.

"Let's do it." Dave gave a thumbs up signal with his right hand.

"And if you need engineering's infinite wisdom, let me know. I'll get them right over to you." Tom saw an opportunity to do his job, which was to get his Team the resources *they* needed to solve the problems.

Seeing that settled, Bobby spoke up, switching gears. "Our goal statement says we're responsible for designing a pull/scheduling system. I guess I'm not exactly sure what that is, but, I do know one thing. We need to fix the way we schedule around here, darn it!" He slammed his fist to the table, feigning anger.

Sally mimicked him, whacking the tabletop. "We do need to crack that vault." She pointed at Bobby, "And you're elected."

"What do I know? I mean, I always thought that if we could keep all of the work in some sort of definite order, in the same order throughout the plant, in a *sequence*, then we'd have a chance of taming the beast." He looked around, got up, and began to pace the room.

Suzanne felt hooked into the creative energy crackling in the room. "Last night I went to the market and bought some cold cuts at the deli counter. It was crowded, and we each had to take a number. This prioritized the crowd milling around in the area. And when my number came up, I became the top priority and was 'processed.' It almost seems like we should number everything here." She stopped and watched the others stand up and gather around the blueprint of their layout. She half-giggled, "I'm not even sure what I'm saying makes sense."

"No, this makes a ton of sense. But, the number has to be assigned at the beginning. We can't keep assigning numbers in the plant at every workcenter or cell. It'd be chaos." Dave bent over and drew a circle with his finger in the air over the layout.

Tommy and Keith both thought of their meeting with Jose. Tom spoke, "Getting the scheduling system right is crucial to our success." He saw Keith nod his head. "Supervisors run around here all day assigning priorities to jobs at each operation. We have to get away from that."

"But the *real* problem is that every department has a different set of priorities. It's pure chance that the requirements for a job come together at the same time in assembly," Keith added. "So what we need is to establish this sequence, this single priority, throughout the plant at every operation in every department."

The Team members were all on their feet, with hands waving furiously in the air as they heatedly discussed this. They were animated and consumed by the challenge. Even Clark joined in. "Hold it, y'all. We need to get back to our seats and get organized. Lots of great ideas here, but we need to write them down so they don't get lost." Clark went to the chalkboard and began scribbling.

ILLUSTRATION 17-1

SCHEDULING SYSTEM CHARACTERISTICS

- Easy to manage and control the volume of plant work-in-process.
- Physically organizes the plant.
- Synchronizes the movement of product.
- For make-to-stock, make-to-order, or both.
- Simple priority change communication.
- Motivates the Team.
- Makes problems visible.
- Simple and inexpensive.

"Here's a list of the characteristics this scheduling system *should* have."

"We're not going to iron out all the details of this right now, so let's break and we'll tackle it during the next several weeks. But, trust me, you're on to a concept that is both powerful and easily workable." Clark put the chalk down and sat. "During the last 20 years or so, companies have spent millions on software and computerized scheduling techniques. You've probably heard the terms MRP II, and material requirements planning? Well, it's pretty hard to find a company, large or small, that has successfully implemented computerized scheduling on the shop floor. I know this company tried several years ago, and it really flopped. On the other hand, I know of several other companies that have done something similar to what we're talking about, a simple manual priority system, and had great success. It's called Production Sequencing."

Clark continued, "In this system, each workcell receives a copy of the sequenced master production schedule. This ensures that each workcell operates under the *same* set of priorities. Then, each workcell has designated inbound and outbound squares. These are physical locations that hold a line item on the MPS. Each Team is responsible to keep their outbound squares full. When an outbound square opens, it signals the Team to produce the next order in the sequence of the master production schedule. And all components needed are already in the inbound square. The end result is that every workcell in the plant is linked together and product is pulled through the factory in the sequence of the MPS." He returned to the board and sketched the plant layout under this system.

The Team agreed that resolving the plant scheduling system would be a top priority next week. In the meantime, Tom would speak with the order entry and planning department supervisors to involve them in the design process.

As the meeting drew to a close, Clark somewhat off-handedly added, "Oh, by the way, Pat asked me to request that you select a Team member to join him at a corporate headquarters meeting in Chicago next month. He'd like you to select the person you think would best serve as a spokesperson for our Teamwork and Total Quality efforts." Clark instructed Tom to let him in on what the group decided, and left the room.

They all knew the importance of the events in Chicago. The discussion about who should go lasted several minutes as it gradually emerged that they all knew Dave would best represent the Team and the workforce. His down-to-earth style and his honest manner were the key factors. But, everyone would help him organize his notes for the trip, because they wanted to be sure that the commitment to improvement was clearly expressed.

While Dave didn't know exactly what his role in Chicago might be he knew his ability to persuade people would be

ILLUSTRATION 17–2

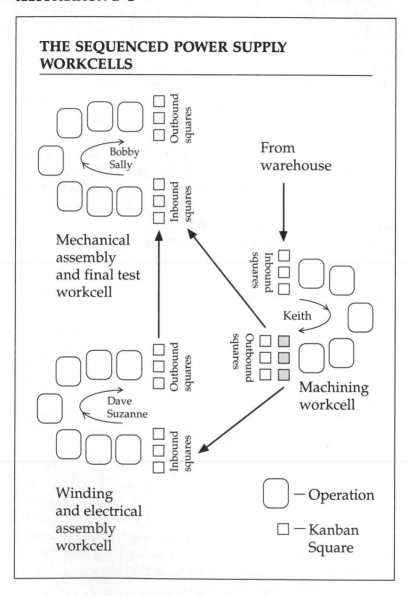

THE SEQUENCED POWER SUPPLY WORKCELLS

Outbound squares

Bobby
Sally

Inbound squares

From warehouse

Mechanical
assembly
and final test
workcell

Inbound squares

Keith

Outbound
squares

Outbound
squares

Dave
Suzanne

Machining
workcell

Inbound squares

Winding
and electrical
assembly
workcell

— Operation

— Kanban
Square

pivotal. He couldn't realize at that moment that his ability to persuade the board of directors would mean the difference between the success and failure of the company.

* * * *

It was Monday morning, and the Team gathered in the cafeteria to prepare for the first day of the implementation of the Power Supply Workcell.

During the last several weeks the Team had worked hard to establish their procedures and rules. Clark worked closely with Tom to write the Team's playbook, which included all areas of Team management. The playbook was the governing rulebook of the Team, its bible. It contained the guidelines that described the specific procedures to follow in each facet of the Team's worklife. They had all come to realize that the written word was vital to properly communicate the rules. Unwritten rules quickly lost their meaning, were open to a wide variety of interpretations, and thus, were essentially unenforceable.

The "Reporting Relationships" section of the playbook described the basic relationships of the Team members, the Team Leaders, the supervisor, and the coordinator. It emphasized the importance of the chain of command maintained under Teamwork. The frequency of formal communications was set down, including weekly meetings between the Team members and the supervisor prescribed to maintain an open dialogue. The general manager or any other member of the Management Team could be invited to sit in by the Team.

The "Pull/Scheduling System" section of the playbook described how the Team would receive the sequenced master schedule from the planning department, and how each workcell would work in the exact priorities of this document. It explained how the open kanban squares on the shop floor would signal the movement and production of orders, and how the MPS would be reissued to each

ILLUSTRATION 17–3

PLAYBOOK COMPONENTS

- Team reporting responsibilities.
- Pull/scheduling system.
- Maintenance management system.
- Housekeeping system.
- Performance measurement and reporting.
- Quality system.
- Inventory management system.
- Performance appraisal and compensation.
- Playbook update procedures.

---

workcell whenever the sequence of orders was changed due to necessity.

The "Housekeeping" section of the playbook described the daily tasks and routines that each Team member must complete to keep the floor and work areas perfectly clean and tidy. The frequency of painting the walls, floor, and equipment was defined. It was decided that the last 15 minutes of each day would be dedicated to performing the required housekeeping tasks. The Team Leader would inspect and approve the neatness of the work area at the end of each day.

The "Maintenance Management" section described the specific checks, lubrications, and other preventive care tasks that the Team members would conduct daily, weekly, and monthly, and how to record these efforts on a log attached to each piece of equipment. In addition, it described the procedures the Team members would follow to *directly* report equipment problems to the maintenance department. The red tape that previously existed was eliminated, and the workers now had the authority to request and approve the work of maintenance. This system had been defined by Ruth Mummer's Work Team.

The "Inventory Management" section of the playbook described how the Team would place requisitions to purchasing and other company departments for components that they stocked on shelves in the workcell.

The "Quality Management" section of the playbook described the most important product specifications and tolerances, and alerted operators to the nuances of product manufacturing that required special attention. This also forcefully explained the authority each Team member had to stop production in order to prevent product not meeting quality requirements from being passed on. A light system was set up so that the Team members could request the assistance of engineers as soon as they ran into a problem that needed their participation. At each workcell a light that could be lit and seen across the plant was put in place.

The "Performance Appraisal and Compensation System" section of the playbook proposed a pay system compatible with Work Teams. The new system centered on performance appraisal for workers that was completed in confidence by Teammates and the Team's supervisor. A worker would be evaluated on such behaviors as attitude, creativity, initiative, attendance, quality, and level of effort, and the weighted average of the grades from each reviewer would determine the worker's pay increase. In addition, the rules regarding "hiring and firing" of Team members were clearly defined. It explained that both the Team and the supervisor would be responsible to select new Team members, and it explained the steps the Team should take in the event a member doesn't fit in the group due to work performance or attitude.

The "Playbook Update Procedures" section described how the Team would meet monthly with the specific purpose to update the playbook so that it *always* reflected the current rules and procedures. It emphasized the need for the Team to continually search for new and better ways in each of these areas to improve productivity and quality performance.

The Power Supply Team presented their playbook to the Management Team at a formal presentation. This was extremely important because it gave the managers and supervisors of each department the opportunity to review the proposal and to voice an opinion about this new system. The Power Supply Team was the first Self-Directed Work Team to undergo implementation, and the other two were scheduled to follow closely behind.

The task of moving equipment was completed over the weekend. The Team members and over two dozen other employees volunteered to assist the outside contractors move equipment. The senior managers, including Pat and the directors, were there in jeans and rolled-up shirt sleeves, working side-by-side with everyone else to get the job done. They wanted to show that *no one* was better than anyone else. Their sweat didn't go unnoticed, and it was one of the key points for discussion in the cafeteria early Monday morning.

Keith was anxious to see his Teammates, and he hurried in from the parking lot to see who had already arrived. While it was still February, the morning felt faintly like spring, and the mildness gave Keith comfort and a sense of well-being.

As he walked into the cafeteria, he was taken aback by the clamor. Usually at this time in the morning, only a few souls would be found clinging to their coffee cups. But this morning, Keith saw well over 50 people gathered, and when he entered, the crowd turned toward him and cheered loudly. They chanted, "Keith, Keith, Keith!" And as Keith drew closer, he saw Dave, Sally, Suzanne, and Bobby, all smiles, standing in the center. Next to them on the table were cupcakes, each with a single lit candle in the middle, and all arranged in the horseshoe shape of the workcells.

Suzanne turned to Keith, "They were already here when I came in!"

A voice from the crowd rang out. "Keith, we all just wanted to let the Team know that we truly appreciate the efforts you guys have all put in. And we just wanted to wish you well and get you off to a good start. Have a cupcake! Cheers!"

The crowd buzzed with chat and jokes about recent events. The Team members joined in the celebration, basking in the brief recognition of a job well done. But they all knew that the challenge of making what they had envisioned, what they had tried to express on paper, work and function in the real world, was just set to begin. Keith smiled at Dave and quipped, "As a great man once said, 'Let's do it!'"

KEY POINTS FOR DISCUSSION

(1) The Team brainstormed a list of characteristics to describe the ideal scheduling system for the shop floor. Briefly discuss and describe the current system used to schedule production in your company. To what extent does it meet the characteristics set out by Keith's Team?

(2) The Team completes a description of the rules for each playbook topic. Briefly review these topics, and compare the rules established by Keith's Team with the rules set by your own.

(3) Pat and Clark, along with other company managers, roll up their sleeves and work side-by-side with the workers to physically reorganize the plant floor. Why did they do this manual work? Discuss whether or not your company leaders should participate in the same way.

Chapter Eighteen

The Search for Leadership

"It makes sense to get people to want to be their best."

B y 11 A.M. that very morning the Team members were fully prepared to hoist the white flag above the work-cells and throw the bloodied towel in the ring. It wasn't merely that there were a few rough spots, a few kinks that needed working out. No, it was quite a bit worse than that. It was nothing short of a total, unmitigated disaster.

The Team readily agreed to take a 10-minute break and retreat to the conference room to figure out what could possibly be done. Keith mused, "Now I know what it must have been like to be on the *Titanic* and hear the band play. The only difference is that we forgot to bring *any* lifeboats."

Everything that could have gone wrong did. They found that because the rest of the plant wasn't yet tied in to the pull system, the availability of components was extremely uncertain. This highlighted the scheduling problem in the rest of the plant. They found that there were strong disagreements on the quality specifications at each step in the process. This highlighted the need to clearly define product quality. They found maintenance unable to adjust to the new system and quickly respond to their problems. This highlighted the need to establish a professional maintenance system with swift response capability. They found that their layout needed further refinements to provide adequate work space. This highlighted the complexity of designing an efficient plant layout.

And as the problems surfaced, the Team members argued among themselves and lost their tempers. This highlighted the need for strong, positive supervisory leadership. These were the "highlights" of an otherwise dismal foray onto the frontline.

*   *   *   *

As the morning progressed and the Power Supply Team struggled, Clark observed from a distance. He watched closely, and took careful note of the interaction and attitudes of the people as they ran into difficulties.

As Clark stood studying the mayhem from across the plant floor, Pat came up to him to get a status report. "So how's our Power Supply Team doing? Production five times what it used to be?" Pat said this with a soft smile, knowing full well that it would take time to achieve smooth operations. They had both been through startup situations many times, and pretty well knew what to expect.

"Well, we've seen it all too many times before. But, man, I just love it, it makes it all worthwhile. It's got to be the reason we put ourselves through all of the other torture. I only wish more executives had the opportunity to watch their people come to life." Clark spoke in a hushed, reverent tone. "You know, this Team is probably the best we've run across. I mean they have set high standards, and so far, they're not lowering them in the face of adversity. I think we'll have them sit down later this morning and sort out all they've learned. Just the quality issues alone will get us real results. They just won't let product pass on if it isn't what they think it should be." Clark wrote a quick note to Glanahan to schedule the meeting.

"How are the peripheral people, like engineering, maintenance, and even dear old Glanahan doing? Is my pet peeve housebroken yet?" Pat barely began that sentence and Clark knew exactly what was on his mind.

"I've got to tell you I haven't *seen* our friend Glanahan around. He's made himself scarce, and although I told him he was expected to be here, he's yet to roll up his sleeves and help his Team." Clark held his hands out palms up, and shrugged his shoulders. "I need to find him and have a chat."

"He better hope you find him before I do." Pat's look was dead serious, and Clark knew he'd better get his errant supervisor back on track. "I want to see that guy make it, but I have some serious doubts."

"The good news is that engineering has been side-by-side with the Team all morning. They're getting answers to questions they've had for 10 years. And they've got a lot of questions. Apparently, the engineering change notice system the Improvement Team put in place several weeks ago has helped organize design info." Clark turned and said good morning to a group of workers heading to the cafeteria. "And for maintenance, I'm not sure they understand that a written request from the Team is *top* priority."

"Heck, this is the first time they've had written requests or work orders from anywhere. Hmmm. Make sure our maintenance manager, Frank, stays close to the action." Pat reached into his pocket and pulled out a coin.

Clark kept talking. "Hey, how's Chicago looking? You were going to get the attendance list?"

"I got it from Honlinks yesterday, and of course, they're *all* going to be there." Pat and Clark both poked their fists at the air, boxing an invisible opponent. "It's going to be the toughest pitch of our business life. If only that old codger Van Dauphin wouldn't show. Well, you and I need to put the finishing touches on the show, and I go with Dave next week."

"Dave's up for it, although he doesn't know exactly what *it* is. And if we told him, he'd fall to pieces." Clark halfheartedly laughed.

Pat made a sweeping gesture with the hand holding the coin from his pocket. "Loser pays for the plant celebration out of his budget, *and* buys dinner out of his pocket. And the winner picks the restaurant." Clark nodded approvingly, and with that, Pat flipped the coin in the air for Clark to catch. Pat called out 'tails,' and watched the coin land in Clark's right hand, as he instantly slapped it onto the back of his left. Slowly, Clark revealed the face side.

"Heads, I win again!" Clark exclaimed.

Pat looked at him with mock sorrow. "Well, it'll be my pleasure, even for an old freeloader like you." Pat turned and hustled into the deep recesses of the plant.

Clark began to head for a phone to page Glanahan, and stopped. He held the coin up for closer inspection. "Hold on. Heads on this side." And he turned the coin over. "That dog! Heads on this side, too!"

*   *   *   *

Pat hustled through the plant, to the maintenance department, stopping along the way to exchange greetings with employees who crossed his path. As he turned the corner in the finished goods warehouse, he saw Glanahan leaning against a skid of boxes, chatting with several workers. Several minutes earlier Pat had heard Clark's page for Glanahan, and now decided to step in.

"Glanahan. I know you're busy helping your Team through their struggle, but if you have a second or two, I'd like to have a word with you." Pat made it clear that the coffee klatsch was over. The three workers scampered back to their duties, and Glanahan nonchalantly approached Pat. He wasn't sure that Pat knew of his lack of participation with the Power Supply Team.

"Clark paged you. Did you respond?" Pat was no-nonsense, and Glanahan suddenly realized something was up.

"Not yet, I was just about to." He looked hard at his pad as though checking his schedule, avoiding Pat's glare.

"Call him right now. Tell him to join you and me in my office in 10 minutes. He'll know what this is about," Pat said tersely.

"That's fine, but I don't." Glanahan was cut short, as Pat stated in a level tone, "You will, my friend, you will." And Pat turned and continued on his original path through the plant.

* * * *

Clark knew Pat to be a great leader and motivator of people. He had inspired Clark and gained his deep respect over the years, and they had grown close. But Pat could be tough, very tough, and those around him didn't like to face this side of the man. There were occasions when Pat would rip into his managers and supervisors, and although there was always justification for the chastising, Clark thought a less head-on approach would better achieve the goal. But somehow, even on those occasions, Pat's approach seemed to get the desired result, which was to modify *behavior*. As he sat across from Glanahan, waiting for Pat to return to his office, he knew Tom was about to meet Pat's Mr. Hyde.

Pat entered his office and shut the door. This was not a good omen. "Glanahan, let me tell you something, if it wasn't for Clark, you'd be out walking the streets right this minute. How *could* you avoid the Team on *this morning*? What else could be more important? What do you think we've been striving for these last several months?" Pat was nearly shouting, his voice at a fever pitch.

Tom had been dreading the day when the Team would actually go into full gear on the shop floor. He found himself torn between the old and new ways. On one hand, he wanted to be the Team leader, to play a more humble, enabling role to his people. He wanted to be part and parcel of the success that would result from change. Yet, on the other hand, when it came right down to it, he couldn't shake the fear that he would be viewed as weak, as no longer the authority figure he had worked so hard for so many years to become. That morning, he had tried, honest to gosh, but he just couldn't bring himself to say to his employees in front of the other workers, "How can I help you?" And as he now sat in front of a fuming Pat, he didn't know how to put his feelings into words.

Tom spoke as though he were muttering to himself, "I've come a long way, I know I'm not there yet. I'm willing to listen. I'll make it, I'll make it."

"You're going to have to prove that to *me*. Pretend I'm from Missouri and *show me* that you can provide the leadership those good people out there need and deserve. You better get back in the game, Tommy." Pat paused to let it sink in. He stood and extended his hand to Tom. "I suggest you both stay here and review the rules for supervisors. Remember you went over them at the supervisors' meeting? Learn 'em this time, and follow 'em." Pat nodded to Clark, and left the room.

*   *   *   *

Clark pulled from his folder copies of "Ten Rules For Supervisors on Self-Directed Work Teams." He handed Tom a copy. Clark spoke in his professorial tone. "Let's go through this again. And you'd better make some notes. Maybe we'll invite Keith to join us, and get the worker's perspective."

Clark paged Keith with the invitation. As the group of three settled down, Clark restated the topic for discussion.

ILLUSTRATION 18–1

> ## ROLE OF SUPERVISORS ON SELF-DIRECTED WORK TEAMS
>
> - Responsible for Team performance and for Continuous Improvement efforts.
> - Provide Teamwork, Total Quality, and process education and training.
> - Provide access to company resources.
> - Lead Team meetings and prioritize Team improvement activities.
> - Provide daily positive leadership and motivation.
> - Resolve interpersonal conflicts among members.
> - Ensure Team playbook is executed and management standards are achieved.
> - Be the Team's focal point of communication.
> - Learn the production process and contribute to continuous quality improvements.
> - Manage the Team; decide upon Team recommendations.

"We want to talk about the role of supervisors on Work Teams." Keith said with exasperation that they had been looking for Tom all morning.

Tom looked at Keith, "I know. I know. I know. I should have been there."

Clark began, "Usually, supervisors avoid Teamwork because they're afraid to lose authority. The fact of the matter is that in this new environment, you can actually gain more 'power' over the people that work for you. The word power is often considered a bad word, but power is only bad when it's used in a destructive or negative way. We all have varying degrees of power in an organization. By power I mean the ability to direct people's behavior and actions, or the ability to directly impact productivity and quality." Clark stopped to watch Tom jot some points down. "Supervisors direct the work force, the people. But it's the workers who directly influence the performance of the plant by determining productivity and product quality. The workers, too, have power."

"Traditional managers, including you, try to intimidate the worker and force them to do what you want them to do. Instead of setting up an adversarial relationship, these 10 rules describe a relationship that is based on cooperation and partnership, with the supervisor as leader, coach, and mentor to the worker. The reason is that *real power* over productivity and quality lies in the hands of the *work force*. Their actions and efforts *directly* affect performance. So it makes sense to get people to *want to* be their best and maximize productivity and quality. And then, once people want to, set up the procedures and physical tools so that they *can do it*. Desire first, followed closely by action."

Keith added, "I think everyone realizes that *somebody* has to be in charge and responsible, and that person has to be the supervisor." He paused, then kidded, "Otherwise, the plant would become a hotbed of revolution and public demonstration. There would be pandemonium in the aisles."

The three laughed. Tom added, "There *are* times when the place looks pretty much as you described." They all referred to the sheet listing the rules. Clark continued, "So, point one, is that you are responsible for Team performance and for continuous improvements. You've got to wear two hats. One, help the Team meet daily production goals, and two, ensure the Team is always seeking new and better ways to meet these goals. But you're the fellow management will hold responsible. And if the Team doesn't get results, you're in it deep.

"Point two is that you're responsible for the education and training of the Team. And it's okay to bring resources from elsewhere to achieve this. But *you* have to keep your people continually reading, thinking, talking, about new shop floor techniques and philosophies. For example, each week pass out a new magazine article and spend five minutes discussing the piece at a Team meeting. You have to be creative and find innovative ways to keep the Team learning new ideas."

"I'm always amazed at how much Tom knows about the production process, and how much some of the less experienced employees don't know." Keith shrugged.

Clark shot in, "What a great opportunity to play leader and teacher. Every day be sure you spend time with the less-experienced workers and talk about the production process. Teach them. Your knowledge will further establish you as a leader. *Knowledge is power.*

"Point three means that *you* are the point man for the Team. You have easy access to the other company departments. So your job is to make these resources available to the Team when they're in need. They look to you, your power and contacts, to get them what they need." Clark continued the lesson. "Point four means that you've got to continue to lead the weekly Team meetings. These sessions have to include a review of the week's performance as well as work on improvement tasks."

Keith looked at Tom. "And right now, we're not wanting for improvement topics. Help!"

"Point five means that you've got to keep your people psyched up. There are times when we all need a lift, positive feedback that sincerely expresses your appreciation. Let's face it, Tom, you know how you feel when you're told you've done a good job," Clark reminded him.

"But you're also responsible for discipline. Deal with problems quickly and directly to ensure they are not repeated."

"I can see how giving positive feedback is an important part of being a good leader." Tom thought back several weeks when Pat had commended him on the design of the workcells of his Team. "Yeah. It feels good, alright."

Clark worked his way through the list, "Point six means that you've got to stay close to the Team and understand the relationships among Team members. And you've got to be prepared to resolve the interpersonal conflicts that are bound to arise. Not everyone is going to love one another, but you've got to keep the individual relationships intact so that their differences do *not* negatively impact Team performance. That's the test of whether or not you should get involved. You've got to build and maintain harmony.

"Point seven means that you've got to help guide the Team to establish policies and procedures that meet the plantwide management standards, and to execute these policies and procedures they've set out in their playbook. This means you've got to be on top of what's going on. You've got to be involved."

Keith added, "We've never had written rules and procedures that had *real* meaning. The playbook represents procedures *we've* created, but now we have to learn how to stick to the rules. Before this, we only had procedures that were written 20 years ago and were covered with two inches of dust. Now, we've got something relevant that we can refer to to direct our daily activities."

"So my task is to know the rules and to be sure they're followed." Tom made notes as he spoke.

Clark continued on, hoping this session would give Tom the additional insight he needed to cast away his fear and anticipation. Knowledge *is* power. "The Team must communicate with other Teams and other supervisors, and there needs to be a single person to represent them to the rest of the world for this purpose. Point eight means that person is you."

Tom picked up the ball, "And point nine means that if there are areas of the production process I'm not familiar with, then I better go learn them. It's funny, but using the workcell concept means that I need to know *all* steps in the production of an item. But there are several operations in our workcell I know little about. In fact, the Team members on those operations know more than I do."

"It's a great technique. But this morning we didn't get too far." Keith looked up at the ceiling and held his fists in the air. "But I have begun learning a lot about the other operations. That'll help me be a better machinist because I'll better understand the impact the quality of my work has on the other operations." Keith looked to Clark for his understanding, trying to be philosophical about that morning's debacle.

"Last point. Go manage the Team. You're the decision maker on the important issues, and you've got to carefully consider the Team's recommendations." Clark closed his folder and stood. "I've done all I can do. Now it's up to you."

Clark left the two men to digest the morning's events. Tom whispered, "We've got a Team meeting in five minutes. My cup is empty, and I'm ready to learn." He put his arm on Keith's shoulder, and they headed back together to the roar of activity in the plant.

KEY POINTS FOR DISCUSSION

(1) The Team experiences a "disaster" as they begin the implementation of Teamwork and the workcell technique even though they had spent much time planning the system. Does this mean that their planning efforts were wasted? Why should you expect start-up problems regardless of the intensity of the design effort? Briefly discuss what problems you may encounter in the start-up of your Team's new systems.

(2) Tom Glanahan couldn't bring himself to assist the Team on their start-up day. Describe the emotional stress that Tom is experiencing. What steps could the Team members take to help their supervisor over these high hurdles?

(3) Review the role of supervisors on Self-Directed Work Teams, and discuss each point with your supervisor. What are the greatest challenges for Team members and for supervisors working under these guidelines?

Chapter Nineteen
Continuing Education

"It was no longer a 9-to-5 job."

I t was 6:30 P.M., and Keith dragged himself from the plant to his old Chevy. He sat in the front seat, and could barely muster the energy and concentration needed to select the ignition key on his ring and start the car's engine. His mind was awhirl, running a thousand miles an hour, playing the day's events over and over.

Although the workday ends at five, they kept milling about for an extra hour and a half, excitedly discussing the workcells and the solutions to problems they'd encountered. A whole new world had been opened, and it fully consumed them to be awakened to a new perspective on the product, the people, and the production process that for so long had remained sealed in a black box.

Keith pulled out from the parking lot and headed toward the bridge that would take him from the city. Today, it appeared different; he saw the intricacy of its design, the strength in its river-spanning girders. He felt an unfamiliar closeness with the great teeming city as never before. For an instant, he imagined that he could feel the throbbing pulse of the invisible people as they coursed through the metropolis. Great silver-gray storm clouds, massed over the skyline, seemed frozen in his rear view mirror and he felt a thrill as if he had discovered a brave new world.

As he continued on into the countryside toward his sister-in-law's home to pick up Crystal, he was shaken from his reverie by the red flashing lights of emergency vehicles at an accident ahead. As he edged closer to the scene, he saw a single vehicle badly smashed, apparently having flipped over and tumbled down an embankment. The ambulance had already left the scene, and the emergency workers were trying to clear the area. The car belonged to no one Keith could immediately identify. "God, I hope everyone's okay, but it looks pretty bad," he thought. And he continued on a bit more carefully.

Keith thought back to the hectic early morning and the Team meeting at 11. "What seemed like a totally lost and hopeless situation was quickly turned into a dozen or so valuable lessons when Tom used these simple words, 'You've learned more about product quality in the last three hours than you have in the last three years.' That transformed it from a negative to a positive experience.

"We listed at least a dozen major problems identified in that three hour period, along with possible actions to resolve them. I have to admit, Tom did a beautiful job of organizing the session and then following up later that afternoon. Heck, by 5 o'clock we were actually producing completed power supplies. And we *knew* each one was right.

"At first I was frustrated, almost angry with Clark, because he sat in the back of the conference room, looking smug, like he was getting a kick out of us floundering around. But afterward, I realized why he was so content. We were *learning*, and he was watching us teach ourselves how to be better operators and Team members. His smile was a proud smile like a parent watching a toddler's first step.

"By the end of the day, we all felt proud of what we had accomplished."

As Keith pulled into Ginny's sister's driveway, Crystal came bounding out as usual. Crystal jumped in the car and gave him a big hug. "I have so much to tell you, Daddy. I learned a lot of new things in school today." She said this almost every day when Keith came to get her, but this time her words took on a whole new meaning.

Keith laughed out loud. "So did I, sweetheart, so did I."

As they drove up the mountain, Crystal excitedly explained her curiosity with astronomy. "Do you know how far away the moon is? Why it's close to two zillion miles away. And we used to send men there to collect rocks! Isn't that great, Daddy?"

Her mind was totally captivated with the notion of space, stars, and planets. "I'm going to read every book about space so I can be an expert. See, I brought some books home with me." And she held up the pamphlets her teacher had handed out.

Keith sat and listened closely to her. It wasn't so much what she said, but how she said it. "What natural curiosity. If only we could maintain the unchained mind of a child and keep ourselves open to new ideas. If only we didn't grow up and accept wholesale the traditions we're force fed, but instead continually sought to challenge the ways of the world. Somehow Pat and Clark created a business environment that *promoted* questions, that made it good to challenge the conventional wisdom. Teamwork and Total Quality turns the old ways on their head, and those guys were the catalysts that created an organizational

ILLUSTRATION 19–1

KEEP LEARNING

"Don't Be Afraid of What You Don't Know."

---

mindset that allowed such significant changes to actually *happen*. The old managers didn't want *anyone* to ask questions. Just do what you're told."

As Keith navigated around the hairpin turn at the steepest slope of the mountain, he asked, "Why do you like to learn new ideas?"

She sat and thought for a moment. "It makes my head feel bigger and better. I feel smart and like I did something good. And, because I'm afraid of what I don't know." She paused to see if her father liked her answer. "Is that good?"

"Sweetheart, you're one very smart and beautiful girl." Keith thought he would put those last words on a plaque and hang it in his workcell. It would read "Don't Be Afraid of What You Don't Know," and he envisioned how it would look in his work area. He thought, "If only our company had fostered curiosity and embraced new ideas years ago, this near catastrophe wouldn't have happened."

As the car finally came to rest in the driveway, Crystal yelled, "I'm going to get the mail today, and then go read my space books. Remember, we sent away for moon goggles last week?" Keith headed inside, and she raced in behind him, dropping the stack of mail on the kitchen counter. They both proceeded with the chores and routine that filled each evening.

Later that night Keith relaxed in his big comfy chair, thinking that he'd never felt a better tiredness in his life. He sat in the still and quiet of the evening, his mind focused on the Team's day. "Our first challenge is to resolve the product quality issues. But it seems that process is never really complete. Clark was talking about continually measuring quality variation using statistics. He said we'll all learn how to do it. In the meantime, we've got to get our pull system working, although that's relatively simple. When we see an empty outbound square, we produce the next order in the sequence of the master schedule. We pull our parts from the inbound squares. And the empty inbound square tells us to move parts from the feeding workcells to the using workcell. One of the real benefits is that only one MPS order goes in a square, so we've limited the amount of work in process in the plant. Suzanne said she's totally confused because everything is so neat and organized."

Keith got up and stretched. He went to the window overlooking the valley below. There was a hint of springtime in the damp night air. "The other Work Teams will be starting next week. Pat and Clark are going to keep this thing going, Team after Team, until we achieve our *best* as a company. It's like I've got a new lease on my work life. I'm *learning* again."

Keith spied the stack of mail across the room. As he flipped through the pile, he saw an envelope with a return address in Palo Alto, California. "It's from Annette. Haven't heard from her and Joe in a while. That guy was a bit goofy, like the lights are on but nobody's home. Sis only usually writes for the holidays or birthdays. I wonder?" He read the letter.

Dear Keith:

Just a quick note to bring you up to date on events here. As you know, my relationship with Joe was shaky at best. Last week we decided to split, and I'll stay here in the house with all four kids. It's really the best solution, and he's going to help financially.

You and I always said that we might need each
other someday. I think the day is here. I know Crystal
would love it here with the kids, and we would make
it a real happy family for us all. Just think it over, and
let me know. There's plenty of room, and the upstairs
apartment would be perfect for you guys.

Anyway, hope all is well. Read your letter about
your company, and it sounds like the Team is fantas-
tic. There was an article in the Sunday paper about
several companies doing the same thing.

Love,
Annette

As Keith lay in bed that evening, his overheated mind
swam with turbulent thoughts. He thought about his duty
and responsibility to his sister and his daughter. He knew
that for Crystal's sake it would be best to join his sister and
her family, to unite with them and improve their family
life. But for the first time since he began working, he felt
like he was a significant part of his company. It was no
longer a 9 to 5 job to collect a paycheck. It had become
much more than that, for he knew that his Teammates
needed him as much as he needed them.

The situation presented yet another tragic turn in Keith's
life, for no matter which direction he chose, there would
result a deep sense of loss and an unfulfilled obligation.

KEY POINTS FOR DISCUSSION

(1) Keith finds that the Teamwork process is intel-
lectually challenging, that it requires Team members to think hard about the people, process,
and equipment used to produce the product.
This form of education has both inspired and
motivated them. Briefly discuss how your Team

will respond to this challenge. Do you welcome the same creative test?

(2) The resources of the company have been made available to the Team. For example, engineers have relocated and moved on to the shop floor. This provides an opportunity for the Team members to interface and ask questions of personnel who would not traditionally be accessible. Do you believe that your company would benefit from a similar setup? Today, to what extent does the workforce of your company know what they need to know?

(3) Keith describes the quality improvement process as never ending. Do you believe this to be true, or is there a finite amount of time and energy that should be spent to improve quality? How will you know when the Team should no longer seek ways to improve quality?

Chapter Twenty
Show Time

"The will must exist to pull yourself up and take the next step."

A t 30,000 feet, Dave and Pat were served the traditional box lunch, which tasted more like the box than the lunch. They'd be in Chicago by 3 P.M., and then head over to the corporate office for the Board meeting by 9 the next morning. The Big Man had a big appetite, and regardless of its culinary merits, the portions were too darn small. "Pat, if you're not going to have that cake, I'd be glad to help you with it." Dave looked as though he were pleading for the last morsel of food on the planet.

"Well, I've got to admit, it looks pretty good. Hmmm," said Pat, and Dave looked about ready to cry. Pat called the stewardess over for help. He whispered so others around them couldn't hear. "Any chance you've got an extra lunch for my friend?"

Dave looked sorrowful. "Yes ma'am. And if there are two extra, I'd be glad to take both of those off your hands." Within a few moments, Dave had the extra meals, and was as satisfied as could be. "Now I'm ready to talk business." He demolished all three boxes, and Pat was glad to have solved his companion's dilemma.

"Let's summarize our presentation. Together, we'll have 20 minutes, and I'll take 15. And you'll wrap up using the last 5 to make your case." Pat pointed to his watch. "Don't go beyond 5 minutes unless I approve. But there might be a lot of questions, in which case we'll stay to answer them."

"Sure. Sure. I got it." Dave nodded his head up and down. He had the same concentrated look as he had had in his high school football huddles.

Pat spoke as though he were sitting alone in a room, trying to memorize his lines. "Now, I'm going to explain the business environment at the beginning of Teamwork, what steps we've taken, highlight our achievements, and then explain our two year game plan."

"Roger Honlinks will love that." Dave said this to bolster their collective confidence.

"He will." Pat said this out loud, then thought, "I hope the rest of them will, too." After a few moments, he said, "But let's talk about your presentation, Dave. Give me the summary again, and then talk through it from beginning to end." Pat straightened in his seat, preparing for the speech.

Dave shuffled through the pile of paper in his lap. It had accumulated during the last week, and most of the papers were notes and ideas given to him by his fellow workers. He finally found his two pages, "Okay. I've got it. First, I'll introduce myself. That's easy. Then I'll explain what it was like to be a worker before Teamwork." He read, "Emphasize *hopeless.* Then I'll explain the opportunities for improvement. Like leadtime reduction and improved customer service. Quality improvement and cost reduction. Productivity increases. And most important, I'll explain that the workers *want* the chance to do this. I'll show them the petition and pledge we all signed."

As Dave spoke, Pat looked at the overhead luggage rack, his thoughts riding on every word Dave uttered. "That's good, Dave, real good."

"Who's going to be there? It's not just for Honlinks, is it?" All along Dave knew it was bigger than that.

This was the question Pat wished to avoid, but knew he couldn't. "Well, no, it's definitely more than Honlinks. In fact, there will be maybe two dozen or so people there." Pat said this slowly and nonchalantly, so as to not frighten Dave. "But you'll have no problem, just get up and talk like you do at the plant meetings."

Dave probed further. "These are real important people, aren't they? This is all really big time to the company, huh?"

Pat responded, "Sure. And you and I will just do the very best we can." He repeated those words to himself over and over as the two grew deathly silent and lost in their solitary thoughts.

There were, however, a few things about Dave that neither Pat nor most anyone else in the plant knew. He was not only an outdoorsman, but he was also very active in the local community. He was a member of the county civic league and he helped manage numerous church events. When he was a child, he learned to love the theater. So much so, that he took to acting, and over the years played major roles in the local theater company. The stage was familiar ground, and he could perform a wide range of characters, from Shakespearean heroes to Willie Loman in Arthur Miller's *Death of a Salesman*.

And once again, the hidden talents of the workers would be put to unexpected good use.

*   *   *   *

It was 6:30 in the morning, and the phone beside Pat's hotel bed rang. He flopped over, and his hand searched for the receiver. Not so much to find out who was calling, but to stop the incessant ringing.

"Morning," Pat spoke in a sleep-slurred voice.

"Hi. It's Dave. I know we were going to meet at eight, but I'm hungry. Can I go get some breakfast, now?" Dave remained silent, anxiously waiting for the answer.

"Sure. Whatever you like. And however much you like. Or need. Have fun. And think about the presentation. I'll meet you in the lobby at 8:30, and we'll head over." Pat hung up the phone and rolled over.

As both men stood in the elevator whisking them up to the corporate office, the nervous tension they both felt was nearly overwhelming. Each of the very few words they spoke was like a razor slashing the dense air surrounding them.

As Pat and Dave entered Honlinks' office, Janice was sitting at her usual post. She became wide-eyed, and rushed to greet Pat. "I'm so excited. I just knew you'd do it." She shook Dave's hand, and offered the two seats.

"Roger is about as nervous as a fox in the henhouse." He keeps saying, "I've got confidence in Mr. Teamwork," and then he says, "And if he blows it, I'll fire him." Janice was whispering to Pat, and Dave sat on the couch out of earshot, trying to concentrate on the day's paper. "Roger is down in the boardroom. And they're all here. They've been there since 7:30 this morning. There's a lot on the table." Janice turned away, as though she wanted to say more, but couldn't.

"It's okay, Janice. I know Van Dauphin and others are campaigning to sell us off. I know that. But I brought a secret weapon." And he pointed toward Dave.

"Oh, is this the director of marketing?" she asked quizzically.

"Not quite. He's a worker in the plant." Pat said this as though it were self-evident.

She stopped in her tracks. "A worker? You mean he's going to talk to the board?" She paused and thought a few moments, taken aback by it all. "Roger knows?" She knew the answer to that question, but she asked it anyway, hoping that it had already been agreed upon. But she knew better.

"He said he'll meet *you* at 8:45 in his office to prep for your presentation." She knew the cards had been dealt, and there was nothing more she could do or say to help.

"Janice. Trust me. It's all fine." He wanted to console his supporter and friend, and lift her up. She looked more frayed than Pat and Dave combined.

At that moment, Honlinks burst through the door in his usual style. "Well, well. If it isn't Mr. Teamwork. Welcome to the land of make-believe. Step into my office." He hardly glanced at Pat, and didn't even notice Dave who had been sitting on the couch, but stood when Honlinks entered.

"Roger, let me introduce you to Dave. He'll participate in our presentation as well." The two men shook hands.

Honlinks responded, "Don't think we've met. Having a director join us always adds a bit more dignity to the pitch." He said this half jokingly, and turned and marched into his office.

Dave and Pat looked at each other, and Pat put his index finger to his lips motioning silence. He then pointed at his chest, mouthing, "Let me handle it," and they both followed Honlinks' steps to his billiard-table-sized desk.

As Roger stood behind his desk, fumbling about in his briefcase, Pat reintroduced Dave. "Roger, let me assure you that our presentation will be quite persuasive. And professional. The case to keep us intact is strong. I'll present the management view, and Dave will present the view of the work force. Dave is a plant worker who's been fully involved in the Teamwork effort."

Honlinks stopped fumbling. He almost stopped breathing. He stopped short of asking Pat to repeat himself, because he feared he would hear the same unbelievable thing again. "Well, I eh, ur, I'm real, uh, glad that you're here, um, Dave. Let's see, um, there were a few things, that eh, um we need to cover, right Pat? Pat, maybe you could join me down the hall for a few moments. We'll be right back, uh, Dave."

He turned to Pat, inviting him to follow through a broad false grin, then gingerly stepped out of his office, with Pat in hot pursuit. He walked ahead, and flung open a conference room door further down the hallway. "In here, Forte."

As soon as the door closed, Honlinks hollered, "Are you Section 8, a complete head case? You brought a worker to talk to the board! This isn't grade school show and tell! I should pack you off on the next plane the heck out of here!" Moments after the initial explosion, a deflated Honlinks sank into a chair at the conference room table. He placed both elbows on the tabletop in front of him, and held his face in his hands, as though he were fit to sob. He whispered, "Forte, I spent three years on the frontline in Vietnam, but *you're* going to be the death of me."

This only strengthened Pat's resolve and confidence. Pat stood behind the seated Honlinks, and placed his hand on his right shoulder. In a display of mock *esprit de corps*, he squeezed hard. "Don't worry, Rog, be happy. We're on in five minutes." And he opened the door and walked back to Dave, leaving Honlinks alone in the room.

* * * *

The conference room that housed the board of directors and their assistants was as finely appointed as Honlinks' office. A huge 40-foot conference table extended down the center of the room, with rows of burgundy leather upholstered chairs down each side. The front of the room was equipped with the latest in audiovisual technology.

The walls were lined with large gold-framed portraits of past and present board members, each in his favorite pose. The earliest dated back to the turn of the century, and the many traditions of the company could be traced back to the company founder. Half of the board members had been from banking, government, and academia. Others represented major industrial companies in the United States and abroad.

The chairman of the board was an elderly English gentleman, knighted by the Queen some 30 years before, whose spark had long since petered out. He had little interest in the decisions of the business, but he considered the fulfillment of his post a duty to the founding family. He relied on the others to provide the decision-making firepower.

The gentleman that wielded the most influence, less for his position than for his ability to persuade, was Van Dauphin. He was a lead banker, and had earned great wealth in Texas land development during the fifties. A cadre of attorneys and accountants seemed to buzz about him constantly. He viewed the world as one enormous bottom line, and if something didn't immediately hit that mark, it was struck from the ledger.

The other board members were a fairly pragmatic group, and they had a realistic view of the company, its history, strengths, and weaknesses. The go-go eighties had burdened the company with much more debt than at any time in its history. And while a number of acquisitions were made in those heady days, the company found itself in financial distress in the subsequent recession. Cash was at a premium, and the board sought to raise the needed funds to service the debt. One painfully easy way was to sell off the bad performers, the businesses that didn't fit the new mold. And for better or for worse, Pat's division had been targeted as the first to be broken up and sold.

There were a handful of board members who were delighted that a division had begun the Teamwork and Total Quality journey. And from what they had heard through Honlinks, they knew that the course that had been set was the correct one. They respected Pat's knowledge and experience. They also knew that to convince the majority of the board to put their faith in this new strategy would be a monumental task. The risk of supporting an unknown entity was too great, and the majority could comfortably rationalize the obvious choice of selling the losers. Turnarounds took too much time.

Honlinks introduced Pat and Dave, and explained that Pat would present his strategy for improvement. "And, Mr. Dave Jackson will provide additional insight into the manufacturing and shop floor issues."

Pat began, "Thank you for the chance to present our perspective and to personally respond to your questions about the future of our business. I realize the nature of the decision facing this group, and recognize your responsibility to the corporation as a whole. But I must tell you, the changes we have undertaken in the last six months represent the tip of the iceberg in their ability to yield financial improvement. But remember the numbers I'm going to review don't reflect the goodwill and improved customer relations that our new level of performance has created. Quite simply, we are now more competitive, and only with your support will this upward trend continue. And more important, these results can be achieved not only at our division, but also at every division throughout the corporation.

"These are not short-term fixes. I'm not talking about a band-aid approach. I'm talking about permanent change in the business culture, and hence, in its performance. But you've got to be in the game for the long haul."

Pat went on to explain the history of Teamwork and Total Quality, presenting case study examples, and drawing on his own personal experiences. He tried to educate each board member, helping them gain a new view of how industrial companies could be managed, by comparing the old traditions with these new ways.

"Let me emphasize that accepting new ways is *not* a verdict against the old. But *you* have a responsibility to keep these businesses current and in the mainstream of management thinking, and today I'm afraid that the majority of this organization is lagging far behind the leaders and doers." He paused to let this sink in. "The reason to do this is not philosophical or moral, although you could argue from that point of view. But the decision to move ahead should be made so that we adopt sound business practices to achieve *lasting and long term* bottom-line results."

Our next two years, should you decide to accept this challenge, will be driven by the following "Ten Points For Improvement." I know Roger gave you our implementation plan, and I believe understanding these points will help clarify our proposed plan of action."

Pat continued, "Please allow me to briefly explain these guidelines. I contend that if our business can achieve, honestly achieve, these standards, then we will perform at the highest level possible given the strengths and weaknesses of our people, machinery, and other assets.

"First, we'll continue to teach our managers and workers leadership skills. Everyone will understand that it is a pattern of behavior that *can* be learned and developed in each of us.

"We're going to be *consistent*, and *quality* will be our number one priority in everything we do. We're *not* going to employ the end of the month rush, and ship garbage to our customers to maximize our monthly revenues. If it isn't right, it doesn't go. Our managers, supervisors, engineers, marketeers, will all live to *serve* the workers, and assist them in solving quality problems."

"Our entire work force will be organized into Teams, Work Teams and Improvement Project Teams, and we're going to . . ." Pat, who felt as though he were on a roll, was suddenly cut short.

Van Dauphin, who had shown fidgety signs of displeasure throughout Pat's presentation, spoke. "Mr. Forte, good

ILLUSTRATION 20-1

TEN POINTS FOR PLANTWIDE IMPROVEMENT

1. We will practice and improve leadership skills, and build relationships on mutual respect, not authority.

2. We will establish a value system based on the belief that quality is fully in the hands of the work force; management is responsible to be consistent, and to provide the resources needed to make quality happen.

3. We will measure quality and performance-to-schedule above all else.

4. We will avoid complicated statistical analysis.

5. We will sequence and pull all production and not use MRP to plan the shop floor; we will build productivity into the master production schedule.

6. We will establish employee Improvement Project Teams and Self-Directed Work Teams to drive the plant and office.

7. We will build an effective maintenance system.

8. We will establish an environment where it is acceptable to openly criticize current ways and to put forth solutions.

9. We will tie compensation at all levels to evaluations by superiors, peers, and subordinates based on effort, quality, leadership, creativity, attitude, and Team skills.

10. We will implement change slowly and cautiously, and link pockets of improvement to achieve our best level of performance.

fellow, please excuse me, but our time is so valuable. If you don't mind my saying so, we can *read* your points. In fact, I think I saw something like this in one of those manufacturing journals. It all sounds wonderful. It really does." His tone shifted from that of a lauded English gent to that of a New York prizefighter. "Forget all this nonsense. When do we get results? And how much will it cost?" Several Van Dauphin supporters echoed his skepticism.

"Mr. Van Dauphin, we're already seeing results." Pat presented the cost savings of the improvement projects, and the projected performance improvements of the Work Teams. "I need two years to complete the task, to drive these changes throughout our company. But the benefits will be reaped continuously. Hold me accountable, and I will come here every six months to present our results. You should see a positive bottom-line impact the next time we meet."

A Van Dauphin supporter piped up, "Mr. Forte, you're suggesting that changing the performance of *operations* is the core of your strategic plan. Usually, the focus is on marketing, new products, and financial matters. This really is most unusual."

"Sir, I realize I'm asking you to change your view of the world fundamentally. But, this is a *manufacturing company.* We're not an advertising agency, not an engineering company, and certainly not a financial institution. We're industrialists. We're manufacturers. And that *happens* on the shop floor. That's where the war is won or lost. As Roger can tell you, while troops need solid support, it's what happens on the *frontline* that determines which army moves forward and which one retreats. As you can see, we're going to build a frontline of supervisors and workers, of Teams with the firepower to blow any competitor away. *That* is our plan."

Another board member asked, "Pat, don't we have the latest in computer technology? It seems we approved a large expenditure in this area not long ago?"

Pat smiled softly, and answered, "Yes ma'am, we do. Do you realize that if you asked me or anyone else what the scheduling system was in the plant, you couldn't get a straight answer? We don't *have* a single, defined system with rules and procedures. Something *that* fundamental doesn't exist! In fact, I would venture to say that most of our competitors are struggling with that same aspect of operations. Material requirements planning, which is the planning system for manufacturing companies, is very difficult to implement on the shop floor. But our Teams have designed a technique to solve this problem. Imagine how much more efficient we'll be once we solve these basic issues!"

Many of the Board members recognized the sense in his words. He convinced them that these were not new and untried strategies, but that numerous companies had successfully employed these methods. In a sarcastic tone, Van Dauphin voiced the question that gnawed at the entire group, "You certainly have a commendable confidence in human nature, but how do we know *our* people are capable of this?"

Pat looked at Dave, who was just finishing a cookie from a spread on a sideboard. "I am very pleased to present to you Mr. Dave Jackson. He is one of the *people* who we'll all be relying on to make Teamwork and Total Quality a success. Dave?"

Dave confidently strode to the head of the long conference table. "Well, thank you for the chance to be here. I'm a ten-year-plus veteran of our company, and I'm intimately familiar with our shop floor. In fact, I know this will surprise you, but I'm a soldier on the frontline. I am a worker."

Dave could see everyone shift in their seats as he said this. They tried not to show their shock, but it was still obvious. Van Dauphin cleared his throat as though suppressing a laugh. Dave looked him straight in the eye.

ILLUSTRATION 20–2

"And I'm *proud* to be a worker. I represent the typical American, the person whose back built this country and made it the greatest nation on earth. These hands build the cars, planes, trains, houses, and everything else. *We* add value."

Dave was a proud man. And he now felt compelled to stand up for his friends and peers. "Look. What we're really talking about is the future of our economy. We're talking about the future of our country, and the quality of the lives our children will live.

"Let me tell you. Teamwork and Total Quality works. I've seen it. You must understand one fact first, that there isn't a worker out there who doesn't *want* to cooperate and make the company a success.

"It's not as though we want to make all the decisions ourselves. But we should be involved in those areas that affect the shop floor. We should have our ideas seriously considered. Doesn't that make sense? Don't you think it's wise to give the people on the frontline a chance to *buy into* the decisions. Especially given that we're the ones that have to make them work? And who else can tell you whether or not a new idea is feasible?

"Look. We have a methodology for Teamwork. We have a *system* to do this. *Your* responsibility is to evaluate the system, audit our progress, and motivate the management to adopt new, contemporary methods. *You've* got to move the company ahead despite all of the resistance and excuses to maintain the status quo. That's how you can help us.

"It's funny. It seems to me that the workers hardly resist these changes. It's management that needs gentle assistance, subtle persuasion, and sometimes the threat of a baseball bat to push ahead and challenge tradition. Stagnation is death. Slow and torturous death.

"Although, at our division, we're lucky to have a general manager who is leading the way.

"Sure, you can decide to sell this plant today. And the next one. But at some time you'll have to decide to sell it all, and invest in some slick real estate deal or the software industry making video games, because the industrial competition will leave you in the dust. I've learned a lot about our competition in power supplies, and what they're able to deliver to the customer in terms of price, quality, and availability is awesome. But our Team will be in the lead within months. We're just lucky we managed to stay within striking distance. I mean, how competitive are the rest of your businesses?

"I'm just a worker. But I know the real enemy is us. And to win, all we have to do is adopt a new way of managing, of working on the shop floor, of leading people. Can our people do it? My humble opinion is, yes. I've seen people who had given up all hope of doing anything more than just collect a paycheck, come around and become real contributors to change. We're all smart, we're all able to pitch in and make Teamwork work. It can work at our company, or at any other company out there. But it takes leadership, guts, determination, and persistence. You can't sell out the first time there's pressure. You can't say 'I told you it wouldn't work' when you trip and fall. The *will* must exist to pick yourself up and take the next step. But you've got to keep challenging traditions. Otherwise, you'll lose hope of ever being better."

Dave's heartfelt words had touched almost every person in the room. Here was an average worker asking for nothing more than a chance to learn and to compete. For the respect that they could plainly see he deserved. The challenge that he laid in front of the board was clear. And the lesson that he taught humbled his students.

The room fell silent. Dead silent. Pat broke the stillness, and quickly moved to the front to thank the group. He and Dave hustled out of the conference room. Honlinks called for a break. He darted after them, but was too late, and caught only a glimpse of the two men with their arms on each other's shoulders, entering the elevator.

KEY POINTS FOR DISCUSSION

(1) Dave presented the workers' point of view to the board of directors. Do you think senior management of your company understands the attitudes and desire of your work force to participate in solving problems?

(2) Pat presents the Ten Points for Plantwide Improvement. Review each of these points, and explain the impact each will have on your company's continuous improvement efforts. Why is each point a critical component of change towards Teamwork and Total Quality?

(3) Pat emphasizes that they are a *manufacturing* company and should focus on manufacturing solutions. What is the strategic emphasis at your company? Do you believe that marketing, engineering, R & D, finance, or some other area is incorrectly favored over another? Does manufacturing receive adequate notice and attention?

Chapter Twenty One

Earning a Purple Heart

"The example you set, the path you cleared, took real courage."

A fter several weeks, the Power Supply Team began to settle into the new way of working. They had slowly adopted and implemented the procedures they had set out in their playbook. And sure enough, what they had envisioned as creative solutions to old problems, had come to life. That's not to say they weren't still running into significant problems. The bugs weren't yet all worked out. But they had become a Team, they had bonded, and were striving to maximize quality and to meet their daily master production schedule. *They* were making it work.

Keith was the emotional mainstay of the group. He had become the motivator, and he helped them through the expected tough days. He had a quick wit, and often poked fun at himself, and goodnaturedly ribbed his Teammates.

His objective was to build camaraderie, to break down the ill feelings between departments. He often toured the workcell to learn more about each operation, and kept asking, "Why do we do it this way?" It caused people to *think* about the accepted patterns, and more than once it sparked an investigation that resulted in a new and better approach.

Keith relished the work day. They had all become deeply committed to the test. And each day they saw themselves getting better, constantly moving along the learning curve, as each small step forward gave rise to another.

Keith had decided to put off answering his sister's letter. He wanted to wait and see how the Team worked out. "I'll get a better feel for the future here before I decide to pack it all up and join her," he thought. But he knew that it was selfish to leave her hanging in a time of need.

It was 6 A.M. this mid-April morning, and Crystal had spent the night with her aunt. She had a fever and Keith thought it best for her to stay put. Keith bundled up against the cold sleet that fell from the blackish clouds overhead. He'd stop and check in on Crystal, then head to work.

The old Chevy sat faithfully in the drive, and Keith was surprised to find his windshield iced over. It took only a minute with his scraper to clear the view and he'd be on his way. The car started right up when he turned the ignition. He patted the dashboard, "Now, now Nellie. I bet I could close my eyes, and you'd get me there."

Heading down the mountain was a bit more treacherous than he had anticipated, and a skid made him pull over for a minute feeling rattled. "If I had any sense, I'd let it warm up a bit and the ice on the road could melt. But I need to be in early today. I told Frank from maintenance I'd meet him to go over a few things in the cell. I'll be okay."

He drove on. He had successfully braked his way down the mountain so far, but as he neared the hairpin turn, he saw that the pavement ahead glistened with a sheet of sheer ice. It was as though someone had laid a plate of glass on the road. It was too late. He braked hard, then pumped the brake pedal, but the wheels locked and lost all traction. The old Chevy sailed forward, gathering momentum. "Oh my God. I can't let it go off the end!" He turned the wheel hard in an effort to smoothly guide the car into the guardrail and stop his slide, but it was to no avail. The car was on a straight and unstoppable path across the road and into the thick jungle of trees and brush that covered the steep side of the mountain.

Keith grabbed the wheel hard, and heard the ripping and tearing of steel as the car catapulted through the guardrail, shearing in half the pine trees standing at the point of impact. It was like some weird amusement park ride that went loop-the-loop. He saw blue sky, then green, then blue sky. The smashing of metal and crumbling of glass seemed to go on forever. He thought, "Just like when they threw rice at our wedding." And then his world became dark and silent.

*   *   *   *

It was 10:30 A.M. and Keith's Team became concerned because he hadn't yet shown up. They sensed something was wrong, and Suzanne called first Keith's home and then his sister-in-law. She finally phoned the state police, who shortly after being dispatched, found the wreckage.

*   *   *   *

Keith received dozens of visitors and well-wishers in his hospital room throughout the late afternoon and evening. His Teammates had rushed to the hospital, and stayed with him until visiting hours ended. They knew it'd be a while before he would be able to return to work, and the broken bones in his arms and leg would require further surgery. All in all, he was lucky to have survived the crash.

It was 11:30 P.M., and he lay in bed thinking about all of the people who had come by and showed their concern. "Six months ago, maybe four or five would have showed up. But now everyone has been brought closer together. It means so much, especially in times like these.

"And speaking of trouble, now what do I do? Well, I'll need some help to get back on my feet, and my sister could use some moral support. Now it makes sense to head out there. I can't take proper care of Crystal like this. I could get us out there somehow and join Annette. Eventually I can get a job somewhere, and the rest of the chips will fall in place."

Keith was drowsy, and kept drifting in and out of consciousness. The pain killers were wearing off, and he felt the discomfort of his battered body growing into intense pain.

"Hey, fella. Better get you a new pair of ice skates. Ones with brakes that work." This was a familiar voice, and Keith momentarily thought he was dreaming. But as he stiffly turned his head toward the door, he saw Pat's wide smile. "I stuck my head in before, and you were dozing. The nurses said you'd be waking soon, so I hung around. How 'ya feeling?"

Seeing Pat at that moment, knowing that it was such a long way to drive from his home, so late at night, deeply moved Keith. It took a few minutes for him to regain his composure. "The bones will heal. I guess my mind got banged up a bit, too." He paused, and continued. "You didn't get much production today. I think half the plant was here."

Pat spoke quietly and soothingly. "That's what it's all about. I want you to know that in all my years I've met few people who had the guts you've shown. You've made a real contribution and changed people's lives. The example you set, the path you cleared, took real courage. I'm proud to know 'ya, Old Man. You'll be up to speed in no time."

"I wasn't going to tell you this, but you cost me twenty bucks." Keith spoke sheepishly. "I figured you were a short-timer, and would be gone in three months. I actually bet against you. I didn't think anyone would *do it.*" Keith hesitated, for he knew that *it* meant saving the company, and the future still was uncertain. The result of the board meeting was unknown. "Well, whatever happens, Pat, we stirred it up some, didn't we?" Keith tried to make a jabbing motion with his hands, and let out a yelp, forgetting his physical condition.

"Listen, I heard you were considering heading out west to be with your sister. While I hate the idea of losing you, I made a few calls today. Old Rog Honlinks, you remember him, well, he told me we have a division with a plant in a nearby town out there. Just so happens they need a *supervisor.* So when you're ready to do some dialing, I've got a number for you to call."

Keith grew very quiet and softly said, "Thanks." He thought for a moment, then asked, "They doing Teamwork?"

Pat grinned, like the cat that just swallowed the canary. "Not yet, but they're going to be one of the next plants to get it underway."

Keith gave him a look that said, "How do you know?"

"Trust me, trust me." The two sat in silence for the next few minutes. It felt good to be in each other's company. Sometimes words aren't necessary.

Pat broke the silence, "I'm gonna run and let you get that shot. If there's anything we can do, just holler. I'll be in touch."

As Pat left the room, Keith called out, "Hey!" And Pat stopped and turned. "Thanks, Mr. Teamwork."

Pat shuffled out and walked past the nurses' station. There were a few times in his life when he found himself overwhelmed by the strength and beauty of a human spirit. This was such a time.

KEY POINTS FOR DISCUSSION

(1) Keith has been given an opportunity for promotion to supervisor. Do you believe he is prepared for these responsibilities? In your opinion, what has Keith done to earn Pat's confidence and respect?

(2) The outpouring of concern and caring for Keith after his accident was much greater than he would have expected before Teamwork. Describe the bond that has been created between the people of the company.

Chapter Twenty Two
The Final Verdict

"Like a long lost boomerang that finally returns."

T he next morning Pat sat in the silence of his office. He hadn't slept much, his mind obsessively replaying the events of the last several days. At Pat's request, Clark was on his way in. "I'll check on our Teams and give Clark an update on corporate."

"How's Keith? I'm going to stop down and visit later this morning." Clark had a look of deep concern on his face.

"He's fine. A bit sore. No, a lot sore, but he's in good spirits. Pat walked to the office door and pulled it shut. "How are our Work Teams doing? What are the current problems?"

"Bob Walner's office Team has cut in half the number of forms we use to process orders and payments, and stream-lined the other half. We're moving an order through in one third the time it used to take. Two days ago they began to report customer satisfaction information to the plant. They have a logsheet of all complaints and associated dollar values. They also decided they want to do a customer survey." Clark spoke as though he were reporting to a Senate subcommittee. He was a faithful and loyal player.

"Next, Ruth's Team has eliminated all of the narrowly defined positions on the winder. The Team members are all working on the machine as a Team. If something needs to be done, the old 'That's not my job' mentality is gone. Jobs classes have been reduced from twelve to three." He paused to consider Pat's reaction, then continued. "The maintenance system, and tool and die system, have been defined and are almost in place. And of course, their playbook is complete.

"Ruth's Team has also begun to collect quality data on the final product off the winders. They selected two quality characteristics, torsion and tensile strength, I believe, and are collecting test data on both. Initial results show standard deviations way beyond anything acceptable. Glanahan is giving Ruth fits, saying 'I told you so' every time they pass in the plant. Anyway, we're going to continue our training sessions on basic statistics for the Team, and it'll wrap up next week."

"And last but not least?" Pat queried.

"Your friend and mine, Mr. Glanahan. They've got their pull system in place, and they've decided to invite other departments to a session to figure out how to sequence these other areas." Clark stood and moved to the window. "They haven't gotten to designing the training and certification program, but they'll get there."

Pat responded, "One thing at a time. Hey, I spoke to Honlinks late yesterday afternoon."

Clark stood at full attention. He knew this was the response from the board.

Pat jumped out of his chair and cheered, *"And they're going to back us! We did it, you old dog, we did it! The sale is off!"*

Like two children on Christmas morning, they whooped and cheered, raising clenched fists in the air in victory. They hugged and high-fived as they did their victory dance.

"And get this. They want to set up a corporate-wide Teamwork and Total Quality committee. It will include every division president and general manager. The initial objective is senior management education, followed by setting up a corporate-wide audit/award program. They want to be able to assess the progress of each division. Sort of like a Malcolm Baldrige Award Program, but the criteria are customized, and include specifics of our business and our philosophy."

Clark sat and stared at the ceiling. "Unbelievable. Bottom of the ninth, two men out, bases loaded, and you smack a homer over the fence to win it."

"And they want *me* to be the committee chairman." Pat jumped up on the table, "You, I, and every bloody person in this place, *pulled it off!*

Clark jumped up on the table with him. He stuck his finger in Pat's chest, "And *you're* buying dinner!"

* * * *

The fax machine at the Detroit plant snapped to attention, sensing a particularly important message on the way. The device's activity had been unusually light, as customer order volume had slowly decreased over the last year. It did save on the cost of paper and wear and tear on the machine. Like a long lost boomerang that unexpectedly returns and strikes its owner in the head, the message, addressed to the general manager, fell into the receptacle.

> As you may know, all plans for consolidation have been permanently put aside. Thank you for your assistance in this matter.
>
> A Teamwork and Total Quality Committee has been established, and as chairman, I am inviting the

division presidents and general managers to join me at my plant on June 3rd to set strategy. I am immediately sending to your attention several books and articles on the subject, and expect you to be an expert by that date.

Give Terry my regards.

Sincerely,
Pat Forte

KEY POINTS FOR DISCUSSION

(1) The board of directors decided to establish a corporate-wide audit/award program for Teamwork and Total Quality. Discuss how you think this should be done. Review the Malcolm Baldrige National Quality Award, and then have your Team outline the evaluation criteria to assess progress in your company. What are the major Teamwork and Total Quality topics for your audit program?

(2) Discuss what you believe the next 12 months will hold for Keith's company. How many Improvement Project Teams and Self-Directed Work Teams do you think would be reasonable to put in place? Describe the extent of change that they will accomplish in this time frame. Then describe the extent of change *your* company will achieve in the next 12 months.

Appendix

You Can't Schedule Production, But You Can Sequence It

Introduction

The shop floor scheduling system is the heart and soul of a plant. It must be a tool that Self-Directed Work Teams can rely upon and use daily to direct their efforts.

Don't underestimate the potential productivity, quality, and cost improvements when the shop floor scheduling system works. That means the master production schedule is continually achieved with little or no expediting. Our experience is that the majority of plants are not satisfied with their current system. Expediting rules! And even worse, the solution remains elusive. The search often includes a bout with Material Requirements Planning that ends in frustration. And kanban is only applicable for parts that are repetitive and produced on a continual basis, which often includes only floorstock components.

This appendix explains the basic concepts embodied in production sequencing. As you'll see, it is a simple system of logic and procedures. No black box. No special software. Just a common sense approach to shop floor scheduling that should be the primary problem solving tool Teams use to search for productivity and quality improvements. It is Team-based in that the system is owned and operated by the Work Teams, and not driven by office planners from the computer room.

Production sequencing was originally conceived by Work Teams that were redesigning their plant. They needed to find a system to link the workcells, and pull both customer orders and stock orders through the plant. Since then, it has proven to be a powerful system that can fill the void between MRP and kanban for any manufacturer of discrete products. Your Work Teams should review this article and consider the merits of this approach. Worker Teams quickly understand the system, and can immediately undertake the challenge to determine the specific application of the system in the plant. Use this to catalyze discussion about the strengths and weaknesses of the existing scheduling system. And then set a plan of attack to finally resolve the scheduling dilemma that has plagued our plants far too long.

"You can't expect every work center/cell/department (WCD) in this plant to meet its production schedule. It's impossible. Too many unexpected things happen that interfere with the weekly schedules issued to each WCD. As managers and supervisors, we make the plant work by expediting production around the problems. We set the priorities hourly, because the priorities change hourly."

Those statements probably sound familiar, because this is how the majority of our production facilities operate. With all of our advanced information technology, engineering expertise and business acumen, we still have not created a methodology that prioritizes production throughout the plant to minimize early and late completion of production at each level in the bill of material (BOM). There is no easy and effective technique for meeting customer delivery commitments.

ILLUSTRATION A–1

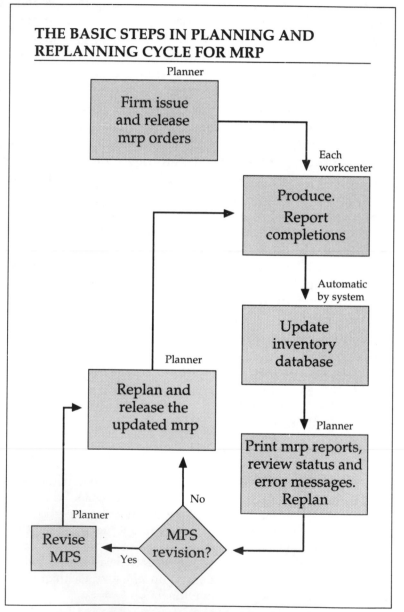

THE BASIC STEPS IN PLANNING AND
REPLANNING CYCLE FOR MRP

Source: Louis W. Joy III, CFPIM and Jo A. Joy, "You Can't Schedule Production But You
Can Sequence It," *APICS–The Performance Advantage*, May 1992, pp. 33–37.

Production sequencing holds the promise of a solution, as it physically organizes the plant and synchronizes the movement of all product. It is based on the pull/kanban system, but is enhanced, and can be used not only in a make-to-stock, repetitive environment, but also in plants that are fully make-to-order or a combination of both strategies. It is simple, motivates shop floor teams, provides visibility of problems and allows for immediate priority change communication and decision making.

What are we doing wrong?

We need a sound manufacturing resource planning (MRP II) information system, but without several of the traditional modules, especially material requirements planning (MRP) used in the traditional way. Using MRP and shop floor control to schedule the shop floor is simply too complicated.

To effectively use MRP, you need a valid master production schedule (MPS) which assigns completion dates to each end item. That's fine and remains a necessity. However, we next explode the BOM and backward schedule each level of the BOM based on routing and planned lead time information. This creates a production schedule or plan for each item, which translates to a production schedule or plan for each work center. We then attempt to prioritize the queues using a dispatch list and set of priority rules. Many plants never get this far. Those that do find the responsiveness of the replanning cycle far too slow to keep up with the changing priorities of the real world on the shop floor.

For the MRP replanning process to work, there must be continuous transactions of the database on the shop floor, as production order completions must be input at each work center. Then someone, typically a planner, must evaluate all of this information, and react to this new status of production. MRP requires that all activities in the plant be reported accurately as well, and this information must be continuously reviewed by the planning department. If you have ever worked with this approach, you know error messages and suggested action reports quickly become voluminous and unworkable.

We have enough difficulty with simple inventory accuracy in the stockroom. How many of our companies struggle to keep

ILLUSTRATION A–2

Basic Information on MPS for Production Sequencing

Customer	Products	Completion Date	Sequence Number
Alpha Co.	A,B,C	Jan. 1, 1992	1
Beta Co.	C,E	Jan. 1, 1992	2
Omega Co.	A,G	Jan. 1, 1992	3
Them Co.	H,K	Jan. 2, 1992	4
Us Co.	A,C,H	Jan. 2, 1992	5
We All Co.	D	Jan. 2, 1992	6
You Guys Co.	B,S	Jan. 2, 1992	7
Ladies Inc.	Q,R,S	Jan. 2, 1992	8

the inventory database accurate? The typical mid-sized plant still conducts the annual physical inventory, very often because there is a lack of integrity in the inventory database. Without an accurate database, MRP cannot work anyway. Who are we kidding?

How does it work?

To illustrate the application of production sequencing, let's first consider a plant that is fully make-to-order. We start by looking at the MPS. We number, in sequence, each customer order, regardless of size, including all customer orders in the MPS horizon. Production sequencing assigns each order a completion date and a sequence number. In effect, we have given each order a priority, even those orders scheduled to be completed on the same day. Note that a customer order may include more than one product.

The master production schedule and implied priorities will drive the plant and serve as the dispatch list for all WCDs.

Each WCD will define a set number of inbound and outbound work-in-process areas. This is usually done by physically taping off squares on the floor. In the example in Illustration A–3, the work cell has defined three inbound and three outbound squares. The rule is that only one customer order per square is allowed.

ILLUSTRATION A–3

Workcell with Inbound and Outbound Squares Designated on the Shop Floor (The numbers represent the sequence number of the customer order residing in each square.)

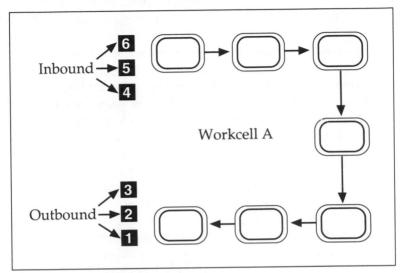

Each WCD is provided a copy of the sequenced MPS without completion dates. The WCD team works only in the sequence of this MPS, and production is authorized only by an empty outbound square. As illustrated in Illustration A–3, work cell Team A will produce customer order number 4 only when customer order number 1 is moved to the next WCD. The empty outbound square is the signal to produce the next order in the sequence of the MPS. In this way, all product moves through the plant in the sequence of this MPS.

A final assembly line, work center, cell, or even final inspection area is designated as the source of the pull signal for the plant. This Team is provided the MPS with completion dates, and is responsible to meet the production schedule. This is the only work team that works to meet a schedule! As you can see, as long as this final area meets the MPS schedule, then all other WCDs have performed as needed to meet customer commitments. Why complicate matters by giving these other teams a schedule when it is not needed?

Let's look at production sequencing again, taking into account the entire plant, as illustrated in Illustration A-4.

In this plant, W/C 1 feeds Final Inspection, as does W/C 2 and W/C 3. W/C 3 also feeds W/C 2. Complicated routings do not create any more difficulty than exists in the traditional plant. In fact, production sequencing eliminates the sorting of product that often takes place due to lack of physical organization.

In our example, Final Inspection has designated five inbound squares. Customer orders number 1 through 5 currently fill these areas and await inspection. When customer order 1 is inspected, a square empties. This is the pull signal for the material handlers to gather all products/components for the next customer order (number 6) and bring them to the open square. The material handlers may use routing information to determine which outbound squares are the source of product for customer order 6, or, they may simply view the outbound squares, which have clearly visible signs that indicate the customer order sequence number assigned to the product. Of course, most material handlers know the plant very well and know where the product is produced!

The material handlers will go to the appropriate outbound squares and move all customer order 6 WIP to the inbound square at final inspection. This opens outbound squares at the WCDs that previously held customer order 6. These open squares are the signal for the WCD team to produce the next customer order.

For example, W/C 1 has customer orders 6,7,8,10 in outbound and 12,15,17,18 in inbound. When 6 moves, W/C 1 will work to complete customer order 12. Note that W/C 1 does not produce anything for customer order 9,11,13,14, and 16, and the team simply skips to the next order on the MPS on which they must work.

If your plant is currently a hodge-podge of complicated routings, and WCDs require four, five or more outbound destinations, then you should challenge the basic plant design and attempt to streamline the flow of product. The effort to design the production sequencing system often highlights the opportu-

ILLUSTRATION A-4
Production Sequencing System (Note that workcenters/cells that serve as supplier to more than one workcenter/cell designate outbound and inbound squares for each destination.)

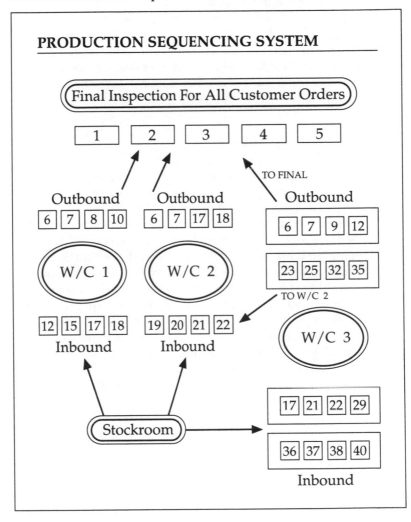

PRODUCTION SEQUENCING SYSTEM

nities for improvement to existing routings and layouts, and serves as a basis for plant design.

In simplistic terms, we have created a giant assembly line, connecting all areas in the plant.

How about a plant that is both make-to-stock and make-to-order? The same rules and approach apply. Each production/stock order and customer order is sequenced in the same MPS. Whether we produce to stock, to customer order, or do both, we still follow the same rules and process each of these orders in the same manner.

What about problems?

As you can see, production sequencing is an organized and logical approach to managing a plant—at least when all goes well and the typical problems that result in expediting are at a minimum. But, what if WCD teams have problems?

One of the real benefits of production sequencing is visibility of performance. It is extremely obvious which WCD teams are keeping up with the production pace set by the MPS and the final production area. The teams that have full outbound squares are maintaining the pace! A team experiencing difficulties, and possibly in need of assistance, has a number of empty outbound squares. As a plant manager or supervisor, you should take a quick tour and see to what extent each team is maintaining full outbound squares. Those struggling to keep up may need help.

Under material requirements planning, the only way to determine how well a WCD is doing is to review the dispatch list and schedule and consider completions versus the plan.

Now, let's say on the tour we find a team that has four outbound squares to maintain, one destination, and only one full square. This team is close to "stocking out." What should we do?

The team may have a mechanical problem, design problem, etc., and we must determine a course of action. There are two and only two alternatives. The first choice is to bring in the necessary resources, i.e., maintenance, engineering, perhaps even team members from other WCDs, to help this team catch up and maintain the sequence. This maintains the sequence of orders and does not affect any other WCD.

The other alternative is selected when it is clear that the team cannot avoid a stockout. The sequence of customer orders must be altered. This must be done not only for the troubled WCD, but also for the entire plant. The planning group must be immediately made aware of the need to reschedule, and a new MPS and revised sequence issued to all WCDs in the plant. All WCDs will reorganize the inbound and outbound squares to this new sequence.

Looking at Illustration A-4, let's say that customer order 6 has been pulled to final inspection. W/C 1 begins work on customer order 12, but quickly realizes there is a serious design problem. The sequence must be changed and customer order 12 must be put behind customer order 22 to allow time for resolution of the problem. W/C 1 will simply hold customer order 12 "on the side" and process 15, 17, 18 and so on up to 22, then fit 12 physically into the new sequence. Remember, do what makes sense; it might not be feasible to physically move 12 into the stockroom so that it can be physically in sequence after 22. These types of rules must be set for each plant. In our example, customer order 12 is already completed by W/C 3 and sitting in the outbound square. W/C 3 may wish to produce customer order 17, put that in the outbound square, and physically move 12 in the now open inbound square after 22. Another choice might be to "hold" 12 to the side, process 17, and move the customer order following 29 into the inbound area, and insert 12 into the outbound area after 22 later on.

Again, do what makes sense; what is important is that all WCDs maintain the synchronization and sequence of orders. The feedback and replanning cycle is quick and easy, and requires the planning group to stay close to the process and know what is going on the floor by maintaining a presence in the plant. Today, planners tend to spend too much time in the office at the PC. Let's change that role. Just-in-Time suggests a light system that signals the status of the WCD, i.e., red light on when there is a problem.

Another benefit is that WCD teams will not seek the notoriety that results when they fall behind and the MPS sequence must be revised! The teams like the positive recognition of "full squares." For a manager or supervisor, finding a team maintaining full squares is an opportunity to give positive feedback. You've just found someone doing something right—tell them. Keeping squares full is the team's primary responsibility, and along with quality, becomes an important performance measure.

Besides, the teams know that when the squares are full, they've done their job, and are free to work on other problems, grab a coffee, or help another team. Under traditional ways, such as MRP, they would just keep working, even if this meant building far ahead of schedule. Even worse, it is not unusual for teams to work outside the schedule and select jobs that will maximize today's productivity, at the expense of the schedule. The result is expediting and more expediting.

All this production sequencing discussion sounds good, but if we have to stick to the sequence, how do we manage productivity?

It's really quite simple. Build productivity into the master production schedule. The MPS should be determined based on a number of factors, including customer requirements and productivity needs. Every MPS has an implied level of productivity for each day, week, and month. Construct the MPS to meet the productivity needs as well, and then meet the MPS. Traditionally, we tend to ignore the MPS and work to maximize daily productivity at each WCD in the plant. This results in costly expediting and late completions, plus a work environment that frustrates the people and negatively impacts quality. Let's break this vicious cycle. Plant productivity will reach new heights when expediting is minimized and organization and order rule. Sequencing the plant seems the best and simplest way to achieve this goal.

Continuous improvement

Implementation of production sequencing should be conducted in the same manner as the implementation of any major change in an organization. Let's look at the four guiding principles:

(1) Use employee teams and get their "buy in"

Whether or not you presently use the employee team strategy on the shop floor, you'll need to assemble employee groups to participate in the implementation. Chances of success are slim without their help as they make the system work, and these teams are the source of critical information, such as routings, that often no one else knows or understands. They must review, design and "buy in" to the new procedures. It is their system, and they will live with it every day. Managers and supervisors provide the leadership and motivation for success, facilitate the design effort, teach the concept and guide the design to ensure it all fits together.

(2) Document and understand the current system

The primary documentation required of the current system is the routings. This information serves as the basis for plant design and the determination of inbound and outbound squares and destinations. Surely, it is best to have this data in a BOM or shop floor MRP II database, but it is okay if it isn't. Just get it on paper and in a clear format that can be used for analysis. Nothing fancy is required.

(3) Use pilot projects and change slowly

Whenever possible, change slowly. Your production sequencing pilot project should include the selection of one or two WCDs. Establish squares and destinations and issue a sequenced MPS to these work areas. Revise and refine the demand procedures based on your experience.

One word of caution. You'll most likely find that while these pilot areas keep the squares full and in sequence, the real throughput benefits of this technique will not be realized until the balance of the plant is also organized. In fact, you should expect many sequence changes to impact the pilot areas because not everyone is sequenced and traditional expediting remains. Also, pilot areas may experience shortage of parts in inbound squares. This only highlights the plant's current problems. Even so, go slowly, and gradually add WCDs to the production sequencing system. Allow people time to adopt the new mindset and to build confidence.

(4) Document the new system and maintain simple, written rules

Every WCD creates a simple manual that explains how the area works. Topics include procedures and rules for:

- Production sequencing system
- MPS change requests
- Performance measurement
- Team rules, (i.e., responsibility of team members)
- Layout and product routings
- Preventive maintenance
- Manual update rules

The manual is typically called a playbook, just like that of a professional football team. It describes how the team works and is used for continuous evaluation. The written word helps us all better understand and communicate. Otherwise, interpretations of the rules will vary greatly among team members. Remember, all changes and improvements to these rules are also recorded in the playbook.

We all know that continuous improvement is the basis for contemporary management. In a production sequenced plant, the objective is to minimize the number of both inbound and outbound squares for each WCD. Like the standard pull/kanban system, the teams should challenge themselves to minimize squares and avoid stockouts. How close can we get?

The number of squares a team begins with should be well in the safe zone. The team may find that they never go below having three of the total seven outbound squares full. The challenge may be to remove two squares, and work to avoid stockouts. In essence, apply the Just-in-Time concept to this system and, in an orderly way, remove the buffer inventory between WCDs. By doing so, you'll reduce the total manufacturing lead time and work-in-process inventory, and will have increased plant flexibility to better meet customer delivery requirements.

What should you do about the MRPII system?

The big question at this point is what should you do with your material requirements planning system? Use it to manage raw material inventories and to time-phase vendor deliveries. You still need to carefully plan raw materials, and MRP can accomplish that requirement quite satisfactorily. And, you should maintain the current pull/kanban system being used to replenish standard, repetitive parts.

Whatever you do, don't try to schedule production. Sequence it!

About APICS

APICS, the educational society for resource management, offers the resources professionals need to succeed in the manufacturing community. With more than 35 years of experience, 70,000 members, and 260 local chapters, APICS is recognized worldwide for setting the standards for professional education. The society offers a full range of courses, conferences, educational programs, certification processes, and materials developed under the direction of industry experts.

APICS offers everything members need to enhance their careers and increase their professional value. Benefits include:

- Two internationally recognized educational certification processes— Certified in Production and Inventory Management (CPIM) and Certified in Integrated Resource Management (CIRM), which provide immediate recognition in the field and enhance members' work-related knowledge and skills. The CPIM process focuses on depth of knowledge in the core areas of production and inventory management, while the CIRM process supplies a breadth of knowledge in 13 functional areas of the business enterprise.

- The APICS Education Materials Catalog—a handy collection of courses, proceedings, reprints, training materials, videos, software, and books written by industry experts...many of which are available to members at substantial discounts.

- *APICS The Performance Advantage*—a monthly magazine that focuses on improving competitiveness, quality, and productivity.

- Specific industry groups (SIGs)—suborganizations that develop educational programs offer accompanying materials, and provide valuable networking opportunities.

- A multitude of educational workshops, employment referral, insurance, a retirement plan, and more.

To join APICS, or for complete information on the many benefits and services of APICS membership, **call 1–800–444–2742** or **703–237–8344.** Use extension 297.

Other books of interest to you from Business One Irwin . . .

FRONTLINE MANUFACTURING

Rules, Tools, and Techniques for Line Workers

Robert A. Forcier and Marsha M. Forcier

The Business One Irwin/APICS Series in Frontline Education Finally, a comprehensive reference for today's frontline worker! This valuable guide simply, but thoroughly, describes basic techniques line workers can use *immediately* to improve yields, attitudes, quality, new product deliveries, job performance, and customer service. (253 pages) ISBN: 1-55623-671-9

QUALITY IN AMERICA

How to Implement a Competitive Quality Program

V. Daniel Hunt

Dramatically improve your firm's market share, performance, and profitability! Hunt, the author of several award-winning productivity improvement books, analyzes the present state of the practice of quality in America and helps you understand the theories, basic tools, and techniques that can improve quality in your organization. (308 pages) ISBN: 1-55623-536-4

SELF-DIRECTED WORK TEAMS

The New American Challenge

Jack D. Orsburn, Linda Moran, Ed Musselwhite, and John H. Zenger

The definitive guide to self-directed work teams! This strategic reference details ways to motivate employees to produce the quality products and services that will keep you competitive in the years ahead.

Inside, you'll find the techniques that have helped General Electric, Blue Cross, and many others improve productivity and quality. (353 pages)
ISBN: 1-55623-341-8

TEAM-BASED ORGANIZATIONS
Developing a Successful Team Environment
James H. Shonk

Identifies the advantages and challenges of empowered work teams and tells how you can manage an organization or department that fosters this type of collaborative environment. You'll discover how to align team and company goals, resolve conflict, and ensure a smooth transition to teams. Includes time-saving examples, forms, and checklists. (168 pages)
ISBN: 1-55623-703-0

Available in fine bookstores and libraries everywhere.